D1176821

For Mam

Also by Jonathan Wilson

Behind the Curtain: Travels in Eastern European Football

Sunderland: A Club Transformed

Inverting the Pyramid: The History of Football Tactics

The Anatomy of England: A History in Ten Matches

Brian Clough: Nobody Ever Says Thank You

The Outsider: A History of the Goalkeeper

The Anatomy of Liverpool: A History in Ten Matches

Angels with Dirty Faces: The Footballing History of Argentina

The Anatomy of Manchester United: A History in Ten Matches

*The Barcelona Legacy: Guardiola, Mourinho
and the Fight For Football's Soul*

CONTENTS

PART I

PART II

183

PART III

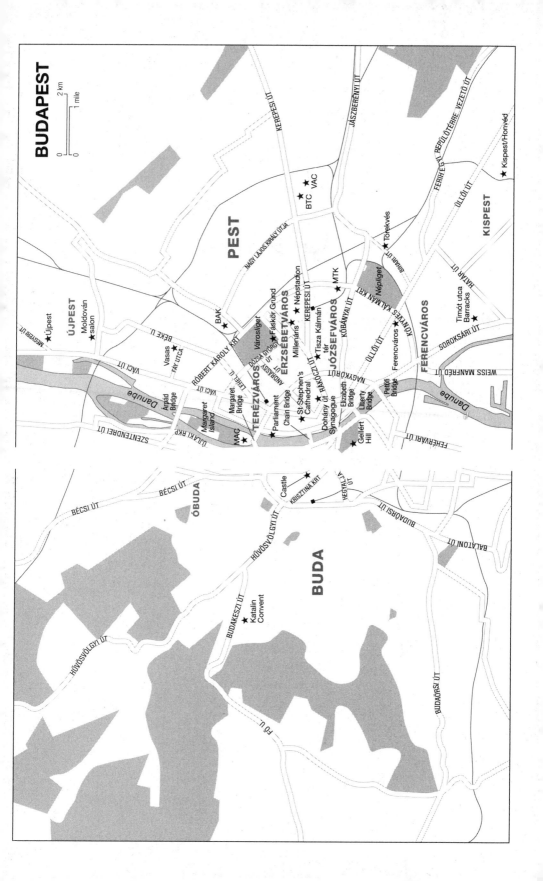

A NOTE ON NAMES

Many of the cities referred to here have undergone multiple changes of name, or are known by different names in different languages. Where there is a common English name I have used that; otherwise, unless there is good reason not to, I have gone with the name it is currently known by in the country where it is now located, providing the Hungarian alternative in parentheses.

With clubs, unless there is a commonly used English variant – e.g. Bayern Munich – I have used the local name, so FC Nürnberg are the team from Nuremberg and FC Hannover 96 play in Hanover.

I

PROLOGUE

THE BACK OF THE GRAVEYARD

A bright October morning in the Kozma utca cemetery in the east of Budapest. The leaves are copper, the sky clear. A grave-keeper gives us a lift to the plot we're looking for, a mile or more back from the road. Nobody comes to this part of the cemetery much any more. The paths are overgrown to the point that this feels like woodland. Branches claw at the sides of the van. We stop, and the grave-keeper points vaguely into the trees. There is a suggestion of a path, but the grass comes to shin height and we have to duck under a fallen branch. Every now and again, a slight raise in the ground or an angular stone hints at what this land is. Eventually, 50 or 60 yards from the main path, we come to a headstone so swathed in ivy that if you weren't looking for it you could easily think it was a tree stump. The grave-keeper wrenches the leaves aside. It's not the one we're looking for.

We'd asked in the cemetery office and, after a quick search on the computer, been given a number. There was the plot, and then two other numbers: how many rows back and how many rows across the grave was. Even near the gate, that was of limited use because it wasn't clear from which corner the numbering started; out in the woodland, the reference was a hint, nothing more. We were also shown the burial card, a rectangle of ancient brown paper, perhaps three inches by two:

3

Péter Pál Hirschl, died 7 July 1940, buried 9 July 1940. It seemed likely nobody had looked at it for 78 years.

We walked on and came to another headstone, the ivy so thick upon it the branches were half an inch or more in diameter. Impatiently, the grave-keeper tore the ivy away. I saw the 'PÁL' first, then the 'PÉTER'. This was it:

Petikém
HIRSCHL PÉTER PÁL
ÉLT 14 ÉVET
MEGHALT 1940 JÚLIUS 7-ÉN
Kisfiam, a viszontlátásra!

פסח[1]

HIRSCHL IMRÉNÉ
Sz. BLEIER ERZSÉBET
1896–1971

Not just the grave of Péter Hirschl, but also of his mother, Erzsébet, the wife of Imre Hirschl, and the message, added after Péter's death at the age of 14: 'My little son, until I see you again!'

To my surprise, I felt a ball of emotion rise in my chest. In part perhaps it was at a life ended so young, and at two lives so thoroughly forgotten, but more than that, I think, it was a selfish feeling, another detail added in uncovering the life of a man who had obsessed me for more than a decade, more confirmation of who he was, that I was chasing somebody who had actually existed – which at times,

---

[1] Only the horizontal bar remains of the last character, but this appears to say 'Pesach' – Passover – which was probably Péter's Hebrew name.

given the way Imre Hirschl seemed always to slither from my grasp, I had almost come to doubt. It was a relatively straightforward matter then, armed with dates of death and burial, to return to the archives to consult Péter's death certificate and find cause of death listed as 'pneumonia and deterioration of the kidneys'. Not much, perhaps, but another fact, another tile in the mosaic.

A curtain fell over Hungary in 1945, beyond which few ventured. Hungary is a country that has forgotten a lot of its heroes, but none have been so thoroughly forgotten – in part, in his case, it must be admitted, through his own obfuscations – as Imre Hirschl. He was a brilliant coach, hugely successful in South America, and yet when he left Hungary in his late twenties, he had never worked in football. He is an extraordinary figure, his life shaped by two world wars, a genius, a charmer and a rogue – and yet he is one of roughly a dozen coaches of similar influence and intrigue produced by interwar Hungary.

* * *

When does a book begin? People ask how long it took you to write a book and you say a year, or 18 months or four years. From signing the contract to submitting the manuscript for this book took roughly two years but, because I was writing *The Barcelona Legacy* during that time, there was probably only around 14 months from beginning the research to submission. In reality, though, the book began long before that.

I first went to Budapest in 2004 when researching *Behind the Curtain*. I arrived by night train – from, I think, Belgrade – and spent my first hours there huddled in a bakery in Keleti station avoiding the junkies on the concourse and waiting for the sun to rise. But the city soon grew on me. There was something in the faded grandeur, the sense of cultures meeting, that appealed. An old girlfriend once said that I make a decision on whether I like a city or not based on whether I have a good meal in the first 24 hours I'm there. It's an observation not entirely without justification and certainly Budapest passes that test: the coffee houses and restaurants are a large part of the appeal.

But the impetus for this book came a little later, in a bar in Rio de Janeiro late in 2006, as the great historian of Flamengo, Roberto Assaf, explained to me how Brazilian football had been changed utterly by the arrival in 1936 of a mysterious figure from central Europe, somebody known in Brazil as Dori Kruschner. He had lasted less than a year before being sacked, but the ideas Kruschner instilled prompted the revolution that led to Brazil winning the World Cup in 1958. The problem was, nobody seemed to know who he was.

It was the Hungarian radio journalist Sándor Laczkó who first suggested Kruschner might actually be Dori Kürschner, a Hungary international who had played for Jimmy Hogan at the Budapest club MTK before succeeding him as coach when Hogan returned to Britain at the end of the First World War. Once that link was made, a whole number of pieces fell into place, shaping the first third of *Inverting the Pyramid*, my book investigating the history of football tactics.

I was aware, though, that there was a piece of the jigsaw missing, that logically there had to be an equivalent to Kürschner in Argentina to explain how the game had developed as it did there. I found him, eventually, in a man I initially called Emérico Hirschl, who had coached Gimnasia y Esgrima La Plata and River Plate with distinction in the 1930s. It was only when I tried to find out more about him for *Angels with Dirty Faces*, my book on the history of Argentinian football, that it became apparent almost everything that was known about him in Argentina was wrong. Piecing together the life of Imre Hirschl, to give him the Hungarian version of his name, cutting through the myth and the lies he told about himself, became an obsession. There is, still, a lacuna between early 1928 and September 1929 when he turned up in São Paulo begging Béla Guttmann, at the time a well-known Hungarian player for a touring US side, for a job as a masseur, but I've pretty much managed to fill the rest in.

The deeper I dug into Hirschl, the more it became apparent that he and Kürschner were part of a much broader culture. It seems reasonable to say, with the possible exception of the astonishing group of coaches and future coaches who came together at Barcelona in the late 1990s, there's never been a more influential school than that which emerged from Budapest in the late 1920s and early 1930s. In part, that's because so many left, some for financial reasons, some because they were Jewish and fleeing anti-Semitism, taking their ideas around the world. But the ideas had to be there for them to take root when scattered far and wide.

In prioritising football, there is a danger of sounding trite, of course. The Second World War, Hungary's precarious alliance with Nazi Germany and subsequent existence as a vassal state of the Soviet Union overshadow everything. Kürschner and Hirschl were remarkable men who got out. Many more did not. This is a football book, but it is also a book about courage and tragedy, about survival and death, about the horror of the Holocaust, the Soviet repression and the awful choices people had to make during and after the Uprising of 1956.

Research has not been easy. A long time has passed, records have been destroyed, people have died. Communities that might have preserved a memory have been wiped out. Some, such as Hirschl, wilfully obscured their past. The Communist government discouraged reflection on what had happened before 1945. As a result, even after research conducted across the globe, from Stockholm to Buenos Aires, from São Paulo to Budapest, there are gaps, doubts and inconsistencies. But what emerges, despite that, is the picture of a culture of extraordinary vibrancy that produced and was propagated by extraordinary men who dealt with extraordinary challenges. The story of Hungarian football is one of tragedy and courage, and of great influence. It's not an exaggeration to say that modern football was shaped in Budapest in the five years of chaos that followed the First World War.

CHAPTER ONE

THE TYPEWRITER SALESMAN OF MANCHESTER

The end is easy. Hungary ceased to be a great footballing power on 4 November 1956 as Soviet tanks rolled into Budapest to crush the Hungarian Uprising, prompting a wave of defections from which the national team has never fully recovered. There were some stirrings after that, it's true, but it was nothing consistent, nothing compared to what it had been, nothing like that period between May 1950 and June 1954 when Hungary were unbeaten, when they won Olympic gold and thrashed England twice. That *Aranycsapat* – Golden Squad – itself appears in retrospect less an indication of the rude health of the Hungarian game than the final spasm of the true golden age of Hungarian football, a period of around a quarter of a century when, against a backdrop of seemingly perpetual economic and political turmoil, they taught the world to play.

Identifying the beginning is rather harder. The Communist version would have it that Hungarian football began its ascent in 1949 when, after the gradual Stalinist takeover and the formation of the People's Republic of Hungary, clubs were nationalised and

Gusztáv Sebes was appointed national coach. And while it is true that the focus of power at a couple of favoured clubs probably did help the development of the *Aranycsapat* in the short term, the longer-term consequences were rather less healthy, and the success of the programme that was instituted was possible only because there was such a fecund culture on which to draw. It's only recently that the official version has begun to be challenged, that people have begun to reach back beyond the Soviet takeover, before the Second World War, and examine the hugely stimulating period when Hungary stood at the centre of the European game, sending out its emissaries to every corner of the footballing world.

So when did that age begin? Did it start in the autumn of 1914 with a knock at dawn on the door of a Vienna apartment occupied by the former Burnley and Bolton Wanderers forward Jimmy Hogan?

Or had it perhaps begun a decade earlier, when Spen Whittaker, the Burnley manager, responded dismissively to Hogan asking what he had done wrong in skying a chance high over the bar. 'Just keep having a pop, lad,' Whittaker said. 'If you get one in ten you're doing well.' That wasn't enough for Hogan, an intense and thoughtful player, possessed of an analytical mind and a thirst for self-improvement. There must, he reasoned, be more to it than luck. Had he been off balance? Had the position of his foot been wrong? From then on, he determined, he would dedicate himself to understanding technique. It was a decision that would lead him to a Viennese jail before the glorious flowering of his ideas not only in Austria and Hungary, but also in Italy, Germany, France, Portugal, Yugoslavia, Sweden, Argentina, Uruguay and Brazil.

But the true beginning, perhaps, was even earlier than that, in 1894, when an ambitious 17-year-old clerk called Edward Shires abandoned his job at a typewriter factory in Manchester[1] and set off to make his fortune – and, as it turned out, shape the club whose players, more than any other, carried the Hungarian game around the world: MTK. 'The island soon becomes small for an English merchant,' he decided. 'I said goodbye to Manchester and settled down in Vienna.' The issue of just how and why Hogan had managed to extricate himself from wartime Vienna for the rather less stressful environment of Budapest, so that his expertise elevated Hungarian rather than Austrian football, is a mystery that for years had not been adequately explained. It is Shires, though, who holds the key.

Shires was a popular member of the British community in Vienna. A photograph taken perhaps 10 or 20 years later shows him in a high-collared shirt, his hair sharply parted on the left, his narrow features a little small for his face which, combined with a slightly raised left eyebrow, gives him a sceptical air. He played tennis and cricket and became friendly with Harold William Gandon, who was a manager at the gasworks. When Gandon won the inaugural Austrian Open tennis tournament in Prague in 1894,[2] he returned

---

[1] In the interview with *Nemzeti Sport* published 15 March 1933 from which the quotes from Shires in this chapter are taken, it is stated this was the Oliver factory. Oliver, though, was a US firm that was not founded until the following year and the account of the company offered in Issue 64 of *ETCetera*, the typewriter history magazine, suggests industrial production, even in the US, didn't begin until at least a year after that. It seems reasonable to speculate that either the journalist misheard or a 40-year lag and the popularity of Oliver, which became a British firm in 1928, led to a mental slip on the part of Shires and that he actually worked at the Gardner's factory on Cross Street. Robert Messenger's meticulous and fascinating blog available at https://oztypewriter. blogspot.com/2015/01/who-was-john-gardner-typewriter.html all but proves that Gardner's went out of business by the end of the decade and Shires refers to the factory as being 'defunct'.

[2] Prague at the time was, as the capital of Bohemia, in Austro-Hungary. It hosted the Austrian Open until 1914.

with a challenge from the local football club, Regatta,[3] to put together a team to represent Vienna. Shires responded enthusiastically, placing an advertisement for the First Vienna Football Club in an expat newspaper. They received numerous positive responses, but also a complaint from the northern suburb of Hohe Warte advising them that the First Vienna Football Club already existed, having been founded by gardeners working on the estate belonging to Nathaniel Mayer von Rothschild, part of the great banking dynasty.[4] Shires merged his team with the Vienna Cricket Club, which had been founded two years earlier by British immigrants including Ernest Blyth, who owned the Stone & Blyth department store with his brother Eddie, and, in December 1894, set up a game against the Football Club, winning 4–0.[5] They went on to beat Regatta 2–1 in Prague. 'They did beat us later in Vienna, but for that match they brought in two guest players from Berlin,' Shires said. 'The point is, now there was a connection between the two cities and this provided an opportunity for further development.'

That development was rapid. Clubs sprung up not only in Vienna and Prague but also in Budapest, which Shires first visited in

---

[3] Regatta was a rowing and skating club. In May 1896, German-Jewish members of Regatta founded Deutscher Fußball-Club Prag. DFC competed in the first German championship in 1903 and reached the final, where they suffered a surprise 7–2 defeat to VfB Leipzig. There was also a team for non-Jewish Germans in the city, founded in 1899 and known as DFC Germania Prag.

[4] His grandfather Salomon Mayer von Rothschild had founded a bank in Vienna in 1820. As the eldest son, Nathaniel was expected to take over the running of the bank from his father Anselm but instead became a philanthropist and socialite who collected mansions and art. His youngest brother Albert took on the family banking business.

[5] The First Vienna Football Club are still going and still wear the yellow and blue kit that reflects Rothschild's racing colours. The football section of the Cricket Club was disbanded in 1936.

1897 as the Cricket Club beat BTC, the Budapesti Torna Club,[6] 2–0 at the Millenáris, the park that was the home of football in the city for years. It was redeveloped for the cycling world championship in 1928 and remained largely unchanged before finally being demolished in 2018. Shires was gifted enough to become captain of the Austria national side, but in 1904, he moved to Budapest because 'my company needed someone to do business in the difficult Hungarian market'.

Shires was a representative of the Underwood typewriter company,[7] but he is generally credited with introducing table tennis to Austria and Hungary and at least part of his job seems to have been importing sports equipment. Naturally enough, having arrived in Budapest, Shires sought out a football club to play for and joined MTK. Magyar Testgyakorlók Köre, the Circle of Hungarian Fitness Activists, had been founded in a Budapest café in November 1888 by a mixture of aristocrats, Jewish businessmen and dissident members of an earlier club NTE – Nemzeti Torna Egylet, the National Athletic Club.[8]

---

[6] '*Torna*' is the Hungarian word for the German '*turnen*', the programme of physical exercise introduced into German schools by Friedrich Ludwig Jahn in the early 19th century. It came to refer almost exclusively to gymnastics and, just as the tenets of muscular Christianity meant sport in British public schools became part of a programme of toughening up young men for the running of the Empire, it was for a long time linked to German nationalism. The term is also present in the official name of Ferencváros – Ferencvárosi Torna Club (FTC).

[7] I am grateful to Gunnar Persson for providing this information. It comes from the Austrian book *Geschichte des Fußballsportes in Österreich*, edited by Leo Schidrowitz and published by Verlag Rudolf Traunau in 1951. It includes details of the business origins of many British footballers. Given Underwood was founded in New York in 1895, it still seems likely the factory Shires quit was Gardner's. It also means it's unclear for whom Shires was working when he first arrived in Vienna. An invoice held in the archive at the Freud Museum in London shows Sigmund Freud bought an Underwood on 12 May 1925, suggesting the business was still thriving.

[8] NTE had been focused on athletics to the exclusion of other sports. BTC, the team Shires's Vienna Cricket Club had played on his first trip to Budapest, and the champions in 1901 and 1902, were an earlier splinter group. 'Athletic' is a loose translation of *Torna* – see footnote six.

Although MTK have always been seen as a Jewish club, the first president, Lajos Vermes, was a Christian,[9] and it was not in any sense exclusive – unlike Vivó és Atlétikai Club (VAC – Fencing and Athletic Club), which was established in 1903 by Lajos Dömény, a law student, as the sporting arm of the Zionist student organisation Makkabea. Like the far more famous and successful Hakoah in Vienna, it was inspired by the theories of Muscular Judaism promulgated by the physician and author Max Nordau and sought both to combat the stereotype that depicted Jews as physically weak and to promote Zionism; one of VAC's founder members was Ármin Beregi, president of the Zionist Organisation of Hungary. Dömény had initially wanted to call the organisation the Jewish Athletic Club but that name was rejected for breaching regulations of the use of denominational names (Makabi Brno was similarly rejected when the name was first suggested in 1914, and there were no clubs with overtly Christian names). The name VAC was chosen because a composite of the initials could be shaped into a Star of David.[10]

At first MTK were dedicated to fencing and gymnastics but in 1901 they branched out into football. They took their place in the first division two years later and in 1904 won their first league title. Shires played eight games for them the following season as the businessman Alfréd Brüll took over as president, then, aged 28, with his health deteriorating, he took on a more administrative role and worked as a referee.

Backed by the wholesaler and sports manager Henrik Fodor, MTK won the title again in 1907–08, but in the years that followed

---

[9] Another early president was another Christian, Kálmán Szekrényessy, who was the first man to swim across Lake Balaton and the inventor of the Hungarian word for bicycle, '*kerékpár*'.

[10] For more on the ethnic and cultural background of Budapest's clubs, particularly MTK and VAC, see Péter Szegedi's book *Az első aranykor: A magyar foci 1945-ig* [*The First Golden Age: Hungarian Football to 1945*] (Akadémiai, 2016).

found themselves unable to topple the might of Ferencváros. Founded 11 years after MTK (although their football section is a few months older than MTK's), Ferencváros carried a vague sense of German ethnicity – their nickname, 'Fradi', is derived from Franzstadt, the German form of Ferencváros, the ninth district of Budapest. 'At the beginning of the century,' said the sociologist Miklós Hadas, although his work is far from universally accepted, 'the concept and connotations of the "Fradi-heart" implied a sensitive, good-hearted, compassionate, enthusiastic petty bourgeoisie who felt Hungarian, as against the coldly calculating, business-like, alienated big bourgeoisie of foreign origin – MTK.'[11]

That may have been the image the clubs had, the one the majority of their fans felt they were expressing, but in practical terms the divide was far from concrete and the players tended to come from similar backgrounds. Between 1900 and 1930, for instance, a quarter of Ferencváros players were Jewish, as opposed to a little more than half of MTK players.[12]

By 1911, frustrated by MTK's inability to end Ferencváros's domi-nation, Shires took radical action and strengthened the club with two imports from Britain. There was the English forward Joe Lane, who joined the club as an amateur in 1911, scored the only goal in the inaugural match at MTK's Hungária körúti stadion,[13] a 1–0 win over Ferencváros on 31 March, and ended up signing professional terms

---

[11] Miklós Hadas, 'Football and Social Identity: The Case of Hungary in the Twentieth Century' in *The Sports Historian*, Volume 20 (2000), Issue 2.

[12] As cited in David Bolchover, *The Greatest Comeback* (Biteback, 2017).

[13] The stadium suffered severe bomb damage during the Second World War and had to be rebuilt in 1946–47. It was later renamed Hidegkuti Nándor Stadion after one of MTK's greatest players, and was used as the Stade de Colombes in Paris during the shooting of John Huston's 1981 film *Escape to Victory*. The stadium was demolished and rebuilt again in 2014.

with Sunderland, who had been impressed by him after playing MTK in a tour match in 1913. And, far more significantly, there was the Scottish manager John Tait Robertson.

Robertson was born in Dumbarton in 1877. A combative half-back, he played for Morton and Everton, won the Southern League in his single season with Southampton, and then returned to Scotland in 1899 where he was part of a Rangers side that won three successive championships. In 1905, as an international career that earned him 16 caps came to an end, he became Chelsea's first-ever signing as they made him player-manager for their inaugural season.[14] Robertson also scored Chelsea's first competitive goal, in a 1–0 win at Blackpool, as he led them to third in the table.

Chelsea were among the favourites for promotion the following season but something went awry. Robertson played in only three of the opening 12 games of the season and his frequent absences began to draw comment. When he failed to show for a board meeting on 6 November, the club secretary William Lewis demanded an explanation, while the directors decided that they should take over team selection.[15] Robertson resigned a week later but early the following month the chairman Claude Kirby received a letter from an H. Raucorn. 'Dear Sir,' it read. 'Knowing that Mr J.T. Robertson was no longer an official of the Chelsea FC, I thought it my duty to inform you that he was in your office after 11pm last Thursday Nov 29th.'[16] What Robertson was doing there is unknown, but the following year

---

[14] They were founded by the entrepreneur Gus Mears, who had bought Stamford Bridge in 1904 with the intention of turning it into a football stadium. When Fulham refused to move in as tenants, he founded his own club.

[15] The minutes of this board meeting are reproduced in Colin Benson, *The Bridge* (Chelsea Football Club, 1987). I'm very grateful to Dominic Bliss for bringing it to my attention.

[16] Reproduced in Benson, *The Bridge*.

he was named player-manager at Glossop, a position he held for two years. He was working as assistant manager of Manchester United when Shires got in touch. Persuading him to accept the job, Shires claimed, was his proudest achievement. 'It was Robertson who did the most for developing football in Hungary,' he said. 'The Hungarians learned more from him in two years than they would have learned from somebody else in ten.'

That Robertson was a Scot was significant. From the first international in 1872, when a physically weaker Scotland side had surprisingly held England to a 0–0 draw through judicious use of coordinated passing, the game north of the border had eschewed the traditional dribbling game, focusing instead on the pass.[17] The success of the policy was seen in Scotland's domination of the early years of their rivalry with England, and by the extraordinary influence of Scottish players and managers on the early years of the English league.[18] By the early 20th century there had been a general acceptance of the efficacy of passing, but the Scots were still regarded as the masters.

Robertson was not impressed by what he found in Budapest. 'The mistake the players commit ... is that they only use one foot,' he said. 'I think a player should be able to use both feet. The aerial game is very weak... The half line does not play well with the backs – when the backs lose the ball, the halves should be there to provide cover. The halves are not working together with the forward line either, and their shots are not good. [Sándor] Bródy [of Ferencváros] is clearly the

---

[17] For much more on this development, see my book *Inverting the Pyramid* (Orion, 2008).

[18] When the English league champions Sunderland beat the Scottish league champions Heart of Midlothian in the first 'World Championship' game in Edinburgh in 1895, for instance, all 22 players on the pitch were Scots.

best centre-half but it does not mean that he would be exceptional – I have not seen a really good centre-half in the whole league.'[19]

But as Shires had hoped, Robertson began to implement the Scottish passing game in Budapest. 'Because of Robertson's work,' Shires said, 'and the example set by Lane, the MTK style was created and MTK became a stronger and stronger opponent for Ferencváros to face...' Many would suggest that MTK already had an image of themselves as a passing side before Robertson's arrival, but even as he built on those foundations, Ferencváros won the title in 1911–12 and 1912–13, extending their streak to five in a row.

That summer, Robertson returned home, for reasons at which Shires only hinted. 'It's a pity that he wasn't teetotal,' Shires said in that 1933 interview – which may explain what happened in those final weeks at Chelsea. 'If he had been, he could still be around now.' The team he had built, though, ended Ferencváros's domination and won the championship in 1913–14. War brought the temporary abandonment of the league and there were three half-length unofficial seasons played, the last of them won by MTK, before a full resumption in 1916–17. The foundations were in place and MTK were ready to ascend to much greater heights.

---

[19] *Sporthírlap*, 13 January 1913.

CHAPTER TWO

THE EVANGELIST AND THE COFFEE HOUSE

As a player, Jimmy Hogan's lust for self-improvement did him limited good. After Burnley, he moved to Nelson, then Fulham, Swindon and Bolton. He was a decent professional, but no more. As a coach, it initially seemed his inquisitiveness and his pedagogic zeal would count against him; those were not characteristics much prized in English football in the early 20th century (or arguably since). He spent a year teaching Dutch students in Dordrecht but when he returned to England to rejoin Bolton as a player, Hogan must have wondered whether he had been right a decade earlier to defy his father's wish for him to go into the priesthood.

Yet the Netherlands had shown him another way: players who learned in a classroom, who wanted to study the game. In 1912, he was given another chance to work with a foreign squad. After Austria had played poorly in a friendly against Hungary, their manager and the head of their football association, Hugo Meisl, who had been an early member of the Vienna Cricket Club, appealed to the referee, James Howcroft of Redcar, for advice on how best to prepare his side before the Stockholm Olympics. Howcroft recommended Hogan.

For six weeks, Hogan worked in Vienna, developing his players' technique and trying to persuade them to add more fruit and vegetables to their diet. In Sweden, Austria beat Germany 5–1 but then lost to the Netherlands to enter the consolation tournament, in which they beat Norway and Italy before losing in the final to Hungary. Hogan felt Austria should have done better, but that summer marked the start of a friendship with Meisl that would have a profound effect both on his career and on the history of football.

Struggling with a knee injury, Hogan knew the 1912–13 season would be his last as a player and began looking for further coaching opportunities abroad. In 1913, he applied for a job as manager of Germany and was one of 21 applicants interviewed by a German schoolteacher at the Adelphi Hotel in Liverpool. Hogan was the German football association's preferred candidate and they wrote to Meisl asking for a reference. Meisl was appalled by the possibility of his friend working with a rival and offered Hogan a role preparing Austria for the 1916 Olympics. He accepted and the Germany job went instead to the former Derby forward Steve Bloomer, who was arguably the most famous English player there had been until Stanley Matthews.

Hogan moved with his wife, Evelyn, the daughter of the licensee of the Dragoon Hotel in Burnley, and his two young children, Joseph and Mary, to Austria. His first training session was something of a disappointment for the Austrian players, who found him difficult to understand and felt he focused too much on the basics. But Meisl was impressed and he and Hogan chatted long into the night about the game. Both were happy enough with the 2–3–5 formation that had been the basic template across Europe for three decades, but they felt football had become too rigid, positions too defined. Both felt that teams needed to encourage interplay and that the best way to do that was to focus on controlling the ball and simple, intelligent passing, rather than dribbling. Hogan always stressed the value of the long pass to unsettle opposing defences, provided it were well directed and not an aimless upfield punt. Although Meisl was a romantic, who saw a value in beauty for its own sake, Hogan was essentially a pragmatist: while instinctively inclined to the Scottish passing approach, he favoured a game based on possession not for how it looked but because he felt it was the best way to win football matches. 'Sometimes I have been accused of being a "short passing" expert,' Hogan wrote in 1954. 'This is just ridiculous! Anybody who saw the Hungarian style or, to get nearer home, my grand Aston Villa side which won promotion and reached the semi-final of the Cup in 1938, must admit that we exploited the short pass, the cross pass, the through pass, the reverse pass – in fact any other kind of pass which enabled us to keep possession of the ball.'[1]

Hogan's reputation soon grew and he began working with the national team twice a week, spending the rest of his time with Austria's leading club sides. So in demand was he that he had to schedule his sessions with Vienna FC to begin at 5:30 in the morning. He was not merely a manager looking to win games, but a guru shaping the entire footballing vision of a nation. 'This was a revelation,' he said. 'To leave my dark, gloomy industrial Lancashire for Gay Vienna was like stepping into paradise.'[2]

Or at least it was until a disaffected Bosnian Serb student called Gavrilo Princip assassinated the Austrian Archduke Franz Ferdinand in Sarajevo on 28 June 1914. Within a month, Britain was at war with Austro-Hungary.

* * *

---

[1] *Sport Express*, May 1954.
[2] Cited in Norman Fox, *Prophet or Traitor?* (Parrs Wood Press, 2003).

Knock. Knock. Knock.

Evelyn Hogan answered the door. Austrian police pushed past her, burst into the bedroom and pulled Jimmy out of bed. He was taken to the local police station where he was questioned and then, as an enemy alien, sent to the Elizabeth Promenade prison where he was held, as he later described it, 'with thieves and murderers'.[3]

A few days later, according to the account given to Norman Fox in his biography of Hogan, Evelyn was allowed to visit. She found her husband, a meticulous man who would never willingly have gone unshaven, sporting thick stubble, terrified by the comment of a guard that camps were being prepared and that he would be moved there as soon as they were ready.

'My wife and children were frightened to death, and had to make a shift for themselves,' Hogan told the *Burnley Express* after the war.

---

[3] Bloomer was arrested in November 1914 and interned in Germany in the camp at Ruhleben, six miles west of Berlin, where his fellow inmates included Fred Pentland, later a highly influential coach of Athletic of Bilbao, the former Sheffield Wednesday forward Fred Spiksley and the former Everton and Blackburn defender Sam Wolstenholme, all of them England internationals, plus the former Tottenham player–manager John Cameron, a Scotland international. They established a football league and staged international fixtures that would draw crowds in the thousands, and wrote the first-ever coaching manual. More details can be found in Barney Ronay's article 'The Bomb and the Bowler Hat' in Issue Three of *The Blizzard* but, once they got beyond the initial hardship, the Ruhleben internees seem to have created a remarkable life for themselves, a thriving (all-male) community in which all walks of society mixed while attending classes in a range of subjects, theatre productions and sporting events. Other than the footballers, the inmates included: 'F Charles Adler, a world-famous conductor and student of Gustav Mahler; Sir James Chadwick, a Nobel laureate physicist who first conceived of the nuclear bomb; Prince Monolulu, legendary horse-racing tipster of the 1920s whose catchphrase was "I gotta horse!", and who via Pathé news films became the most well-known black person in the Britain of the times; "Bertie" Smylie, fabled sombrero-wearing alcoholic editor of the *Irish Times*; and Geoffrey Pyke, writer, inventor, garden-shed genius and a man who once demonstrated his invention of aircraft carriers made out of ice to Winston Churchill in his bath.'

'I eventually got out of this prison but the Austrian FA broke my contract and left us to starve. Our story of hardship is too long to relate in detail. Suffice it to say that the American Consul sent my wife to England in March 1915 and I was saved by two Englishmen who had obtained their freedom by giving £1,000 to the Austrian Red Cross.'[4]

Those Englishmen were the brothers Eddie and Ernest Blyth, the latter of whom had been a founder member of the Vienna Cricket Club. For several months, Hogan worked as an odd-job man on the Blyth brothers' estate while teaching their children tennis, reporting regularly to the police station.

A century on, the chronology is a little hard to piece together. The Habsburg Empire, attempting to conduct the war honourably, reported all prisoners to the International Red Cross in Geneva. Sure enough, in a document[5] written in a mix of French and German, Hogan is recorded as an *anglais* of '33 *ans*', his profession given as *'Fussballtrainer'* who is *'confiné a Wien'*. The document is handwritten and unfortunately is not dated. Hogan turned 33 on 16 October 1915, which only makes sense when the technical difference between *'confiné'* and *'interné'* is considered. Confinement was used for enemy aliens who were not considered a serious threat and essentially meant they were restricted to one part of the country and had to sign in at a police station.

It's likely that Hogan was 'confined' – that is, released from jail and working for the Blyths – from late 1914. The implication of his interview in the *Burnley Express* is that he had been let out of prison by the time his pregnant wife returned home in March 1915. She gave

---

[4] *Burnley Express*, 12 March 1919.
[5] I'm grateful to Professor Matthew Stibbe of Sheffield Hallam University, an expert in civilian internment in the First World War, for tracking this down for me.

birth to their third child, George Frank, in Haslingden, Lancashire, that summer, which suggests Hogan had been released by, at the very latest, December 1914.[6]

A letter from the Austrian Ministry of Interior to the provincial governor of Lower Austria dated 23 July 1914,[7] makes clear that measures to restrict freedom of movement and place suspect foreigners under police surveillance were enacted almost as soon as war had been declared and on 18 August 1914, 95 enemy aliens were arrested in Lower Austria and interned at Schloss Karlstein. Those interned at that stage, though, tended to be Russian rather than French or British, people of whom there was a reasonable suspicion they might be spies or who held political views that were considered dangerous. It was only in November, after the Germans had rounded up 4,000 British men, and in response to the detention of Austro-Hungarians in Britain, that there was an order in Austria to round up Britons 'whose continued residency or employment in our lands is a matter of luxury only', rather than being considered a 'necessity'.[8]

In that *Burnley Express* interview, Hogan said he 'was allowed to continue working for a time' after war was declared, which perhaps fits with the November date but, if that is when he was picked up, he was held for slightly less than the two months suggested by Fox on the basis of interviews with Hogan's family.

Even the November arrests were relatively small-scale. In May 1915, the US ambassador in Vienna, Frederic C. Penfield, stated in

---

[6] I'm indebted here to the work Dave Rose did checking birth records in Lancashire.

[7] Held in the Niederösterreichisches Landesarchiv St Pölten and cited in Stibbe's essay 'Enemy Aliens, Deportees, Refugees: Internment Practices in the Habsburg Empire, 1914–1918' in the *Journal of Modern European History*, Nov 2014, Vol 12 Issue 4.

[8] Cited in Stibbe.

a letter to his counterpart in London, Walter Hines Page, that only 75 out of an estimated 1286 British subjects had been interned in Austria, and only three out of an estimated 512 British subjects in Hungary.[9] In that sense, Hogan was unfortunate to be picked up at all – particularly given that the work he was doing was for the benefit of Austria – and the subsequent leniency with which he was treated was in keeping with the general policy. That is not to say, though, that life was easy for Hogan even after he had been released from prison. Like many of those similarly confined within Austria, he found himself essentially trapped without any income and was fortunate that he had the Blyths to support him.

* * *

Hogan, Shires explained, 'wrote to me from captivity asking for help'.[10] Shires approached Brüll, who by then had gained international recognition as a sports administrator, not only in football but in swimming and wrestling, and he, supported by the Cambridge-educated Hungarian nobleman Baron Dirsztay, a vice-president of MTK, interceded with the Viennese authorities. According to the champion sculler W.A. Berry,[11] Brüll was 'one of the biggest-hearted men living', who made it his mission to help out any Englishman in trouble, but he must also have recognised an opportunity that couldn't be missed. Either way, Hogan arrived in Budapest late in 1916. He felt instantly at home, describing Budapest as 'the most beautiful city in Europe'.

The Budapest into which Hogan was thrust was, despite the war, a bustling, modern capital. Hungary had been granted internal

---

[9] Cited in Stibbe.

[10] In *Nemzeti Sport*, 15 March 1933.

[11] In an interview with the *Yorkshire Post* on 30 December 1918.

independence from the Austro-Hungarian Empire in 1867 and Budapest in its current form had been created six years later by the unification of Pest, Buda and Óbuda, sparking a programme of urban renewal, much of it funded by Jewish capital, unease at which hinted at a fault line that ran through Hungarian society.

Independence had brought the abolition of laws that denied Jews full political and civil rights and in 1892 the Diet (the Hungarian legislature) had passed a bill recognising Judaism as 'an accepted religion'. By 1899, there were 170,000 Jews living in Budapest, around a quarter of the total population. Only Warsaw had a larger Jewish population. According to the historian and ethnographer Raphael Patai,[12] in that half century leading up to the First World War, Jews had never felt so at home in Hungary. That acceptance was seen clearly in the way an 1890s statue of Miklós Toldi, a 14th-century Magyar warrior and Hungarian hero, was modelled on David Müller, a Jewish gymnast of the late 1880s and one of the founder members of MTK.

At the same time, the government had instituted a conscious policy of Magyarisation as it sought to unify an ethnically diverse people: as well as Jews, Hungary comprised significant numbers of Germans, Slovaks, Croats and Romanians as well as ethnic Hungarians – although it should be stressed that Hungarian identity was seen as something that transcended ethnicity. The success of that policy can be seen in the population's gradual shift from speaking German to Hungarian, the conversion of hundreds of Jews each year to Christianity and a trend for altering surnames: between 1881 and 1919, 45,000 Hungarians changed their names to something less conspicuously Jewish (although that, of course, suggests a perceived need to change). By 1915, one in three Jewish men were marrying Gentiles,[13]

---

[12] In Raphael Patai, *The Jews of Hungary* (Wayne State UP, 1996).
[13] Cited in David Bolchover, *The Greatest Comeback*.

an indication of the secular nature of society.[14] Theodor Herzl, the Pest-born father of modern political Zionism, was so dismayed by the widespread assimilation that he described Hungary as 'the withered branch on the tree of world Jewry'.

But suspicion of Jews, particularly as representative of foreign capital, remained, a contradictory relationship that found expression in the coffee houses for which Budapest was famous around the turn of the century. In 1900, it's estimated there were around 500 coffee houses in the city.[15] An 1891 guidebook declared, 'Budapest is the city of coffee houses. Whoever wants to depict the image of the capital must paint the portrait of its coffee house.'[16]

The coffee house was the symbol both of Budapest's modernity and of its Europeanness. The journalist Ödön Salamon, in an 1896 essay, wrote of visitors looking in vain for the 'barbarism and Orientalism' of Hungary and finding only well-dressed men and women in the latest Parisian styles.[17]

But the coffee house was more than just somewhere for fashionable Hungarians to be seen, it was a democratic space in which different classes gathered to discuss the issues of the day: politics, art, music, literature, gossip and football. 'There is no salon that competes in elegance to the coffee house of Pest,' wrote the journalist Sándor

---

[14] Actual religious conversions were limited: in 1944, when such details took on a deadly significance, the fascist authorities calculated the number of ethnic Jews in Hungary at 870,000, of whom 800,000 were religiously Jewish. In other words, only around 10 per cent converted to Christianity.

[15] According to Mary Gluck, 'The Budapest Coffee House and the making of "Jewish Identity" at the Fin de Siècle', *Journal of the History of Ideas*, April 2013, Volume 74, no 2.

[16] Viharos [Ödön Gerő], *Az én fovárosom* (Révai Testvérek, 1891).

[17] *Budapest a nyugat nagyvárosa'* in *A mulató Budapest* (ed. Henrik Lenkei, 1896) cited in Gluck, 'The Budapest Coffee-house'.

Bródy.[18] 'Its atmosphere can be compared to the purest mountain air and its waitress is the equal of a marquise. To be in intimate contact with thousands of people, with every group and class, who discuss their most intimate affairs in front of one's eyes – this constitutes the very definition of heaven for the writer.'[19] In that, Bródy hints at the self-mythologising nature of the coffee house: what happened in them was widely reported in newspapers and magazines because they were frequented by writers and journalists.

As the writer and journalist Tamás Kóbor put it, the coffee house was 'Janus-faced': they may have looked on to the glittering boulevards of the new Budapest, but they backed on to the grimy alleys of traditional working-class neighbourhoods. For Kóbor, the coffee house was explicitly an escape from the poverty of his early life in the tenements of Terézváros. He wrote a series of pieces in the literary magazine *A Hét* [*The Week*] between 1892 and 1893 about coffee houses: 'The coffee house,' he observed, 'has become an inescapable part of our lives, the externalisation of everything that is inside us, of everything that we long for. Smoke saturates its atmosphere and its characteristic beverage induces sleepless restlessness. It is a place where flirtation imitates love; where haggling pettiness accompanies the search for truth; where the division of labour and the fragmentation of ideas rule triumphant; where the four-penny literature and the sixteen-penny paradise flourish.'

---

[18] Not to be confused with the footballer of the same name, who played for Ferencváros, represented Hungary at the 1912 Olympics, was held as a prisoner of war in Russia from 1914 to 1920 and then became manager of IFK Göteborg in Sweden (and was held up by John Tait Robertson as the best player in the league). He also had various stints as manager of Ferencváros between 1920 and 1937 and died in 1944.

[19] Quoted in Gábor Sánta, '"*Vigasztal, ápol és eltakar*": *A budapesti kávéházak szociologiai és pszichológiai természetrjza a századfordulón*,' *Budapesti Negyed* 12–13, nos 2–3 (1996).

For all the artistic celebration of the coffee houses, the freedom of thought and the social fluidity they encouraged, though, there were those who had reservations. The coffee houses were noted, for instance, for gambling on cards, dominoes and billiards and as places that encouraged sexual licentiousness. The coffee house was also, as the historian Mary Gluck put it, 'emphatically a Jewish-identified public space' as exemplified by, for instance, Kóbor's articles or *A kalábriász parti* [*The Card Game*], a one-act play by Antal Orozzi first performed in 1889 that celebrated the conversation of a group of Jewish regulars. Although usually performed by Jewish companies, there were fears among some Jews at the time that it promoted anti-Semitism. That would become an increasing problem as the political situation deteriorated at the end of the war.

Those characteristics, inevitably, shaped the football they produced – and Hungarian football, at least initially, had its roots in the coffee houses, which were rife with football debate. Ferencváros, for instance, would meet at – and for a time had to store their goalposts in – the Gebauer Coffee House, which offers one of the many theories for the origin of their colours. One of the founders of the club, Kornél Gabrovitz, was said to have been in love with the daughter of the owner of the Gebauer and to have asked her to choose the team kit. She opted, the story goes, for green to reflect the baize of the billiard tables in the coffee house and her favourite colour, lilac. After a few washes, though, the lilac faded to white, leaving the green and white they wear today.[20]

---

[20] This is the version given in Béla Nagy's 1995 book *Fradi – Football Century*. Another variant, perhaps the most plausible, has Ferencváros consciously replicating BTC, both in their official name, FTC, and in their colours. BTC wore white with red details and, it's suggested, Ferencváros opted to take white and the other colour of the Hungarian flag, green.

The location itself was a significant fact. In Britain, football tended to be discussed in pubs by men standing up with a pint in their hand. In the coffee houses, the tendency was for customers to sit down at a table, and so it became possible to illustrate tactical arguments using the simple props of a cup, a spoon or a sugar bowl. Once that level of abstraction was reached, it was a short step to begin drawing diagrams, something that would have seemed preposterous to most in Britain at the time. When the English footballing visionary and managerial great Herbert Chapman began organising tactical discussions with his Huddersfield Town team in the early 1920s, it was regarded as an outrageous eccentricity.

The background of those involved in the discussions was important as well. Football in Britain had begun in the universities but by the 1880s, after the coming of professionalism, had become an overwhelmingly working-class game. By the Danube, though, there was a great mix. While football was a predominantly male sport, photographs of the stands at early games show significant numbers of women, most dressed in fine clothes and extravagant hats. As the sociologist Péter Szegedi notes, ticket prices were so high that, for the majority of people, going to a match was a treat, certainly not, as it was in Britain, a routine to be engaged in every other Saturday.

Intellectuals and writers began to take football seriously and, although their understanding of football may not in essence have been any different to the pub-goers of Britain, they expressed it differently, in diagrams and abstract thought. That facilitated the transfer of knowledge and that, combined with a less conservative outlook and a mindset that was far less conditioned by decades of playing the game in a particular way, made Danubian football ripe for revolutionary theorising.

Yet the coffee houses were not the only influence on Hungarian football, and probably weren't even the most significant. It's striking how little direct evidence there is that the Budapest coffee houses were engaged in sophisticated tactical discussion, certainly by comparison with what was going on 150 miles up the Danube in Vienna where, by the end of the 1920s, coffee house writers were openly lobbying for certain players to be selected for the national team.[21]

That said, given how central football was to everyday life in Hungary,[22] it is inconceivable that there were not lengthy discussions in the coffee house about the game, but, as Péter Szegedi observed, what we don't know is to what extent they were talking about how to set about winning games.

For Szegedi, as he outlines in his book *Az első aranykor* [*The First Golden Age*], the greater reason Hungarian football developed as it did was the *grunds*, the lots left vacant as Budapest underwent rapid expansion where children would gather to play. These became venerated, most notably in Ferenc Molnár's 1906 novel *A Pál utcai fiúk* [*The Paul Street Boys*] which tells of a group of children who defend their *grund* from another gang that seeks to take it over. While some of the portrayal is clearly sentimentalised, certain *grunds* became so famous for the standard of football played on them that managers from major clubs would go there to scout young talent.

---

[21] See, for instance, Roman Horak and Wolfgang Maderthaner's essay 'A Culture of Urban Cosmopolitanism: Uridil and Sindelar as Viennese Coffee-House Heroes' in *European Heroes*, edited by Richard Holt, JA Mangan and Pierre Lanfranchi, (Routledge, 1996). Viennese coffee house engagement in football probably reached its apogee in Friedrich Torberg's poem 'Gedicht vom Tode eines Fussballers' (1945).

[22] The social historian Dániel Bolgár has put forward what he called his 'conflict theory', by which he argues that sporting success is driven by a manageable level of conflict within a circumscribed space. That is to say, the MTK–Ferencváros rivalry had serious roots – racial, religious and class-based – but was never taken so seriously that one side would take up arms against the other. For Bolgár, it was precisely the all-consuming nature of that 'conflict' that elevated football in Budapest.

The *grunds* were seen as the ideal environment to develop technique. 'That,' Ferenc Török wrote in his biography of Gyula Mándi, an MTK full-back who played 32 times for the national side, 'was because the cloth ball couldn't bounce and they had to guide it, dribble with it or shoot in a way that it would not or just hardly touch the sandy, uneven ground with grassy patches, otherwise it would have got stuck immediately.'[23]

But the *grunds* also taught character. 'Matches played at Tisza Kálmán tér provided my father and his mates with a fantastic basis for football,' said Attila Mándi, Gyula's son. 'Since the occasional teams only had a goalkeeper as an emergency player, almost everybody had to defend and attack, too. This also meant that nobody on the square could act like a star. If anybody put on an act, the others either excluded him or taught him a lesson pretty soon.'[24]

The similarity in the roughly contemporaneous development of football in Budapest and Buenos Aires at the time is striking. Both cities were undergoing rapid urbanisation, both came to lionise the vacant lots of the new city – *potreros*, as Argentinians call them – that encouraged technical virtuosity, and both were sustained by the rivalry between a team of the middle class (River Plate/MTK) and one of the working class (Boca Juniors/Ferencváros). Where they differed most, perhaps, was in their attitude to Britain: Argentinian football was set up in opposition to those who had taught them the game; Hungarian football happily followed where an enlightened British coach led.[25]

* * *

[23] Ferenc Török, *Mandula* (Nyik-Ki, 1999).

[24] Cited in Török, *Mandula*.

[25] For much more on the cultural origins of Argentinian football, see my book *Angels with Dirty Faces* (Orion, 2016).

The MTK squad Hogan inherited was formidable, featuring three of the all-time greats of the Hungarian game: Kálmán Konrád, Alfréd Schaffer and Imre Schlosser. To them, he added two teenagers who would become greats. Hogan was walking through Városliget in central Budapest one day when he saw György Orth and József 'Csibi' Braun kicking a ball about. 'They were studying English and were keen to speak to me to practise,' he explained. 'I pounced on them and said, "They are mine, my very own."'[26]

They weren't, or at least not immediately. Braun had been born into a large Jewish family in the northern village of Putnok, about 25 miles from Miskolc, in February 1901. His father Lőrinc (or possibly Lipót) was a trader in crops but subsequently moved to Budapest. There was an elder brother, Gyula, who was signed by Törekvés and moved to Vasas in 1917, while Braun was playing for VAC when he was spotted by Hogan.

Orth had been born two months later. He had never known his father and was raised by his mother, Marika Müller, and her sister-in-law, Térez Szántai, who was separated from her husband. Marika, who worked as a washerwoman, was 40 when Orth was born and had a ferociously close bond with her son. They were desperately poor: friends would share their lunch with Orth or he would not have eaten during the day and he was only able to complete primary school because neighbours clubbed together to pay for the books required for the final year.

Orth was the archetypal player from the *grund*. He played for a team called SKI that was sponsored by the owner of a coffee house on Aradi út, a man called Steiner, who would give them coffee and brioche as bonuses. 'The pillar of the team was Orth,' wrote Pál

---

[26] Cited in Fox, *Prophet or Traitor?*

Fekete in his 1962 biography.[27] 'It was amazing how this ordinary, soft-spoken boy, who immediately withdrew at the sound of a harsh word, transformed on the pitch. In his patched-up shirt he shook off all his inhibitions and feelings of anxiety when he made for goal with the match ball Steiner had given them… [He] stood out in the field even against those of his mates who were more muscular, older and more experienced than him. How come he had these skills at such a young age? It is hard to tell. Perhaps the boy, who was smart, eager to learn and industrious at school too, owed his versatility to the fact that he had a good grasp of things, a great sense of the ball and he practised continually.'

SKI became Terézvárosi Sport Kör and, when Orth was 12, they played a game against another *grund* team called Nemzeti Sport Ifjak for the coveted prize of a real ball. The game finished 3–3, but NSI decided to give the ball to Orth, who had scored a hat-trick. Orth moved from team to team. He played for a club called Sunderland[28] on Fáskör Grund, the legendary venue for youth games at the corner of István út and Aréna út (today Dózsa György út and Ajtósi Dürer sor). Orth then joined Erzsébetváros Athletic Club (EAK) and, in the summer of 1915, when Orth was 14, they played against MTK.

On the sideline stood Sándor Reiner, the manager of Vasas, who was renowned for his capacity to identify talent from the *grunds*. MTK's leadership asked him whom he was watching, but he refused to answer. Within a few minutes it was obvious. Alfréd Brüll asked the club doctor to find out the name of the tall blond boy – he was already almost six feet – who was running the game.

---

[27] Pál Fekete, *Orth és társai* (Sport, 1963).

[28] His future MTK teammates György Molnár and Vilmos Nyúl were also in the side.

The doctor told the club manager to ask Reiner but when he did, Reiner shrugged, pretending he'd never seen him before. When the MTK directors retired to a nearby restaurant for tea, Reiner signed Orth for Vasas.

The family moved to Terézváros, where they lived in a one-room flat. At least in their new accommodation, though, they had two beds, rather than sharing one, and a sofa as well as the trough in which Orth's mother washed clothes, an occupation that left her back permanently bent. To help them out, Reiner arranged for her to wash Vasas's kit from time to time. That December, Orth's side reached the final of the Vaslabda championship, a youth tournament played twice during the war for the prize of an iron football [the *vaslabda* after which the championship was named], but he was sent off for throwing a ball in the face of the referee.

Soon Orth was called up to the first team, for a game against FVTK, only to be dismissed 20 minutes into his debut; the romantic version of the story says he deliberately got himself sent off because he hadn't wanted to betray his teammates at youth level by leaving them behind. It wasn't long, though, before he had moved even further away, joining MTK. It was a move that saved his mother from penury, securing for her during the difficult days of the First World War regular deliveries of flour, sugar and coal. The club president, Alfréd Brüll, meanwhile, paid for Orth to complete his education, then found him a position in a bank. For many footballers, that was an honorific position, but Orth seems to have taken the job seriously, arriving at his desk in the correspondence department at 8am sharp and making up the time when he had to leave early for training.

Orth made his debut for MTK on 1 July 1917 and that November he was called up to the Hungary national side for the first time.

Braun had played his first game for MTK two weeks before Orth. He was a rapid right-winger and also a fine header of the ball, a player of supreme physical gifts who could run 100m in 11.8 seconds (at a time when the world record was 10.6s) and jump 6.06 metres (when the world long jump record was 7.61m).[29]

'They were both intelligent lads attending high school in Budapest,' Hogan said. 'Every day after school I had them on the field, instructing them in the art of the game. The Hungarians mature very quickly and they soon moved into the MTK first team.'[30]

Hogan led MTK to the title in 1916–17 and 1917–18, but trophies were only part of it. Braun and Orth were typical of a football culture that was keen to learn, free of the preconceptions and scepticism about self-improvement that even then were beginning to hamper the English game, and Hogan was keen to teach.

Blessed with great players and a fertile environment, Hogan nurtured a radical football culture in Budapest, from which grew one of the greatest national sides of all time, the *Aranycsapat*. Asked, after their 6–3 win at Wembley in 1953, how Hungarian football had become so good, Sándor Barcs, the head of the Hungary delegation, replied, 'You had better go back 30 years to the time your Jimmy Hogan came to teach us how to play.'

But it wasn't just the Hungarians who benefited. The players and coaches who grew up in the Budapest of the 1920s and 1930s, driven abroad by political and economic turmoil, curiosity and, in some cases, anti-Semitism, would have a profound influence over the global development of the game. The ideas that continue to drive football today were developed in Budapest in the 1920s and spread by that diaspora. Whether it began with an Austrian policeman's

---

[29] Details recorded in *Nemzeti Sport*, 9 January 1941.
[30] Cited in Fox, *Prophet or Traitor?*

knock at the door, a player frustrated by his manager's lack of interest in his determination to learn or a young Mancunian quitting his job in search of better things, it is a story that impinges on every major football nation.

CHAPTER THREE
REVOLT INTO STYLE

From its very early days, MTK had been a club with a clear sense of identity, a team that was stylish as well as successful, a team that lived in the memory for how it played long after the results of specific games had been forgotten. Self-image is often self-perpetuating – this thing is characteristic of us, and therefore it is good, and therefore we will continue to do it – and as Péter Szegedi noted, MTK's middle-class origins perhaps naturally inclined it to a version of football that privileged style over sweat.

But there were also more practical reasons. MTK's first match against foreign opposition came in April 1903, when they played the Southern League champions Southampton. It might not seem a particularly auspicious occasion given the game was played, the club secretary Henrik Fodor remembered, 'in pouring rain and an icy, freezing cold wind' and ended 15–0 to Southampton, but 'the defeat had a productive effect on the young team so eager to be taught, since it was from this excellent English team that they first saw and learned playing with short, flat passes, which in turn made them able to perform so excellently years later'.[1]

---

[1] In *25 év. A Magyar Testgyakorlók Köre története 1888–1913*, ed. Henrik Fodor (Minerva, 1913).

Another major factor was Imre Pozsonyi, one of the early greats of the sport in Hungary. He played for a Hungary national side in 1901 in games against Richmond (lost 4–0) and Surrey Wanderers (lost 5–1), and then in a 5–0 defeat to Austria in Vienna in 1902, becoming one of the early stalwarts of the MTK midfield. Pozsonyi seems to have given up playing the game in 1903, when he was just 23, and trained as a referee, becoming in the seasons that followed one of the most respected officials in the country. He later developed into a successful coach, winning a Polish championship with Cracovia in 1921, a Catalunyan championship and the Copa del Rey with Barcelona in 1924–25 and Yugoslav titles with Građanski Zagreb in 1926 and 1928. He subsequently worked with the Mexican side Real Club España before moving to New York where he died in 1932.

Pozsonyi had seen English teams play in Vienna and Prague and appears very early to have been fascinated by the mechanics of the game. He instilled his ideas at MTK, with the heavy defeat to Southampton reinforcing the wisdom of what he was saying.

MTK ended up third in that 1903 season, but already their style was being recognised as something different and perhaps more sophisticated than that practised by other teams in Hungary. 'MTK owe their success solely to the fact that the team puts the emphasis only on team-play and always works with flat passes,' wrote Mihály Baross in one of a series of articles in *Nemzeti Sport* around the turn of 1903–04 that considered tactics.[2] He picked out Pozsonyi and Jenő Károly, who later managed Juventus, for particular praise.

This approach meant that 'MTK are the slowest among the Hungarian teams,' he said, an obvious contrast to the chaotic style of just a few years earlier. 'The principle that if you can't take the

---

[2] This quote and the one that follows from *Nemzeti Sport*, 24 January 1904.

ball, push the player over had too many followers at the beginning,' Baross wrote. 'A great weight, when it took on a lighter team, totally squashed them and paralysed all kinds of combinations.'[3]

Baross concluded that the 1904 championship would probably be won by Ferencváros or BTC. 'However,' he added, 'the teams that are developing a passing style, namely MFC, MTK, the 33s and MAC are becoming more and more dangerous opponents for the old, proven teams.'[4] He was more right than he knew and MTK went on to win the league that year.

It was from that team that the legend of MTK grew. The journalist Lajos Pánczél, for instance, wrote in a typically lyrical piece in *Ujság* in May 1931 of the reverie into which he was plunged in the restaurant car of a train heading for Zurich by the mention of the name of probably the greatest MTK player of the pre-First World War years, the centre-half Dori Kürschner.

'The name heard so long ago,' Pánczél said, 'makes memories flash through my mind, those of the old great MTK: Kertész I,[5] Révész, Csüdör, Domonkos, Károly, Béla Sebestyén and ... Dóri Kürschner. The more intense the remembering, the clearer the picture I get of the figure of the first great centre-half of Hungarian football – or as chroniclers of football have concluded – of the first thinking footballer, who retired from playing when he was at the peak of his skills.'[6]

Kürschner was born in June 1885, although whether in Budapest or Austria is unclear.[7] Between the ages of six and 16 he went to

---

[3] *Nemzeti Sport*, 27 December 1903.

[4] *Nemzeti Sport*, 24 January 1904.

[5] There is a habit in early Hungarian football of differentiating players who shared a surname not by use of their forenames but by giving them a number.

[6] *Ujság*, 21 May 1931.

[7] It wasn't until October 1895 that a law was passed stipulating that all births had to be officially registered, and as he was a Jew there is no record of baptism.

school in Austria and in 1901 his family moved to Budapest. 'I was an *echt* German when I came to Pest and I thought I would never learn to speak Hungarian,' he said. 'But I started to speak it while playing and unconsciously, without even noticing it, whatever they had beaten into me in the Austrian school during those ten years there was killed by passion for the Hungarian teams and I am more Hungarian in my soul than I am in my tongue.'[8]

Football was a constant for him from an early age. 'First, I kicked every peach stone, then I kicked my cap and after lots of kernels and all kinds of things I kicked a size 3 ball,' he said. 'But how many missed afternoon teas this first size 3 ball cost me and how many little joys of life I sacrificed for it.

'My first bitter experience was the realisation that sometimes incessant attacking is harmful and has sad consequences. What happened was... our team had a great advantage over the other one so the goalkeeper – imitating the English way[9] – was camping out somewhere on the imaginary halfway line. But when very late at night we wanted to go home, we fell into despair as we realised that during

---

[8] This quote and those in subsequent paragraphs taken from *Sporthírlap*, 25 December 1910.

[9] This is, at first sight, a slightly surprising observation. Certainly by the time Hungary beat England 6–3 at Wembley in 1953, Hungarian goalkeepers were regarded as being far more adventurous and far more prepared to leave the confines of the six-yard box than their line-bound English counterparts. Before 1912, though, when the law was amended so that goalkeepers could handle the ball only in their own box rather than anywhere in their own half, there were some goalkeepers, most notably Leigh Richmond Roose of Stoke City, Sunderland and Wales, who were famed for their willingness to bounce the ball up to the halfway line to initiate attacks. It may be that the Roose-style goalkeepers were not quite so unusual as is often considered. For more on the evolution of goalkeepers, see my book *The Outsider* (Orion, 2012); for more on Roose specifically, see Spencer Vignes's biography, *Lost in France* (History Press, 2007).

our ongoing attacks the clothes we had put down as goals – the best part of which was my beautiful brown shoes – had been stolen!

'However, even as I was getting all the punishment for the many ruined shoes I was still daydreaming about playing on the Mili one day.' The 'Mili' was the Millenáris, the home of football in the city, where BTC had played that first game against the Cricket Club of Vienna in 1897 and where a Hungary national side had played Richmond and Surrey Wanderers.

Kürschner started playing for Erdőtelki FE, a small Budapest club with a ground on Lehel út. One afternoon in the summer of 1903, he was spotted by Imre Pozsonyi who, perhaps already contemplating the end of his own career, eased Kürschner's passage to MTK, where he started out in 1903 playing as a left-winger for the reserves. The following season, though, he was elevated to the first team, replacing Pozsonyi for a 2–0 win over MAC (the Magyar Atlétikai Club) on Margitsziget, the island in the Danube between the Margit and Árpád Bridges. 'He is very young and slightly built,' said the report in *Ujság*, 'but he already shows the signs of being a classy player.'[10]

Like all footballers in the amateur era, he was forced to take on a trade and in 1911 he and his MTK teammate Gyula Kertész set up a photographic studio.[11] They had a number of photographs published in *Sportvilág*, but the studio closed the following year and Kürschner began selling sporting goods.[12]

Kürschner won two league titles with MTK before leaving the club when John Tait Robertson did in September 1912. He joined Aradi AC, a team based in what is now Oradea in north-western Romania that was, effectively, an unofficial professional club, playing

---

[10] *Ujság*, 21 March 1904.
[11] Confirmed in *Fővárosi Közlöny* [*Official Journal of Budapest*], 26 September 1911.
[12] Reported in *Vasarnápi Ujság*.

exhibition games for money. Kürschner spent at least a year there, but what he did during the war is less clear. At some point he returned to Budapest, and may even have been working with Hogan as coach of a team that was by then packed with stars.

The biggest of them was the centre-forward Alfréd Schaffer, the 'Football King', who had joined from BAK in 1914. He wasn't quick but he had a remarkable capacity to read the game, which meant that he was able to get away with spending much of his time off the pitch in coffee houses, bars and restaurants. In 89 games for MTK over five seasons, he scored 154 goals. 'His former teammates talk about him as "a statue",' a later profile said, 'to whom you could pass from 30m as he stood out on the pitch.'[13]

Schaffer would become a mystery in his death, but he was also a mystery in his birth. Although it's widely believed that he was born in Bratislava (at the time known as Pozsony; the modern name was only coined after the First World War) on 13 February 1893 and that his parents moved to Budapest while he was very young, research by Gyula Pataki for the television channel Digi Sport suggests that he was actually born in the Hungarian capital (specifically Óbuda) on 19 February that year, while his gravestone, in the Bavarian spa town of Prien am Chiemsee, lists his birthplace as Budapest. What is known is that Schaffer's father, Károly, was an ironmonger from the village of Rusca Montană (Ruszkabánya in Hungarian) in what is now Caraș-Severin county in south-western Romania. Both Károly and Schaffer's mother, Maria Streitmann, were ethnic Germans and Schaffer spoke German at home. He was one of five brothers, two of whom died in childhood.

'For me,' said Bruno Kreisky, who was chancellor of Austria between 1970 and 1983 and watched the forward play at Wiener

---

[13] *Nemzeti Sport*, 10 July 1935.

Amateure in the 1920s, 'Schaffer was a role model. From the way he kept the ball until someone was better placed and then passed it on so the other player could be successful, I learned a lot. You don't always have to do it yourself, you should be good enough to prepare someone else's success.'[14]

Photographs show Schaffer as a heavy-set figure, his hair variously scraped down to his head or springing up in unruly curls, and other than a confidence to his stare, there is little about his appearance to suggest the evident force of his personality. Schaffer was a difficult man, pernickety and quick to anger, and not afraid to let others know what he thought. He demanded high standards, and was rendered tolerable by the fact that he himself usually lived up to them – and that he was very good company. He was not only a great footballer but also an extremely good cook, as attested by a number of players in Hungary's 1938 World Cup squad who tasted the calf stew he cooked for them in Lille, when he was assistant coach to the national side.

'He makes you laugh,' explained a profile in *Nemzeti Sport* in 1935. 'He is a great storyteller, with strong charisma. He has a great sense of humour. It is not a finessed, polished and sharpened humour, but a sincere one, not from the mind but from the heart. When smoking cigars, he chooses from among his stories. He says he could tell anecdotes for six weeks without stopping... This man has an aura. He made half of it with his foot, half with his personality.'[15]

An interview in the hugely popular *Színházi Élet* [*Theatre Life*] magazine gives some indication of his character. 'I am a bohemian,' he said. 'I divide women into two groups. The first is those who are unavailable to me. They are of no interest to me, as I do not sigh in

---

[14] Cited in the APA story, 'Euro 2016: *Alfréd Schaffer: Ein schillernder Legionär aus Ungarn*', 10 June 2016.
[15] *Nemzeti Sport*, 10 July 1935.

vain. The second is those who are available to me, and I deal only with them. From this group, there has never been a single person from whom I received a rejection, because even if there's a remote chance of a rejection, that lady is assigned to the first group.'[16] In November 1920, he had become engaged to a woman called Olga Bernstein, whose father owned a factory in Munich manufacturing cigar- and cigarette-holders. They never married.

The magazine asked if he was happy with his life. 'If I don't think about it, then yes,' he replied, presumably jokingly. 'But sometimes, when I'm bored, I remember how terrible it is that I have nothing to worry about, that I have everything I want, that I have no unreachable goals in my hands. In those moments, I am truly bored and I tinker with the idea of ending it, of stopping playing, but then I remember my mother and go to training.'

Then there was Imre Schlosser. With his high forehead and unconvincing moustache, he too doesn't look much of an athlete but he remains statistically the greatest goalscorer in Hungarian history, 13 times a league champion and seven times the league's top scorer. Schlosser began on the *grunds*, playing for teams called Aston Villa and Remény [Hope] before signing for Ferencváros in 1906 at the age of 17. He scored a barely credible 215 goals in 129 games for them before walking out on the club after they had denied his family additional complimentary tickets for a game. In the argument that followed, a director called him 'a puppy', at which he decided to punish the club by joining MTK. 'I secretly shed a lot of tears for the abandoned green-and-white colours,' Schlosser later admitted. 'I still admire them and it will remain that way. It's easy to understand because I really got to know the true spirit of the club and my football

---

[16] *Színházi Élet*, Issue 43, 1925.

career came from there. I always felt real joy when I put the green-and-white striped shirt on.'

So scandalous was his move considered that questions were asked about it in parliament. The incident was indicative of Schlosser's temper, which had boiled over two years previously at the notorious 1913 Hungarian Cup final, when he was part of a Ferencváros side that also included István Tóth and Jenő Medgyessy. Playing a BAK team featuring Schaffer, Schlosser was enraged by a blow from an opposing player called Ludwig,[17] and he kicked out at the midfielder Kálmán Szury for which he was extremely fortunate to avoid dismissal. Ferencváros won 2–1, but on the pitch after the final whistle, Schlosser's wife insulted the fiancée of the BAK goalkeeper Ferenc György, who then sought Schlosser out in the dressing room. Schlosser responded aggressively, but took a punch squarely to the chin, after which his teammates bundled György from the room. The furore was so great that news of it reached London, where the *Daily Mirror* ran a cartoon imagining the Hungarian take on other sports: men battering each other over the head with croquet mallets, tennis racquets and billiard cues while a golfer tries to tee off as his opponent bites his calf.

It wasn't just Ferencváros who were upset by Schlosser's move. So too was Schaffer, put out by the fact that he was no longer the obvious star at MTK. The two had been on good enough terms to use the informal 'you' but when Schlosser bumped into Schaffer in the Kristály Café after signing his contract with MTK, his new

---

[17] This player remains a mystery. Even Tamás Dénes, Mihály Sándor and Éva B Bába's magisterial five-volume history of Hungarian football, *A magyar labdarúgás története* (Campus, 2016), cannot provide a forename, while his only other appearance in any newspaper is a five-line report in *Sporthírlap* on 17 February 1913 detailing BAK's 3–0 defeat to MAC, in which he was sent off in the second half.

teammate coldly used the formal pronoun. From then on, their relationship remained frosty.

On the pitch, though, the combination worked and MTK scored goals at an extraordinary rate. By the time Schlosser left MTK for WAC in 1922, he had scored a further 135 goals in 115 games. He remains the all-time leading scorer in Hungarian league history, while his international career brought 58 goals in 68 games. Having Schlosser, Schaffer and the subtly skilled Kálmán Konrád in the same forward line, supplied by Orth and Braun, was preposterous. In that 1917–18 title-winning campaign, MTK dropped a single point in their 22 league games, scoring 147 goals and conceding just ten.

When the war was over, Hogan returned to Lancashire, where he took a job in Liverpool, working as a dispatch foreman for Walker's Tobacco. With a wife and three children to support, though, money was tight and Hogan was advised to ask for a handout from the Football Association, which had established a fund to support professionals financially disadvantaged by the war years.

Perhaps his instincts would always have led him abroad, but what made sure he would abandon England was the FA's response to his application. He believed he was due £200 and borrowed £5 to cover his travelling expenses to London. The FA secretary Frederick Wall, though, disdainfully told him that the fund was for those who had actually fought. Hogan pointed out that he had been interned and had had no opportunity to sign up. Wall gave him three pairs of khaki socks, sneering that 'the boys at the front were very glad of those'. Hogan was furious and never forgave the FA. Within weeks he had moved to Switzerland and taken charge of Young Boys of Bern.

* * *

When Archduke Franz Ferdinand was assassinated in 1914, Austro-Hungary had a population of 52 million spread over a little more than a quarter of a million square miles. Hungary itself comprised 21 million people and around 125,000 square miles. The prime minister, Count István Tisza, hesitated but joined the war on the side of the Central Powers after Germany had promised to neutralise the Kingdom of Romania. The multi-ethnic Austro-Hungarian army largely fought on the Italian and Eastern Fronts, with around 350,000 Hungarian nationals being killed.

With the war effectively lost, on 25 October 1918 an opposition National Council was founded by Count Mihály Károlyi, whose scepticism towards the conflict had given him popular appeal. In the early hours of the morning of 31 October 1918, pro-Károlyi protesters wearing asters seized public buildings. They were backed by sections of the army; the post office, for instance, was overrun by a group of soldiers led by the BAK midfielder Ernő Erbstein. This was what became known as the Aster Revolution.

The prime minister Sándor Wekerle was forced to resign and Tisza, the former prime minister, was murdered. The following day, the last emperor, Charles I, in his capacity as king of Hungary,[18] appointed a coalition government led by Károlyi. He headed a Provisional Government until 16 November, when the Hungarian Democratic Republic was proclaimed.

Károlyi turned out to lack anything like the diplomatic or political skill required to cope with extraordinarily difficult circumstances. His first big mistake, perhaps, was to give in to suggestions within his own cabinet that, because the Armistice had been signed between Austro-Hungary and the Allies, it was necessary for an independent

---

[18] He was King Charles IV of Hungary.

Hungary to sign a fresh agreement. At a meeting in Belgrade with the Allied Commander in the Balkans, General Louis Franchet d'Espèrey, he found himself treated with contempt, and far harsher terms imposed than had been in the initial Armistice. Even more misguided was his decision on taking power to disband the Hungarian armed forces in line with his pacifist beliefs. That left Hungary unable to defend itself through the winter of 1918–19 as Romania, Yugoslavia and Czechoslovakia helped themselves to more territory.

With no formal peace treaty in place, the Allies maintained a blockade, worsening food shortages that were exacerbated by an influx of refugees from Transylvania and Galicia. To make matters even worse, the creation of Czechoslovakia blocked the supply lines of coal from Germany, leading to energy shortages. That in turn meant the railways could no longer function, which had a devastating impact on industry, leading to mass unemployment and spiralling inflation.

Domestically, Károlyi was repeatedly undermined by the Social Democratic Party, who blocked his attempts to transfer rural lands into the ownership of peasants, so the only land transfer that ended up taking place was the property he gave away from his own estate to set an example to others. Sigmund Freud, living in Vienna at the time, was in no doubt that the murder of Tisza and the accession of Károlyi were terrible missteps. 'I was certainly no adherent of the *ancien regime,*' he wrote in a letter to the Hungarian psychoanalyst Sándor Ferenczi, 'but it seems doubtful to me whether it is a sign of political shrewdness to beat to death the smartest of the many counts and to make the stupidest one president.'[19]

---

[19] Sigmund Freud; Sándor Ferenczi; Eva Brabant; Ernst Falzeder; Patrizia Giampieri-Deutsch, *The Correspondence of Sigmund Freud and Sándor Ferenczi, Volume 2: 1914–19* (Harvard University Press, 1993).

In January 1919, Károlyi reversed his decision on the army and began to build up troops again as he considered an alliance with Russia. In March, the French army ordered Hungarian forces to retreat from their advanced positions. That was seen as a sign that the borders would be pushed back when a peace treaty was finally signed, which placed Károlyi in an impossible position, unable either to accept or resist the French demand. The prime minister Dénes Berinkey resigned on 21 March, at which Károlyi announced that only the Social Democrats could form a new government. Unbeknown to him, though, the Social Democrats had merged with the Communists led by Béla Kun. Later that day, they announced the resignation of Károlyi and the foundation of the Hungarian Soviet Republic.

Technically, the government was led by the president Sándor Garbai, a Social Democrat, but power lay in the hands of Kun, the commissar for foreign affairs who remained in regular contact with Lenin. In March, Kun began a purge of Social Democrats as he sought to establish a 'dictatorship of the proletariat'. Inevitably, that led to conflict and violence. A failed coup attempt on 24 June was followed by what became known as the Red Terror: widespread reprisals including the execution by revolutionary tribunals of anybody suspected of involvement with the coup.

Kun had promised to restore the historical boundaries of Hungary, hoping for Russian help. With the Bolsheviks still fighting a civil war, though, that was not forthcoming. Nonetheless, the Hungarian Red Army marched into what is now Slovakia and planned a campaign to reclaim land from Romania. There were early successes in the north, but having driven back Czechoslovakian troops, the army proclaimed not a new boundary but the Slovakian Soviet Republic. That was perceived as a betrayal by nationalists both in the army and at home. With morale plummeting, Hungarian lines were breached by the

Romanians on 30 July. Kun and other leading Communists fled, and Romanian troops arrived in Budapest on 6 August.

A counter-revolutionary nationalist government had been operating in Szeged in the south of the country since 19 May and in the vacuum it claimed power. On 16 November, Admiral Miklós Horthy, one of the commanders of the National Army, entered Budapest riding a white horse. A lifelong naval officer, Horthy had ended the First World War as commander of the Austro-Hungarian fleet.

The National government instigated what became known as the White Terror, launching reprisals against those perceived to have backed Kun's regime. As Kun's father and many leading Communists had been Jewish,[20] Jews were an easy scapegoat, blamed not only for the Red Terror but also for defeat in the First World War.[21] A tide of anti-Semitism was unleashed.

However much the position of Jews had improved in Hungary in the late 19th century, it would be misleading to suggest that anti-Semitism had somehow disappeared. When the lawyer Győző Istóczy felt his appointment as a judge had been hampered by Jews in the 1860s, for instance, he campaigned for parliament on an expressly anti-Semitic platform. After being elected to the Diet in 1872, he

---

[20] Seventeen of the 30 People's Commissars of the Hungarian-Soviet Republic were Jewish, while eight of the 20 members of Károlyi's National Council had been, so claims that Kun's government was disproportionately Jewish were only partially true. The link between Communism and Judaism wasn't entirely specious though. Karl Marx was of Jewish descent – both his grandfathers had been rabbis – and, whatever anti-Semitism the far left would later perpetrate, as Orlando Figes points out in *A People's Tragedy*, his history of the Russian Revolution, at least at first Marxism was attractive to Jews because of its transnational nature; precisely, in other words, the aspect that turned Hungarian nationalists against Kun's government.

[21] This despite the fact that at least 10,000 Jews had been among the Hungarian dead.

called on the Ottomans to offer up land in Palestine for the establishment of a Jewish state so that Hungary could deport its Jews or at least encourage them to emigrate.

Istóczy was the public face of a more widespread undercurrent. When the body of a 14-year-old girl was found on the banks of the River Tisza in 1882, it was rumoured that she'd been killed by Jews who needed her blood to practise secret rituals – a variation of the blood libel that had been levelled at Jews for centuries. Three Jews were accused and although they were eventually acquitted 18 months later, the incident led to riots in Budapest in 1883. Istóczy then established the Anti-Semitic National Party which received 14 mandates in elections a year later.

There was also an unfocused late-19th-century economic anti-Semitism that associated Jews with the negative aspects of capitalism and industrialisation. Scott Spector, professor of History and Germanic Languages and Literature at the University of Michigan, argues that the very notion of a Jewish modernity was initially anti-Semitic and associated the perceived decadence of the age, as manifested in the coffee houses, with the supposed inherent racial characteristics of Jews.[22] Károly Nendtvich, a professor at the Higher Technical School in Budapest, for instance, wrote explicitly about the corrosive effect of the 'greed' of Jewish doctors and lawyers. The rise of a cheap mass-circulation press meant these ideas were disseminated like never before.

White Terror units went from village to village seeking Jews and Communists to murder. The worst atrocities came after Budapest had fallen to the National Army in 1919. Many fled but it's estimated around 1,000 Jews were slaughtered.

---

[22] In 'Modernism without Jews: A Counter-Historical Argument' *Modernism/Modernity* 14, no 4 (2006).

Although the frenzy of violence subsided, the atmosphere had changed. Horthy's government had, on 4 June 1920, agreed the Treaty of Trianon, by which Hungary surrendered two-thirds of its pre-war territory as borders were redrawn, theoretically along ethnic lines although there was clearly also a significant element of political expediency as neighbouring countries claimed cities and railway lines. The result was that more than 3 million ethnic Hungarians, around a third of the total, ended up living outside Hungary. There was a significant economic impact as well, with vast quantities of raw materials lost to Hungary.

The following month, Horthy appointed as prime minister Count Pál Teleki, a distinguished ethnographer whose maps had been used in the redrawing of the borders.[23] In 1920 the Hungarian Parliament passed the *numerus clausus* law, the first anti-Semitic legislation in post-World War I Europe. It stipulated that the ethnic make-up of universities should mirror that of the population as a whole and insisted that no new students should be accepted into universities unless they were 'loyal from the national and moral standpoint'. That the law was aimed at reducing Jewish influence over those professions that required a degree to practise was clear, as was the impact: the proportion of Jews at the Budapest Institute of Sciences fell from 34 per cent in 1913 to 8 per cent in 1925.[24]

Teleki's government also began a programme of land reform, dividing almost 1,500 square miles from large estates into smaller holdings to quell rural discontent. Teleki's government fell in March 1921 after Charles, the former emperor of Austria and king of Hungary, tried to reassume the throne. That split the right between

[23] Not to be confused with the Bocskai forward of the same name who played for Hungary at the 1934 World Cup and also won one cap for Romania.

[24] Cited in Bolchover, *The Greatest Comeback*.

conservatives who favoured a Habsburg restoration and nationalists who sought the election of a new Hungary-born king.

Count István Bethlen, a conservative affiliated to neither side, took advantage of the dispute to seize power as leader of a new Party of National Unity. A skilful political operator, who rigged rural elections and promoted his own supporters to key civil service positions, he ended the campaign against the Jews by offering pay-offs and government jobs to the radical anti-Semites, and brought the Social Democrats and trades unions onside by legalising them in return for promises not to call strikes or mobilise the peasants. By so doing he created an unlikely alliance of Jewish industrialists and the old Hungarian gentry that the historian Ignác Romsics suggests delayed the development of fascism in Hungary by a decade.[25] As Bethlen sought to end his country's international isolation, Hungary joined the League of Nations in 1922.

Nonetheless, such was the perception of danger even as late as 1922 that Sigmund Freud banned his daughter Anna from travelling to Hungary for fear of anti-Semitism. 'Papa is, as far as Budapest is concerned, completely intractable,' Anna wrote to her friend Kata Lévy. 'He prophesies, as I want to travel there, all evil from declarations of war to persecution of Jews and will not let me go.'[26]

Yet anti-Semitism in Hungary remains a complex subject. Despite the legislation, the vast majority of Jews clearly felt comfortable in Budapest once the White Terror was over. So profound had the process of assimilation been in the 19th century, in fact, that even to speak of a separate Jewish identity in Hungary can be misleading.

---

[25] Ignác Romsics, *Bethlen István. Politikai életrajz 1874–1946* (Magyarságkutató Intézet, 1991).

[26] Letter from Anna Freud to Kata Lévy, 2 July 1922, Freud Museum London, BL/02/012.

Hungary had always been a multi-ethnic country: Jews were one group among many, albeit a wealthy and well-educated one that some found it convenient to blame for various ills and some thought too influential in certain aspects of culture. That there was an underlying anti-Semitism in certain quarters is undeniable but, at that stage, the practical impact on the lives of Hungarians was limited.

* * *

After Hogan's departure, MTK turned to one of the greats of their past and appointed Dori Kürschner. MTK again romped to the title, winning 18 of their 22 games and scoring 116 goals. That summer, 1919, MTK went on a tour of Austria and Germany, beginning with a match in late June against Rapid Vienna and ending in August in Karlsruhe. For many, it was a welcome respite from the turmoil at home and, as the tour went on, more and more players joined local clubs and the travelling party became gradually smaller. Kalmán Konrád and his brother Jenő were both signed for Wiener Amateure by Hugo Meisl, as was the half-back Péter Szabó, although he seems only to have played one league game for them before moving to Nürnberg.

Even as they were shedding players, it was obvious how good MTK were. There was a printers' strike when they played in Munich, leading the Bayern president Kurt Landauer to send horse-drawn carts through the streets bearing hand-drawn posters advertising the game, but still a record 10,000-strong crowd turned up at Marbachstraße to watch MTK win 7–1. 'The visitors have developed a wonderful technique,' the *Münchner Neueste Nachrichten* reported. 'Their playing ability is exemplary in every way. They are unmistakably fast in both their running and their treatment of the ball.'[27]

---

[27] Cited in Dieter Schulze-Marmeling, *Der FC Bayern, seine Juden und die Nazis* (Werkstatt, 2013).

Bayern decided then that they had to adapt to the Danubian school. 'All those who have seen MTK play,' the journalist Walther Bensemann wrote in *Kicker*, 'will have realised that there is currently no continental club that comes so close to the playing strength of the English league clubs... The class of Hungarians is dazzling... [It's like] the Scottish game with all its finesse and precise ball handling.'[28]

Alfréd Schaffer was the player who really caught the eye and he signed for Nürnberg on the strength of his performance. 'The player,' *Sporthírlap* noted tartly, 'who was always merry and had a somewhat adventurous nature, probably did not need a lot of convincing to stay on German soil. From what we have heard, he was offered a well-paid job, which soon convinced him that Nuremberg was the right place for him.'[29]

Four months later, *Sporthírlap* ran a feature on 'the beautiful days' being enjoyed in Germany by Schaffer and Szabó. 'They live so well in Nuremberg that they do not even think about coming home,' it said. 'They rent a delightful apartment, live like princes, spend their time on the development of their physical and spiritual well-being. They don't go to offices; they deal only with football. The way of life Schaffer and Szabó have, without any ordinary source of income, confirms the assumption that the two players ... make their living only from football.'[30]

Kürschner also left MTK's tour to stay in Germany, joining Stuttgarter Kickers for a monthly salary of 1,000 marks and a bonus of 3,000 marks if he won the regional championship. There was a palpable sense not merely of talent being lost but also a legacy being wasted – not that anybody could really blame players or coaches for

---

[28] Cited in Dieter Schulze-Marmeling, *Der FC Bayern, seine Juden und die Nazis*.

[29] *Sporthírlap*, 1 September 1919.

[30] *Sporthírlap*, 16 February 1920.

seeking better money and a more stable life away from Budapest. As *Sporthírlap* said, 'It is going to take a lot of experimenting for [MTK] to finalise a permanent team.'[31]

And yet MTK did continue to prosper. In part that was because the club's allure meant they could continue to attract players. In 1919, for instance, they signed the 20-year-old full-back Gyula Mándi, who had grown frustrated at his inability to break into the Ferencváros first team. Noted for his positional sense and passing ability, and sporting a widow's peak that would become more pronounced as the years went by, he would be a stalwart for 18 years. Although not a star like Schaffer or Orth, Mándi nonetheless married an actress from the National Theatre, Edit Fazekas. He was prone to jealousy and, after hearing that the famous actor Árpád Lehotay had made approaches to her, went to see him and laid him out with a single punch. At the end of that season, he removed his wife from the National Theatre.

In 1921, after the centre-half Ferenc Nyúl had departed for the Romanian club Hagibor Cluj (Kolozsvár), MTK replaced him with the elegant Béla Guttmann, who would go on to become perhaps the most highly regarded Hungarian coach of all time. A difficult, irascible personality, he had been born in Budapest in 1899 to Abrahám and Eszter, who had moved to the capital from Tiszaszalka, a village in the north-east of the country. Abrahám worked as a clerk in a lamp factory and then he and his wife set up a dance school. They were far from wealthy. As a child, Guttmann later recalled, he often went around 'with empty pockets and a hungry stomach'.[32] When he was 16, he qualified as a dance instructor.

Football, though, was the stronger draw and, in 1917, at the age of 18, he joined his elder brother Ármin at Törekvés, a club based

---

[31] *Sporthírlap*, 1 September 1919.
[32] In *Régi gólok, edzősorsok* (Lapkiadó Vállalat, 1984).

on the railway industry (the name means 'endeavour' or 'aspiration'). Guttmann slotted into the half line before the White Terror forced their flight to Novi Sad (Újvidek in Hungarian). Although Vojvodina, the territory of which it was capital, had been ceded to Yugoslavia at the Treaty of Trianon, it was still predominantly Hungarian-speaking and its football still fell under the jurisdiction of the Hungarian Football Federation (Magyar Labdarúgó Szövetség – MLSZ). While there, working at the dance studio he and his brother had established, Guttmann played in a handful of friendlies for Újvideki AC and also turned out in a league game for Pécsi MFC.

That became problematic when he moved back to Budapest in 1921 as the violence receded, because the regulations stipulated that nobody could play for more than one club in the same season. Guttmann joined MTK and seems to have hoped nobody had noticed his game for Pécs. The MLSZ, though, had. Guttmann was summoned before a disciplinary commission and was fortunate to get away with a warning. It would be far from his last clash with the authorities.

Guttmann made his international debut against Germany that year, one of eight MTK players in the XI, and scored in a 3–0 win. But when Nyúl returned from Romania, Guttmann lost his place at MTK and, on 28 January 1922, the day after his 23rd birthday, his transfer to the Viennese club Hakoah was announced. 'I was in a terrible financial situation,' he subsequently explained. 'I didn't have any sure source of income. Back then MTK didn't pay their players enough to make ends meet. I spent many a sleepless night tossing on my pillows asking myself, "What will happen to me? What kind of future am I going to have?" These were questions that I couldn't answer then. I was in despair, and though my heart ached, after long brooding there was nothing else left but to leave for a foreign country.'[33]

---

[33] *Sporthírlap*, 11 October 1924.

It wasn't just the players they brought in that made MTK great, though. As Péter Szegedi pointed out, there were times when MTK effectively functioned without a coach, as though their method was so good that the players could essentially play by instinct. Yet there was a clear awareness of the value of a coach, seen by the fact that in 1921 MTK advertised for one in the British newspaper *Athletic News*, leading to the appointment of the former Manchester United full-back Herbert Burgess. But whether because of coach or culture, or some combination of the two, the championships kept on coming. In 1919–20, MTK won 26 of 28 games on their way to another title. They won 21 games out of 24 and conceded just nine goals in 1920–21, won 16 of 22 in 1921–22, 17 of 22 in 1922–23 and 19 of 22 in 1923–24. They were unstoppable.

CHAPTER FOUR
THE REGRETFUL HERO

The star of that MTK side, without question, was György Orth. He was an extraordinary talent, described by Hogan as 'the most versatile, greatest and most intelligent player I have ever seen'.[1] So versatile was he that he began his career at left-back before moving further forward and ended up playing for his country in five different positions, including – temporarily – as a goalkeeper. He was also a gentle, polite soul and a great conversationalist; by the end of his life he was fluent in five languages.

Orth's teammate György Molnár worked with him at the bank. They became great friends and made an agreement that if both were interested in the same woman, neither would pursue her; their friendship was too great to risk being spoiled by romance. By 1921, Orth and Molnár were both regulars in the MTK first team. They travelled together on tours. In Paris, they went to the Louvre together. In Berlin, they found a bar with a violinist and together sang English songs learned from Jimmy Hogan. Not that Orth touched alcohol, despite Schaffer's repeated attempts to ply him with champagne to see what he would be like drunk: he saved money to give to his mother

---

[1] Cited in Fox, *Prophet or Traitor?*

and drank only mineral water and raspberry juice. His favourite food was pasta and, although he later became a heavy smoker, in those days his only vice was ice cream.

'As a footballer he was quite self-critical,' said his former MTK teammate Gábor Kompóti-Kléber. 'He was never satisfied with his game.'[2] That suggests an intense, brooding figure, and he certainly became that later in life, but the young Orth, according to Tibor Hámori, one of his biographers, was 'unusually polite, open, straight and informal. He lived a healthy life as a true sportsman. He hardly ever went out at night; he did not enjoy club life. He had no harmful passions, but he adored women.'[3]

Orth was injured during a friendly between a Budapest XI and a Berlin XI at Üllői út in 1922, one of a number of injuries that had begun to afflict him. That night, a dinner was held for the two teams at the Hotel Britannia. There was a cabaret led by the great comedian Béla Salamon and Orth got talking to the elder sister of one of the performers. She was Vilcsi Mihály, a well-known actress in her own right. The following year they married, one of the first great celebrity events Budapest had known since the war.

'It will be on 12 May at 12 o'clock in the Terézváros Church, a wedding that will undoubtedly be talked about all over Budapest,' *Budapest Hírlap* reported excitedly.[4] 'The key figure of Hungarian football, György Orth, so well-known and popular across large areas of the world and not just at home, will marry Vilcsi Mihály. In the end, life is just a big football match. Happy is the man who can score goals and the most beautiful goal is a wedding. We hope for György Orth that this goal is not prevented by any opponent.' They divorced in 1927.

---

[2] In *Nemzeti Sport*, 1 February 1943.

[3] In *Régi gólok, edzősorsok*.

[4] On 8 May 1923.

The previous April, Orth had fought a duel to defend Mihály's honour. They had been having lunch at the New York Café and as they left at about 3pm, Mihály had gone into the street while Orth put on his coat. When Orth came out, his wife was talking to four men, one of whom made a lewd suggestion. Orth punched him, at which a fight broke out. The fencer Attila Petschauer, later an Olympic gold medalist,[5] joined in on Orth's side. A police officer called Antal Horváth became involved and, for reasons that are not entirely clear, the brawl ended when he and Orth agreed to fight a duel. Accordingly, they met at the Fodor fencing school, with medical professionals, police and journalists in attendance, exchanged a couple of thrusts with practice swords, declared it a draw and made their peace with each other. Nonetheless, duelling was illegal, and the following March, Orth and Horváth were sentenced to one day in jail. Orth served it in June 1927.

Orth never seems to have been entirely comfortable with his status as a celebrity, but nonetheless gave up his job in the bank in 1924 and, trading on his name, became co-owner of a sports shop at 34 Király utca. By the end of the decade, he had moved premises to the classy surrounds of Andrássy út. A brief profile of him in *Színházi Élet* [*Theatre Life*] magazine listed his one hobby as 'driving his own car'.[6]

But by then, weariness had long since gripped him. In 1923, he had been tempted by Austria, spending a brief time on loan at First Vienna. In *Orth és társai* [*Orth and his Mates*], a 'close friend' described visiting him at his home on Munkácsy utca. It was very different to the one-room apartment where he'd been brought up, with armchairs, porcelain figures and, Orth's real pride, a bookcase

---

[5] Petschauer won gold in the team sabre at both the 1928 and 1932 Games, and took individual silver in the sabre in 1928. He also won three silvers and three bronzes at the world championships.

[6] Issue 31, 1929.

stuffed with books, and yet there was a sense that, not quite 23, he was old beyond his years, unsure, disillusioned, tired. 'They kept inviting me, promised me everything...' he said. 'But here, there is this eternal partial safety as far as our livelihood is concerned... They depicted a better future for us abroad. But still, they are foreign people... Here I am surrounded by my friends... I'm in a difficult situation... I am a man and thus selfish...'

Orth leafed through a photo album, seemingly overcome by regret and doubt, assailed by advice from all around, but he decided in the end to remain at home. 'Do you know what it means to look at old pictures?' he asked. 'Pictures taken at school or during the tours. In Vienna, in the Ring Café, when I was speaking in German I still felt as if Csibi Braun had been standing next to me and Gyuri[7] Molnár, too... And as though I hadn't been wearing a suit but a blue and white jersey... Always blue and white... And when the waiter put the coffee in front of me I remembered good old Spitzer-*bácsi*,[8] the kit man, who knows how many bandages my leg needs. And you and everybody, who were rightfully angry with me at times but who carried me on their shoulders when I deserved it... And the little boy who asked me in Szabolcs utca, weeping, "Mr Orth, are you really leaving?" I would be much better off in Vienna, but I have made a decision to stay in Budapest... Believe me, I've had to argue, threaten and beg to be able to stay at home... I know, a lot of people don't like the way it is happening... But there's no other way for me. Because of joining Kégler as a partner in his business [the sports shop] I do not have any more fears about the future. Whoever knows me also knows that it's not that I *can* work but that I love to work, too... Sometimes I was at the bank until 5am even though I could have easily avoided working...

---

[7] Gyuri is a diminutive of György.

[8] The term literally means 'uncle' but is used affectionately for any older man.

I'm happy that it all has come together like that, because this way I can prove that I am worth something not only as a footballer, but as a simple, working citizen too, and that I'm not bad at working, either.'[9]

* * *

Jimmy Hogan returned to MTK in 1925 and made Orth his captain. With their great mentor back in position, there seemed no reason why MTK's domination should not go on. But football that summer had undergone a change far more radical than its instigators can ever have imagined. Concerned by a fall in the number of goals scored and the prevalence of the offside trap, the Football Association in England had amended the offside law so that, as remains the case today, only two (in practice, usually the goalkeeper plus one other) rather than three defensive players were required to play a forward onside.

That had a profound impact on the game's tactics. The 2–3–5, or pyramid that had dominated for almost half a century rapidly became obsolete. Without the old offside trap to offer defensive protection, teams in England initially pulled back their centre-half to become a third back and then, realising the shortfall that left in midfield, formalised a process that had been going on for years by pulling the two inside-forwards back to create a 3–2–2–3 shape, the W-M. Elsewhere the shift was less radical, and in Italy Vittorio Pozzo had great success, both with Juventus and the national side, by playing his centre-half in a half-withdrawn role, a sort of W-W – what he called the *metodo* as opposed to the *sistema* preferred in England.

Pulling back the centre-half in turn had a significant effect on style. It soon became apparent that the symmetry of the formation meant the game became a series of individual battles, as left-back

---

[9] Cited in *Orth és társai*.

picked up right-winger, right-half picked up inside-left and so on. Most significant was the way that the battle between centre-forward and centre-half, no longer a central midfielder and creative hub but a combative central defender – an 'overcoat' for the opposition centre-forward, as the terminology of the time had it – became a physical contest. That's why the classic image of the English centre-forward is a powerful, physically imposing figure such as Nat Lofthouse or Tommy Lawton, and also why for years there was not merely no sense in England that a central defender should be able to pass the ball out from the back, but a scepticism about those who did. The reaction of the rest of the world to the change in the offside law was less dramatic and, particularly in central Europe, the notion of the centre-half as a deep-lying creator lingered, but everybody had to adapt.

The amendment seemed not to faze Orth; if anything he began to play even better. Orth's relationship with Hogan was close. It's too simple, perhaps, to say that having a father figure in his life settled him, so he no longer fretted over whether to leave Budapest and his beloved mother to seek his fortune elsewhere, but at the beginning of 1925–26, Orth was superb. And then, on 8 September, came a friendly against Wiener Amateure.

With ten minutes remaining and the score at 2–2, the MTK and Hungary defender Imre Senkey picked up possession. 'From the left-back position,' he said, 'I hit a long ball towards Orth, who was standing or more like positioning himself side-on, waiting for the pass. He wanted to shoot at goal with his left foot or lay it off to [the forward Rudolf] Jeny. But before the ball got to him, [Hans] Tandler, who was known for his cruelty, jumped at his knee with both feet. You could hear the crack even from the grandstand. Orth collapsed on the ground immediately and was writhing in anguish, his knee totally deformed, his ligaments torn. It was a horrible sight!'[10]

MTK players rushed to their captain. Molnár, Orth's great friend, squared up to Tandler. They later ended up playing together for the New York Giants, where Tandler insisted the foul had been accidental.[11] The game was abandoned and an ambulance was summoned, but it took 25 minutes to arrive. As Orth was loaded into it, Hogan burst into tears. He had seen serious knee injuries before and he knew that at 24 his protégé was done. At the Hochenegg clinic, a Dr Kasper said he had never seen a knee in such bad shape and pronounced Orth's career over.

Without Orth, MTK's form faltered. Frustrated, he raged against his younger teammates. 'They are soft,' he said. 'Their condition is poor... When I was a young player, it wasn't dancing that occupied my thoughts and I didn't spend my free time in the Tabarin [a nightclub near Keleti station]. Today they talk about dancers, horses and jazz... I would listen to Jimmy-*bácsi* for hours when he was telling us how this or that great player played.'[12] He was the oldest 24-year-old in the world.

MTK finished the season second behind Ferencváros. Their years of dominance were over. Everything was changing. The following season, professionalism was introduced into Hungarian football and MTK decided to change their name, emphasising their patriotic commitment by becoming Hungária until 1940.[13] Orth's absence

---

[10] Hámori, *Régi gólok, edzősorsok...*

[11] Tandler subsequently became manager of Nice and Galatasaray, jobs he combined with running restaurants. When Austria Vienna visited Istanbul in 1956–57, he laid on for them a banquet of Viennese specialities.

[12] Cited in *Orth és társai.*

[13] For the avoidance of confusion, I have continued to refer to them as MTK, the name to which they kept returning and by which they are known today.

was not the only factor, although it was a significant one. For nine years, theirs had seemed an unbeatable system. Players came and went, coaches changed, and at times disappeared completely, and yet the fluent game based on dominating possession remained remorselessly successful.

CHAPTER FIVE

SHAPING VIENNA

As soon as the First World War was over, the influence of Hungarian football began to spread. Almost from its beginnings, its importance was traced as much through its diaspora as through what was happening in Budapest. 'The Austrians were better than the Hungarians until about 1912,' said Edward Shires. 'Then, because the great Ferencváros had come into being, the Hungarians overcame their neighbours and this advantage of theirs was secured by the great team of MTK later on... It cannot be denied that the "Austrian school" we have today [1933] has grown out of the seeds sown by Schaffer, but first of all by the Konráds.'[1]

Ultimately, for Shires, the credit belonged to John Tait Robertson. He remembered his arrival at MTK in 1911. 'Robertson got here on a Sunday and he immediately wanted to see a match,' he said. 'I took him to the Millenáris where the youth team were playing. Robertson watched the game for a quarter of an hour then pointed at one of the lads. "See that one? I'm going to make a player of him." The lad was Kálmán Konrád, a member of MTK's forward line, and he later became the master of Vienna.'

---

[1] In *Nemzeti Sport*, 15 March 1933.

Robertson was also convinced of his influence. After watching Rapid Vienna draw 3–3 with Rangers at Ibrox in January 1933, he spoke of being 'proud' of how good the Austrians had become 'because I feel I have contributed to it'.[2]

The Konráds were not the first Hungarians to play in Austria, but they were the first Hungarians to become major stars in Vienna. Kálmán Konrád was born in 1896 in Bačka Palanka, a small town in Vojvodina in what is now Serbia, two years after his brother Jenő. Their father was a shoemaker, but so poor were they that they would play football barefoot in the street. When the brothers were still young, their parents moved to Budapest. Jenő, a centre-half with a robust tackle and the capacity to initiate attacks, joined BAK before he was signed for MTK by Robertson in 1911, at the age of 17. He became a regular, while Kálmán was drafted into MTK's youth side.

Robertson returned to Britain in 1913 and was replaced by Bob Holmes, who had played for the Preston Invincibles of 1888–89 and managed Blackburn Rovers to the league title in 1912. Jenő took his school-leaving exams that year so was in and out of the side, playing seven matches, but Kálmán made his breakthrough at centre-forward, scoring 14 goals in eight games as MTK ended Ferencváros's run of five straight league titles.

At the outbreak of war, Holmes returned to England and Jenő Konrád volunteered for the army, becoming a cavalry officer, although he always said he spent more time walking alongside his horse than riding it. He was able to play some part in the three unofficial half-season championships of 1914–15 and even made his international debut in a 2–1 win over Austria in May 1915, but as his involvement in the fighting became more serious, his opportunities to play were

---

[2] Cited in Shires's interview with *Nemzeti Sport*, 15 March 1933.

diminished. Disillusionment rapidly set in and he warned his brother not to enlist.

Jenő was subsequently captured by the Russians and held as a prisoner of war in Siberia. He 'loved the peasants', his daughter Evelyn said, enjoying long evenings spent sitting around the fire as they asked 'profound, soulful questions' discussing 'the meaning of life'. After the February Revolution of 1917, the guards threw down their arms and Jenő, travelling by train, on horseback and on foot, slowly made his way to Moscow, where a rabbi helped him return to Budapest. It was then, Evelyn said, that her father began to lose his hair: he went to war with 'thick black curls' and came back 'almost bald'.

Even before that, though, Kálmán had begun to emerge as the better player and had made his international debut six months before his elder brother, also in a 2–1 win over Austria.

After persuading the Konráds to leave MTK's tour and stay in Vienna in 1919, Meisl found Jenő a job as a stockbroker and Kálmán a position in a bank; both had previously worked in banks in Budapest.

They stayed with Julius Fröhlich, an Amateure fan who went to games with his daughter Gertrud, who was 11 when the Konrád brothers moved in. Fröhlich was a businessman, his wife ran a green-grocer's and they lived on Franzensbrückenstraße near Praterstern, above a sports shop owned by Arthur Baar, a long-term director of Hakoah who had a number of stints as manager. Like MTK in Budapest, Amateure were associated with the secular and assimilated parts of the Jewish population.

'The arrival of the Konráds has transformed Amateure into technically the best side I have ever seen,' said the Swiss pundit Max Sexauer.[3] 'Their team play is virtually flawless and a true pleasure for

---

[3] In the Swedish newspaper *Idrottsbladet*, May 1921, cited by Persson in 'The Exile', *The Blizzard*, Issue Twenty-Three.

the connoisseur. But they would rather lose a game than deviate from their lovely gentlemanly transitional tactics.'

Sexauer identified Jenő Konrád and György Orth, who had joined First Vienna on loan in 1923, as being rare in Danubian football in the way they were celebrated for their defensive characteristics. Kálmán Konrád he described as being 'the supreme champion of football strategy', although there were times when he was criticised in the Viennese press for seeming to believe his left foot alone was enough to win games.

Béla Guttmann had no doubt of Kálmán Konrád's qualities. 'Among all the players in Vienna I think Konrád II is prominently the best,' he said. 'What Gyuri Orth is for MTK "Csámi" is for Amateure. He makes a team he plays for two levels higher. And it's only Buchan that can be put in the same category with Orth and Konrád. Scarone, Petrone, Rydell, Andrade and the rest may have the same virtuosity, but what lifts Orth, Konrád II and Buchan above them is artistic intuition and the depth of content. Only the young Slózi [Schlosser] and Spéci [Schaffer] could be compared to them in this respect.'[4]

For Evelyn Konrád, the way her father and uncle played said much about their respective personalities: Jenő was 'hard but fair' while Kálmán 'specialised in the undetectable tackle'.

---

[4] *Sporthírlap*, 22 December 1925. The other players Guttmann refers to are: Charlie Buchan, the intelligent and innovative inside-right who had left Sunderland for Arsenal that summer and was one of the main inspirations for Herbert Chapman's adoption of the W-M; Héctor Scarone, an inside-right for Nacional and Uruguay, who won two Olympic golds and a World Cup; Pedro Petrone, a scheming centre-forward who supposedly refused to head the ball in case it disturbed his heavily brilliantined hair, but nonetheless was a great goalscorer and also a double Olympic gold medallist and world champion; Sven Rydell, who was Sweden's all-time leading scorer until Zlatan Ibrahimović surpassed his record in 2014; and José Andrade, an intelligent midfielder in Uruguay's great side, who was one of football's first great black stars.

At a ball for medical students in 1921, Jenő met a beautiful 16-year-old called Greta. 'Theirs was a real love-match,' said Evelyn. 'When my mother was 18, my grandmother sent her to Berlin to stay with her younger brother Hermann to try to forget my father. She was looking for a more professional man for her daughter, not an athlete.'

Hermann, though, was perhaps not the ideal figure to advise respectability in relationships. Unbeknown to the family, he was living with an actress several years his junior and enjoyed a social life far livelier than his sister evidently expected. 'Berlin,' Evelyn said, 'was much more of a city than Vienna.' Hermann took her mother to a nightclub, where she happily danced with an admirer, only later to discover her partner was a woman in a man's clothing. Appalled, Evelyn said, Greta 'took a very hot shower – the Viennese bourgeoisie was very conservative in those days'. When Greta returned to Vienna, she married Jenő, who eventually became very good friends with her mother.

The football went well, at least for a while. Outside of Britain, there was little doubt that the game practised in Vienna and Budapest was the best in Europe. Amateure played a number of friendlies around Europe, overcoming Athletic twice in two days in Bilbao and then beating Barcelona before losing to them in a brutal rematch. Schaffer, drawn by his friendship with the Konráds, joined from Sparta Prague in 1923. After leaving Nürnberg, he had initially joined Wacker Munich, where he developed a taste for Bavarian beer and began to put on weight. Schaffer remained proudly Hungarian, as became clear when he went to watch a water polo match featuring the Budapest side MAFC. He supported the Hungarians vociferously and became increasingly angered by the referee, threatening physical violence. When other spectators tried to calm him down, he replied, 'Whomever I punch in Munich should feel honoured.'[5]

---

[5] Cited in Fekete, *Orth és társai*.

Schaffer asked for a signing-on fee of 25 million kronen and a monthly salary of 3 million kronen, as well as ownership of a fashion store.[6] Schaffer was a star, the 'Football King' and made sure everybody knew it. During games he would run to the stand behind one of the goals and shout, 'I bet I will score the winning goal. Who will bet against me?' Few would.

The definition of amateurism had become so flexible as to be meaningless, and the Austrian league officially turned professional a year later. It says much for the esteem in which Hungarian football was held that the two best-paid players were the former MTK centre-half Béla Guttmann at Hakoah and Schaffer at Wiener Amateure. Their status, though, infuriated the Konráds. Hugo Meisl, who was always an idealist, had assumed they would be happy to remain in their jobs and effectively play part-time but they saw no reason why they shouldn't be earning the same as other stars.

Neither played for the first half of 1924–25 and both joined First Vienna during the winter break. First finished third behind Hakoah and Amateure, Kálmán scoring six goals in ten games for the club. Jenő, though, struggled with a knee injury, managed just four games and retired at the end of the season. Both returned to Amateure that summer as Schaffer departed for Sparta Prague, with Jenő named as co-coach of the first team.

---

[6] As reported in *Nemzeti Sport*, 12 February 1923, although two days later *8 Óra* gave his monthly salary as 5 million kronen.

CHAPTER SIX

THE BLACK BOOK

The production and export of players and coaches had made clear that Hungarian football was a significant force in global terms, and so they travelled to the 1924 Olympics in Paris with high hopes. Their squad featured nine MTK players, including József Braun, György Orth, Gyula Mándi, György Molnár and Vilmos Kertész, as well as Béla Guttmann, who had left MTK in 1922, the Ferencváros midfielder Zoltán Blum, who had played at the 1912 Olympics, and the Makabi Brno striker Ferenc Hirzer,[1] who would later join Juventus and score a club record 35 goals in 26 games as they won their first league title in 20 years.

Performances in the year leading up to the Games had been good. Hungary had won four in a row, including a 7–1 demolition of Italy. Although May 1924 brought a draw against Austria and a 4–2 defeat to Switzerland, Hungary still seemed a genuine medal contender, a status underlined when they hammered Poland 5–0 in the preliminary round, each goal scored by a Makabi Brno player. Hirzer and Zoltán Opata, who had played for MTK, both got two, while the scoring had been opened by József Eisenhoffer, a Ferencváros forward

---

[1] Hirzer was also known as Híres, but he is usually referred to by the Germanic form of his name.

74

who was on loan in Brno before a move to Hakoah. He had been born in Kispest and in 1922 had married an Orthodox Jewish woman, Rózsika Reiner, adopting her faith. Guttmann claimed Eisenhoffer's move to Hakoah was delayed while he completed the process of converting from Christianity to Judaism to join a club committed to promoting the Zionist cause.[2]

In the first round proper at the Stade Saint-Ouen in northern Paris, though, Hungary suffered a scarcely believable defeat. Ibrahim Yakan put Egypt ahead after four minutes and Hussein Hegazi[3] doubled their lead five minutes before the break. Yakan's second, 13 minutes after half-time, confirmed the upset. Egypt, it's true, were probably better than most expected, but when they lost 5–0 to Sweden in the following round it made clear what everybody had suspected at the time: Hungary had been dreadful. Their team of stars had failed utterly to perform.

Nemzeti Sport referred to it as a 'catastrophic defeat' and called it an 'event that will be mourned forever, that can never be avenged'. *Sporthírlap* was inclined to blame bad luck, pointing out Egypt had only had three shots on goal. The intense heat and injuries that cost them the attacking powers of Molnár and József Takács offered some excuse, but not enough. There were stories of thousands of people hearing rumours of the defeat and taking to the streets in Budapest to find newspapers to confirm the bad news.

The wider response was fury. Károly Demény, the executive vice president of the National Physical Education Council (OTT) blamed encroaching professionalism, claiming that the 'true amateurs' of Egypt had shown more enthusiasm. Ferenc Zuber, the secretary

---

[2] In *Régi gólok, edzősorsok*.

[3] He had been the first African player to play in England, joining Dulwich Hamlet in 1911 and playing one game for Fulham.

general of the OTT, compared the defeat to the sack of Rome by barbarians, a natural punishment for a decadent culture. Imre Szigeti, the great director of Ferencváros, who was one of the prime movers behind the introduction of full professionalism, was more understanding, blaming an excess of fixtures after the winter break that had left the players lacking the necessary 'freshness'.

There were quibbles about the selection, but perhaps more revealing was the fact that at least some critics chose to blame a supposed lack of patriotic feeling among the squad. 'Our national team members do not represent Hungarians, the Hungarian nation nor Hungarian sport,' Gyula Gömbös, who would later become prime minister, told parliament. 'They represent international professionalism.'[4] Ostensibly he was talking about those players who had moved to Austria to take advantage of the advent of a professional league there, but references to international capital were almost invariably a dog whistle for anti-Semitism.

Whether the players were principally to blame, though, was far from clear. Such was the humiliation of the defeat that the MLSZ commissioned a special report into the Olympics, taking testimonies from every player and collating them into what became known as the Black Book. It makes for remarkable reading.

Having become used to a professional environment and being treated as a star at Hakoah, Guttmann was appalled by Hungary's preparations. Everything, he felt, was done in a rush, while the travel arrangements meant players did not arrive for games in peak condition. 'I was ill, very ill when I arrived in Zurich,' he said, referring to the friendly defeat to Switzerland, the first sign that something was amiss, 'but it's no wonder since I had been lying on the floor of the

---

[4] All quotes in this paragraph from *Nemzeti Sport*, 30 May 1924.

train all night and I had put a suitcase under my head as a pillow. I played badly in Zurich, and the reason I've mentioned my sickness is not because I want to find an excuse for my shameful performance. I was bad, but the whole team was bad, too...'[5]

Then there was the attitude of certain of his teammates. 'It was painful,' he said, 'that instead of finding a supportive company of friends, [Henrik] Nadler, Kertész II and Blum continually cracked jokes at me and nagged me with their remarks ... they grated on my nerves ... I returned to Vienna from Paris broken and sick in both body and soul.'

But he wasn't the only one to complain about having to travel third class, while almost every player protested about the Haussmann Hotel in Montmartre, a district more geared to the socialising of officials than the preparation of a sporting team. Orth suggested that poor facilities were a result of cutbacks forced by the 'unfavourable financial circumstances created by the Peace Treaty in Trianon'.[6]

'The two Fogls[7] and I got a small room which was in a terribly neglected state,' said the goalkeeper János Biri. 'It opened to a separate, tiny wash-basin alcove. There was one single bed in the room – this is where the Fogl brothers were to sleep – while there was a terribly crooked iron bed put in the alcove for me to sleep on, on which poor Jóska[8] Fogl must have felt like sleeping on a ladder (because in fact it was him who got to sleep on it). Luckily, upon my complaint, the leadership got me another room, which I shared with [József] Takács, and the two Fogls remained in the first room. It's true that they could

---

[5] *Sporthírlap*, 11 October 1924.

[6] *Fekete könyv* [*Black Book*], compiled by György Pálfi and János Vachó (Hungarian General Sports Library, Issue 1).

[7] The Fogls, József and Károly, for years formed a formidable defensive pairing known as the *Fogl-gát* [Fogl-gate] for both Újpest and Hungary.

[8] A diminutive of József.

not sleep but instead caught a dreadfully huge rat, which they nailed to the doorpost. Having seen the rat, the leadership got them another room in another hotel. The food was also atrocious, so much so, that some people didn't even complain, they simply did not eat.'

Or perhaps the food was just French. Csibi Braun spoke of meagre breakfasts of 'coffee and bread and butter' and 'half-raw bloody meat for lunch' as a result of which he lost nine pounds in weight. 'The food was bad,' said Zoltán Blum, 'but only because it was French. It was okay for me, I am used to all kinds of cuisine, but for the Fogl brothers, who eat big portions, it was both little and unfamiliar.' Blum spoke for the majority when he insisted that 'Hotel Haussmann, the rats, the food, the travelling were just episodes which may be sensational news for the press, but they cannot be called mitigating circumstances.' He felt the atmosphere in the team had been wrong, that Orth had been played out of position and that Guttmann, out of form, shouldn't have played at all. There was a general sense of a split between the professionals who played abroad and the amateurs still playing for Hungarian clubs.

Guttmann's argument, though, was that his lack of form was a result of the conditions, and so the argument rapidly becomes circular. He would later tell the story as though it had been he who had led the rat-catching missions around the hotel. And perhaps he did; it's entirely possible there were multiple hunts – there seems to have been no shortage of rats.

Whatever the precise truth, the fallout had consequences, and it was never the officials who paid. None of Guttmann, Weisz or Eisenhoffer played for their country again.

CHAPTER SEVEN

THE AGE OF THE CARP

The 1924 Olympics may have been a huge disappointment – and the league's adoption of professionalism in 1926 meant no team was sent to the 1928 Games – but Hungary's status as a football power was made clear both by how many players it continued to export (even if, as Péter Szegedi pointed out, from 1923 or so the big three of MTK, Ferencváros and Újpest tended to hang on to their stars) and by the foreign tours made by its top clubs. Perhaps the most influential was Ferencváros's 1929 tour to South America. Uruguay had won the football tournament at the previous two Olympics, beating Argentina in the final in 1928, and they would win the first World Cup final against the same opposition the following year. Beyond Britain, which remained largely disdainful of international competition, *rioplatense* football was widely acknowledged as the best in the world.[1]

Ferencváros set off from Genoa on the *Julius Caesar*, planning to be away for three months, arriving in São Paulo at the end of June. They were managed by their former forward István Tóth, who in

---

[1] After Uruguay's success at the 1924 Olympics, for instance, the journalist Gabriel Hanot, a former France international who would go on to be both France manager and editor of *l'Équipe*, dismissed the suggestion that British football might still be pre-eminent by saying, 'It is like comparing Arab thoroughbreds to farm horses.'

Hungary is invariably known by his nickname 'Potya', a corruption of the word for 'carp'[2] that refers to his chubbiness. He remains one of the club's greats, a short, stocky forward whose photograph is prominently displayed at their stadium. He is often seen accelerating away from a defender, while head-on photos show a round-faced man, hair scraped across his scalp from a parting that begins over his left eye.

The son of a railway official and a train conductor, he grew up in Nyolcház, a huge housing complex near Keleti station, and spent most of his childhood playing football on a patch of wasteland in the middle of the development. After beginning his career at BTC, he followed a breakaway from the club that established the Nemzeti Sport Club in 1906 and spent six years there as he completed an engineering degree, before signing for Ferencváros in 1912. He made his international debut against England in 1909 and went on to play 19 times for his country, scoring eight goals. He was part of the squad that went to the 1912 Olympics, although he didn't play at that tournament, and won the Hungarian championship in 1913.

After the war, in which he fought on the Italian Front, being promoted to the rank of lieutenant, Tóth returned to Ferencváros, for whom he would play 197 matches, scoring 63 goals. So noted was he for his lack of height that contemporary cartoons depicted him darting between the legs of opposing goalkeepers. He was also renowned for the spirit in which he played the game and was awarded at least three medals for fair play in the early 1920s.

As an amateur, Tóth also needed a profession, and from shortly after the First World War he owned a dairy in Egyed near Csorna in the north-west of the country, although the day-to-day management

---

[2] The Hungarian for carp is 'potyka', but the 'k' became silent over time, resulting in 'potya' – or blunder.

of the business seems to have been taken on by his father-in-law. In 1926, at the age of 35, just as professionalism was introduced, Tóth retired from playing and was named coach. Ferencváros had won the league in his final season as a player, breaking the MTK stranglehold at last, perhaps not coincidentally just as a change in the offside law shifted the emphasis of the game away from the sort of neat passing combinations on which MTK had always prided themselves.

Benefitting from the new environment, Ferencváros won the league in each of Tóth's first two seasons as a manager as well. Central to their success was a player who Tóth, his eye for talent unerring, had signed within days of his appointment as coach, a midfielder who was ideally suited to the changed role of the centre-half and who would go on as a coach to become one of football's greatest tactical innovators: Márton Bukovi.

Bukovi was born in Budapest on 1 December 1903[3] to a Jewish father and Catholic mother and grew up in the Józsefváros district of Budapest with his brother and four sisters. His surname then was spelled 'Bukovy' and, after his parents married in 1912, he took the surname of his father Fülöp, a football coach at a local level, and became Martón Selinka, although he seems never to have used that variant in his football career; I have stuck with 'Bukovi' throughout for ease of understanding.[4] He was registered as a Catholic and there is a cross on his gravestone in the Rákoskeresztúr cemetery, but at

---

[3] That's according to his birth certificate, discovered by Gyula Pataki in January 2019. In an interview he gave to the Croatian newspaper *Šport* in 1936, Bukovi said he was born in Piešt'any (Pöstyén) in what is now Slovakia, the home of his mother (and probably his father). Why he would lie is unclear; perhaps he was simply embarrassed that his parents were unmarried at the time.

[4] In addition, his name was often written as 'Bukovai' during his playing career and he officially changed his surname to 'Bokodi' in 1935, reverting to Bukovi in 1958.

least one of his sisters was registered Jewish by religion. His wife, Aranka Klein, was Jewish.

Complicating the matter further is the issue of his nationality. After the end of the First World War, Bukovi, along with around a million other Hungarians, became a Czechoslovak citizen and although he later took Hungarian nationality, it's probable that when he made his international debut for Hungary in 1926 he was technically still a Czechoslovak.

Both Bukovi's parents died in the Spanish flu epidemic that followed the First World War. He became an apprentice silversmith and after qualifying worked for a company that manufactured snuffboxes. He played for Magyar Labdarúgók Köre, a third-division team that merged in 1920 with Magyar Football Club, and after they went out of business, he was signed, following interest from MTK that was not followed through, by the second-division team Ékszerész SC [Jewellers Sports Club]. There he was coached by Gyula Feldmann and Vilmos Kertész,[5] both former internationals who had played for MTK. 'They had caught something from Jimmy Hogan,' Bukovi said. 'They sparked my sympathies towards MTK, along with György Orth, whose understanding of football was somehow closest to my own.'[6]

He stayed there until 1924–25, when they won the second division, only to be denied promotion following a match-fixing scandal that led to Ékszerész and the clubs who had finished second and third being excluded from the league for a year.

Bukovi moved to Italy for a year, playing for Alba Roma in 1925–26 and, after failing again to land a contract with MTK, was

---

[5] Kertész was the middle of three brothers – the others were Gyula and Adolf – who played for MTK and for that reason he is often referred to as Kertész II.

[6] In the seventh part of a long series of interviews with him published by the Croatian newspaper *Šport* in 1945.

signed by Ferencváros, where Tóth made him captain and installed him as centre-half. Tóth, Bukovi said, 'strived to make training more versatile ... to free us from the cliché. What I like the most about him was that he constantly searched for new combinations, read English handbooks and always had something new to implement in training.

'Every Friday I went to lunch at his house and we talked football for a long time. His wife must have been bored to death! But Tóth had one weakness, the same one as all coaches at the time: he never revealed to a player how he should play his role, he simply trusted the player's imagination, ingenuity and skills. We had too many combinations in our game. We passed the ball too much and too short, the way to the opponent's goal was too long and it ate up valuable time. Without a true system and some collective play that was agreed upon, everything depended on loose mutual agreements between two or three players, never among the entire team.'

Nonetheless, Bukovi was a tremendous success. 'I don't believe Hungarian football has ever had such a profoundly accomplished expert,' wrote the journalist László Feleki on Bukovi's death in 1985, referring both to his playing and coaching abilities. 'Tóth-Potya can undoubtedly be mentioned on the same page, but from the earlier generations only Schaffer can be compared to him. As to what a player he was, perhaps a single statement is enough: he was the best Hungarian centre-half of all time...

'Bukovi was known as an attacking midfielder but a centre-half was the real key player of the old style of football, this ever-moving defensive organiser, but also a player with great skill on the field who started the attack and dominated the pitch. Long after teams in England had been playing with three defenders, Bukovi glittered in Central Europe in the old-fashioned way.'[7]

---

[7] *Képes Sport*, 5 May 1985.

Yet enormously gifted as he undoubtedly was, Bukovi remained humble. A profile in *Színházi Élet* magazine in 1929 described Bukovi as '25 years old, unmarried. Opposed to alcohol, does not sing … has a passion for jewellery'.[8] A year earlier he had said that his long-term ambition was 'to open a knitwear and wicker shop'.[9]

Tóth was a very fine judge of talent and a great motivator but his influence stretched far beyond his successes with Ferencváros. He established the first course for teaching coaches in Hungary, compiling a sort of coaching manual and standing at the centre of a network of key football figures. He played the piano and harmonica well, occasionally performing in clubs, theatres and music halls, had several high-society friends and seems to have been regarded as the life and soul of the many parties he organised or attended. In addition, Tóth's sister Irén married Gyula Feldmann.

Eight months older than Tóth, Feldmann had been born in the southern city of Szeged, near the modern-day borders with Serbia and Romania. His parents had moved to Budapest when he was a child, living near the Tóths in Nyolcház. Feldmann and Tóth had played together at Nemzeti and then Ferencváros, before Feldmann joined Hogan's MTK in 1917, a few months before his 27th birthday. There, he confirmed his reputation as a clever defender, with pace, technique, positional sense and a calm temperament. He was also one of the first Hungarians to master the sliding tackle. After winning four league titles, and doing some coaching at Ékszerész, he left to become player-coach of Makabi Brno, where he worked with Árpád Weisz, Ferenc Hirzer and József Eisenhoffer, spreading the MTK style. He then had two seasons in Germany with Bremen and Braunschweig, before returning to Budapest to take charge of MTK.

---

[8] *Színházi Élet*, Issue 31, 1929.
[9] *Nemzeti Sport*, 9 July 1928.

Feldmann's family was so horrified by his marriage to a Gentile that they disowned him and, as a result, when he was in Budapest he ended up sharing a house with Tóth, even though they were coaching the city's two bitterest rivals. Inevitably, that led to complications. On one occasion, a friend of Feldmann's had arranged a trial at MTK for a talented young player of his acquaintance. When the player knocked at his door, though, Feldmann was having his afternoon nap. Tóth answered the door, sized up the situation and persuaded him to sign for Ferencváros instead. That player was the great József Turay, who would go on to play 115 games for Ferencváros, winning three league titles and breaking hearts with his smouldering looks. He would also be part of the Hungary side that reached the final of the 1938 World Cup, although by then he had moved to MTK, for whom he played 155 times and won another two league titles.

There were clearly no hard feelings, though, and in 1932 Feldmann and Tóth bought a house together on Telepes utca in the district of Zugló.[10] Tóth's grandson remembers the building, which was demolished in 1998, having eight apartments on four floors, most of which Tóth and Feldmann rented out. It was seized by the Communist state in 1952, although Tóth's family was permitted to carry on living there.

Tóth's half-sister, meanwhile, was married to Hugo Steiner, an early secretary general of the MLSZ. He had been the chief accountant at a fabric factory and, after receiving a pay-off, set up a banking foundation to lend money. He went bankrupt, though, and he too ended up living with Tóth and Feldmann on Telepes utca. For a time in the late 1920s, Tóth stood at the very heart of Hungarian football.

---

[10] Reported in *Nemzeti Sport*, 9 August 1932.

CHAPTER EIGHT

THROUGH THE STORMY OCEAN

Ferencváros's 1929 tour of South America was primarily about making money, but it was also a further stage in Tóth's education. The first game was played on 30 June against a São Paulo XI in front of 50,000 fans. 'Ferencváros had a good day,' Tóth noted in the report he sent back to the club, 'and played football with lots of passes on the ground. The pace of the game was very high. The Brazilian team mounted ferocious attacks, especially in the second half, but Ferencváros were able to score twice on the counter.' They won 2–1 and, while it's never wise to read too much into a single match, a pattern was immediately established of the Hungarians, playing on the break, being a little more direct and incisive than the Brazilians.

Tóth wrote after that game of the 'great round of applause' the 'local fans' had given his side and the crowd seem to have been even more enthusiastic four days later as Ferencváros drew 1–1 against América in the first game a Hungarian club had ever played under floodlights. 'We played some fantastic, some would say artistic, football,' Tóth said. 'The fans have certainly never seen anything like this and gave a standing ovation to some of the Ferencváros moves.'

Ferencváros, though, lacked 'killer instinct' and they conceded a late equaliser.

Their form got even better as they then played a Rio XI, withstanding an early barrage before taking the lead 'against the run of play'. 'The players are bubbling over with joy,' Tóth wrote, 'showing all the skills that can be imagined in football. The impact is devastating... Dribbles, elegant first touches, wonderful combinations and high pace – this is what typifies our game! Virtuosity, not football!' Having gone 3–0 up, though, 'they started to play art for art's sake instead of scoring more'.

Many tours of South America by British teams had been characterised by complaints about the refereeing and allegations of various types of skulduggery against the home sides. The first week of the Ferencváros tour had been free of that, but everything changed at half-time in that third fixture. 'The second half turned into a nightmare,' Tóth wrote. 'The referee shocked the team with outrageous decisions. Teófilo kicked the ball out of [the goalkeeper Ignác] Amsel's hands as he lay on the ground and scored! Unprecedented! Seeing this the Brazilian players went berserk and respected no man, no god. The referee wouldn't stop the madness. Hesphanol tried to destroy [the winger Vilmos] Kohut with a two-footed tackle but he evaded it and the Brazilian hit the ground so hard that he hurt his own leg. The game finished 3–3. There is no question it was a profanation of football.'

Ferencváros lost the fourth game of the tour 2–0 to the Brazil national side. 'It happens when you play against 12 men. Artur Morales [the referee], shame on you! Turay was injured after a horrendous tackle while Kohut was sent off. Nobody knows why. Ferencváros were superior in terms of ball-handling, though.'

However much rancour there may have been by that stage, Ferencváros had made an extremely positive impression. 'The Hungarian team plays the best football we have seen,' the *Gazeta de Notícias* reported as Ferencváros returned to São Paulo, 'including professional teams from England. They are flourishing tactically and this is their main source of power. Their moves are witty, ingenious and unexpected but they come naturally for Ferencváros.'[1] It's true that the two English teams to tour Brazil in the 1920s, third-division Plymouth (in 1924) and second-division Chelsea (earlier in 1929), were not of the highest standard but given English football had been professional for 40 years and the respect in which the British game was still held, that was significant praise.

Ferencváros's fifth game, though, brought another defeat, 5–2 to Palestra Italia, who were coached by another Hungarian, Jenő Medgyessy, a former teammate of Tóth. He had been a Ferencváros player for 12 years, winning four league titles, before being forced to retire in 1919 from injuries sustained in the war and seems to have been involved, in some capacity at least, in arranging the tour. Medgyessy had moved to Brazil in 1926, becoming coach of Botafogo, where his name was transmuted to Eugênio and he acquired the nickname 'Marineti'. He then spent two seasons at Flamengo before moving to São Paulo, where he took charge of Palestra Italia. A couple of months after the tour, Medgyessy would help welcome to Brazil another Hungarian, one who would have a profound influence over the game in South America, Imre Hirschl.

Tóth seems to have taken defeat to his former teammate well enough. 'Palestra are a team with outstanding quality,' he wrote, 'and their victory was well deserved. Even so, we had a great time at the banquet.'

Then it was back on the boat and south to Uruguay where Ferencváros met the national side in a game attended by the president of the republic, Juan Campisteguy. The forward Géza Toldi recalled[2]

---

[1] *Gazeta de Notícias*, 12 July 1929.

[2] In his book *Fodboldnavn paa flygtningepas* [*A Footballer's Name on a Refugee Passport*] (Martin, 1962), written in Danish with the journalist Axel Hansen and published when he was coaching the Aarhus team AGF.

Ferencváros playing superbly and leading 3–0 after 90 minutes, but the game then going on and on as Uruguay fought back and scored twice. Eventually, after more than ten minutes of injury time, the referee could prolong the game no longer. 'The tour,' Tóth observed, 'is beginning to seem like a handicapped competition. The teams in South America possess a high understanding of the game and are technically gifted so it can be imagined how hard it is to play against them considering the constant support they receive from the referees – as though they are given a goal or two in advance... Our victory is the true testament of the quality of Hungarian football. It might be true that South American football is faster but Ferencváros can compensate for it tactically and when our opponents have run out of puff we are usually able to take control of the game.'

Ferencváros beat a Montevideo XI 4–1 before a rematch against Uruguay that they lost 3–0. Tóth remained sanguine. 'They did not know what to expect from us beforehand,' he wrote. 'However, we showed something they have never seen. Not only were we able to challenge them but everybody could see that our style was superior and we could out-pass the mighty Uruguay, the two-time Olympic champions, by showing the true values of Danubian football... nowhere else was our team appreciated this much. Uruguay showed great interest in getting to know our team better... I believe it's the greatest recognition a football team can have.' The Hungarian ambassador wrote enthusiastically to the foreign office in Budapest: 'Ten diplomats couldn't have achieved what this team has done to promote Hungary down here.'

The tour moved on, across the River Plate to Buenos Aires. A storm blew up and Tóth was disturbed to hear a banging coming from the bottom of the ship. There was a group of Hungarian musicians on board and Tóth asked them what the noise was. They told him not to worry: there were some holes in the hull and what he could hear was a pump that was getting rid of any excess water. Tóth, though, did worry and ordered that all the balls the club had brought with them should be inflated and tied together in a large net to offer a buoyancy aid should the worst come to the worst. In his diary, he referred euphemistically to 'the long journey through the stormy ocean'.

Despite the difficulty of the journey, Ferencváros beat River Plate 4–3 in front of an 'ecstatic' crowd of 20,000, before heading back to Montevideo where they lost 2–0 to Peñarol. 'The game was refereed by one of the Peñarol board members so the result needs no further explanation,' Tóth wrote. Then it was back to Argentina for a 2–1 win over Racing in which 'the English referee was a real gentleman'.

What happened next is unclear. Tóth in his diary claims Ferencváros were so popular they were asked to stay on and play additional matches but Toldi described financial problems caused by ticket forgery that may have meant they had to play additional games to pay their way. The problem in trying to ascertain the truth is twofold. While there's no reason to doubt the fundamental truth of Tóth's diary, it's equally clear that he glosses over certain events. Toldi's account, meanwhile, is short on detail and at times seems a little fanciful. He describes, for instance, the referee in one game trying to strangle a Ferencváros player and having to be restrained by directors of the home team who later admitted he suffered from occasional psychotic episodes. Discreet as he was, Tóth would surely have mentioned such an extraordinary incident.

Whatever the real cause of the games, Ferencváros lost 2–0 to an Argentina national team. 'No regrets!' Tóth insisted. 'We showed our very best against a formidable opponent and the game was a close encounter throughout. What's more, as far as combination skills are concerned Ferencváros were slightly better, while the same can be reported about the Argentinian defence – they were massive and could neutralise most of our attacks. I thought it was going to be a goalless draw but in the final moments we could not physically keep up with the pace of the game and conceded twice.'

They then beat Racing 2–1 before returning to Brazil where, exhausted after seven weeks of travel, they lost 2–1 to a São Paulo XI. The trip had been such a success that Imre Szigeti, the director in charge, suggested an 'eternal tour' staying in South America for at least another two years.

That plan was vetoed, but Szigeti did stay on, making off with the proceeds of the tour with the result that the club had to wire over further funds to pay for their squad's voyage home. Szigeti bought a pair of cinemas and later, having Hispanicised his forename to Américo, coached Nacional of Montevideo to two Uruguayan league titles,[3] another Hungarian making his name as a coach in South America.

---

[3] He won both the 1933 and 1934 league titles, although the 1933 title wasn't clinched until 18 November 1934. Nacional had finished level on points with their great rivals Peñarol at the top of the table and although their goal difference was far inferior, that was not used as a decider. Instead the championship went to a play-off, played on 27 May 1934. After 70 minutes, with the score at 0–0, a shot from Peñarol's Brazilian left-winger Bahía went wide but bounced back into play off a medicine box belonging to Nacional's team doctor. The inside-left Juan Peregrino Anselmo gathered the ball and teed up Braulio Castro to score. The goal was initially given but Nacional protested so furiously that three players were sent off and the referee hospitalised. One of the linesmen took over, but decided it was too dark to carry on and abandoned the match. On 30 July, the Uruguayan federation ruled out the goal and ordered that the final 20 minutes be played on 25 August. The game finished goalless and was still goalless after 30 minutes of extra time. That meant another play-off, on 2 September, and when that also finished 0–0, a third play-off on 18 November. Peñarol twice took the lead but went down 3–2 as the forward Héctor Castro, who had lost his right arm in a circular saw accident at the age of 13, scored a hat-trick. Nacional claimed the 1934 title a week later.

CHAPTER NINE

THE UNBEATABLE JEWS AND THE GREAT DEPRESSION

Small steps can have profound consequences. When the journalist and librettist Fritz Löhner-Beda[1] and the dentist Ignaz Hermann Körner founded the football club Hakoah in Vienna in 1909, they had a clear sense of purpose; it was not just another football team. But still, it would have seemed incomprehensible then that within two decades, their club would have helped popularise the game in the United States, would have hollowed out central Europe of a number of its star players, and would have sown seeds in South America whose harvest is still being reaped. Few teams can ever have had such an impact on the global game; certainly none that only ever won one championship in their homeland.

Löhner-Beda and Körner were Zionists and had been much taken by Max Nordau's arguments for Muscular Judaism. The name Hakoah itself is the Hebrew word for 'strength'. As one of the original

---

[1] He was born Bedřich Löwy in Wildenschwert, Bohemia, in 1883, but his family changed their name to the less overtly Jewish Löhner after moving to Vienna in 1888. 'Beda' was a pen name he adopted based on a diminutive of his first name.

members of the club, Robert Stricker, put it, 'A people who get used to being insulted are lost.'[2]

Hakoah joined the Austrian league in 1910 and played their first second-division season in 1916–17. They finished second in their first season and topped the table in 1919–20 to earn promotion to the top flight. They celebrated by appointing as coach the Englishman Arthur Gaskell, who had played alongside Jimmy Hogan at Bolton Wanderers.[3] He lasted only a matter of months, though, before the money ran out and he had to be released from his contract. Fritz Konus Kerr, a first-team player, replaced him and led Hakoah to a very creditable fourth.[4]

Guttmann signed that summer, despite being far from devout. According to his wife's nephew Pál Moldovanyi, 'He didn't really care about religion. He even liked bacon! It must have been descent and not religion that was important to him. If he was asked the question, "Are you a Jew?", he never denied it, but he didn't attend a synagogue. He wasn't interested.'[5] There's an obvious comparison there to be drawn with the Konrád brothers who apparently preferred Wiener

---

[2] Cited in Bolchover, *The Greatest Comeback*.

[3] He had also, in 1913, managed the first Russian side to win an international match, when they beat Norway 3–0 with a team that included nine Russians, WC Charnock (one of the brothers who owned Morozov Mills in Moscow and founded the club that would become Dinamo to try to stop his workers drinking themselves senseless with vodka every time they had a day off) and an M Parker. It is not considered an official fixture.

[4] For these managerial details, I am reliant on the research of the Swedish writer Gunnar Persson, who has continued to try to piece together the confused history of Hakoah even after the publication of his peerless history of the club, *Stjärnor på flykt*.

[5] In an interview conducted by Zsolt Gyulás and included as an appendix to the Hungarian edition of Detlev Claussen's biography *Béla Guttmann, a világfutball edzőlegendája* (Akadémiai Kiadó, 2015). The original German edition was published by Berenberg in 2006.

Amateure to Hakoah in part because they felt uncomfortable with the latter's overt Zionism; Guttmann, in such matters, was perhaps simply more pragmatic.

He had, after all, been gifted a dance school from which to derive an income while he played on an amateur basis. By 1924, he already had signed a huge professional contract, but was insisting he didn't really enjoy football and would soon give it up. 'I'm 25, and perhaps I will continue to play for three or four years, but football is not my purpose in life. I am a serious businessman...' he said. 'I think with horror of the times when I spent my days monotonously, in boring idleness. Well, that was horrible, I wouldn't have been able to go on with that lifestyle for long! Football all day long, then a walk, then the cinema or the theatre in the evening. Phew... I didn't feel like doing anything. I was disgusted with everybody but mostly with myself.'[6] When the journalist who conducted that interview, Henrik Garfunkel, had arrived at the dance studio he had found Guttmann, brush in hand, clad in an overshirt smudged with paint. He sent Garfunkel to a nearby coffee house and arrived, immaculately dressed, a few minutes later. The scene is so perfect that you wonder whether Guttmann, a great player of the media game, might have staged it.

At the same time as Guttmann was signed, the long-time vice-president of the club, Arthur Baar, became coach but it was after the arrival of Billy Hunter as manager in 1923 that things really took off. Hunter had also played with Hogan at Bolton and had managed Dordrecht for two years before being named national coach of the Netherlands in 1914. At the outbreak of war, he returned to the UK and enlisted, serving as a corporal on the Western Front. He had been coaching Lausanne in Switzerland before being enticed to Vienna.

---

[6] *Sporthírlap*, 11 October 1924.

Hunter's footballing principles seem to have been similar to Hogan's and, with him and Baar as joint managers, Hakoah soon became noted for their fluent style of play. In September 1923, for instance, they travelled to London and beat West Ham 5–0, a barely credible result given the standing British football still enjoyed. 'They passed the ball smoothly and made good use of the space,' the *Daily Mail* reported approvingly.[7] It's debatable, though, whether the coaches were the main influence at the club. In December 1925, Guttmann described how 'with unflagging energy I was trying to sow the seeds of the school and system that I had come to know in MTK under the hands of master Hogan as the only right and follow-able one in football.'[8] (This, frankly, is a little confusing. Records are incomplete but, although Hogan did return to Hungary at times after quitting MTK in 1918, it's hard to see when Guttmann could have played under him; the phrase 'under the hands' is presum-ably intended metaphorically, a suggestion that Hogan's influence remained strong.)

The following season, as the Austrian league became the first outside Britain to legalise professionalism and Eisenhoffer joined from Ferencváros via his loan at Makabi Brno, Hakoah were cham-pions for the first time – although before the title was sealed, the money had run out again and Hunter, who secured a job managing Turkey, had been replaced as co-coach by the former Wiener AC half-back Gustav Huber.

Hakoah, though, were not just about winning silverware. They weren't even primarily about winning silverware. They existed to promote Zionism and to raise funds for the cause – and that was something that brought problems. It would be an exaggeration to

---

[7] *Daily Mail*, 4 September 1923.

[8] *Sporthírlap*, 22 December 1925.

suggest they suffered anti-Semitic abuse at every game, or even at most games, but it was a frequent enough occurrence that they took to travelling with members of the boxing and wrestling sections of the club for protection. Körner, for instance, was attacked by a Wiener AC player in 1923, while in 1925, Guttmann punched the First Vienna midfielder Leopold Hofmann after the final whistle, later claiming he had been responding to a racial slur.

Hakoah's season as champions was difficult. Results fell away and rifts began to emerge in the squad, exacerbated by the change in the offside law. Hakoah, like MTK, appear to have found their close-passing style less effective in a new environment that encouraged a more physical approach. Guttmann, never a man to let a perceived slight pass, was furious. 'What I built up with my sweat over four years,' he raged that December, 'unskilful hands successfully destroyed in the course of only a few months.

'First of all, they made sure I lost my authority before members of the team. At open meetings with the players, section head Baar regularly used a tone of voice with me, which – even though I am an employee of the club today – I must define as ungrateful, insensitive and unjustified.

'The second step from section head Baar affected me more deeply than these personal offences. He completely forsook the method, which I, following the Robertson, Hogan and MTK school, intro-duced at Hakoah and the usefulness of which I proved, and voted for the so-called snapping style – with its pointing, instep-using[9] and mindless running to and fro – and demands the team develop it as the method of reaching your goals in the face of the current, changed system of the game according to his views.

---

[9] Guttmann is presumably using the term to mean a direct style – that is, one that required long kicks with the instep rather than short sidefoot passes.

'But most of our players are players with technique and tend towards using combinations and besides that, as for their physique, they don't have the prerequisites to play the hurry style. So it's no wonder that they do not play any style at all any more. In my experience everything has stayed the same with the new offside rule, teams must play as they used to, it's only the full-backs that need to be faster and the two insides that need to have great knowledge and determination. The new system, or rather lack of system, became the cause of our repeated defeats which this season we have suffered with the same team that could hardly be beaten last year.

'They blame me for these defeats at the club saying that I am being lazy just to prove to them that the new system is wrong. Of course, these opinions have been echoed in the team and the undermined spirits have been damaged even further by the effects of financial difficulties, which Hakoah hasn't been able to escape. Now we have a team with a bunch of unmotivated players who are also out of form, in addition to some low-quality players.'[10]

Guttmann, who was always on the verge of leaving any club he was at, spoke of quitting and returning to Budapest, but was persuaded to stay on for an ambitious fund-raising tour of the USA in the summer of 1926. It was a huge success, in many ways too great a success. Forty-six thousand turned out at the Polo Grounds in New York to see the 'Unbeatable Jews', as they were billed, take on a composite team of Indiana Flooring and New York Giants that went by the name of the New York All Stars Select XI. It would remain the largest crowd at a game in the US until the glory days of the New York Cosmos half a century later. Hakoah won eight and drew three of 13 fixtures and impressed so much that no fewer than

---

[10] *Sporthírlap*, 22 December 1925.

ten of their players were persuaded to return to the US before the start of the following season.

The American Soccer League (ASL) had begun in 1921 and expanded from eight teams to 12 in 1924, but it was the arrival of Hakoah that gave it life. Football, it suddenly became apparent to US entrepreneurs, could generate real interest and make real money. The dominant force was Fall River Marksmen (named after their owner Sam Mark), who played in North Tiverton, Rhode Island, where there was no law prohibiting clubs from charging spectators for admission on a Sunday, giving them a significant advantage over many of their rivals.

What the Hakoah tour had made clear was that there was potential for growth among Jewish supporters in New York. For Nat Agar, the owner of Brooklyn Wanderers, and Maurice Vandeweghe, the owner of New York Giants, it became imperative to sign Hakoah's stars. Guttmann, typically self-confident and keen to pursue his own interests, led the exodus, and was followed to the New York Giants by four teammates, including the former Ferencváros and Makabi Brno winger Ernő Schwarz. József Eisenhoffer, the former VAC and Hungary goalkeeper Lajos Fischer, the former Ferencváros, Makabi Brno and Hungary winger Sándor Nemes (also known as Alexander Neufeld) and two others joined Brooklyn Wanderers.

It wasn't difficult to see why they were tempted, particularly given that Austria was gripped by hyperinflation. At New York Giants, Guttmann was on $350 a month, having negotiated a signing-on fee of $500. The average private sector worker in the US at the time was making roughly a third of that. Guttmann had been one of the best-paid players in Austria, but he had made nothing like that, even if you included the income from the dance school he had established in Vienna.

Agar made further signings from VAC and DFC Prag, and then made a bid for Kálmán Konrád, offering him $500 as a signing-on bonus, plus $75 a week, roughly double what an English pro earned at the time. Konrád was under contract with Wiener Amateure and so risked being held in breach of that if he left, but he decided to take the risk. He had moved out of the flat on Franzensbrückenstraße but remained close to Gertrud Fröhlich, who had recently turned 18. He met her in a café on Schwarzenbergplatz and told her he would be leaving. He promised, though, that if she agreed to marry him he would return after a year. She accepted.[11]

Amateure received no compensation and also lost Hans Tandler, the defender who had injured György Orth so badly, and the striker Viktor Hierländer to the ASL. Given the lack of protest and given they were 100,000 schillings in the red, it may be that Amateure saw the advantage in clearing some big salaries from their books. Konrád, as it turned out, was a flop in the US. According to his son Peter, he disliked the way Wanderers trained and struggled to adjust to poor-quality pitches. Hampered by injury, he played just 27 of 44 league games and scored only two goals. Konrád was nevertheless able to save roughly $50 a week. He returned to Europe in 1927, by which time Wiener Amateure had been renamed FK Austria. They lacked the money to sign him, though, and so he went back to Budapest, joining MTK after Alfréd Brüll paid Meisl $2,000 in compensation.

Some familiar faces remained. At centre-half, remarkably, was Orth. After his knee injury he had spent three months in a sanatorium before checking out. When he danced a waltz with his wife at an MTK ball, it began to seem possible that he might,

---

[11] Gertrud's cousin Helene Weigel was a well-known actor and director, and was married to Bertolt Brecht.

unthinkably, recover. In June 1926, ten months after rupturing ligaments, he returned to training.

The forward Ferenc Hirzer, meanwhile, was back from Juventus, where he had scored 50 goals in 43 games. Ferencváros may have won the championship in the previous two seasons, but MTK were still an extremely good side. Konrád, though, continued to be restricted by injuries and played only 13 of the 22 league games that season, while Orth was nothing like the player he had been. Although Hirzer scored 22 goals, MTK finished behind Ferencváros who lifted a third straight title. Orth retired at the end of the season and was named MTK coach. Konrád also quit, tired at 32 of battling injury. Brüll, having gone to such lengths to sign him, was furious and made all the more so when Konrád then sued the club over outstanding payments.

Such was the financial might of the ASL clubs in general that in January 1927 the national associations of Austria, Hungary, Czechoslovakia and Yugoslavia made an official complaint to FIFA about New York Giants, Brooklyn Wanderers and other sides encouraging European players to break their contracts. The USFA managed to head off calls for them to be suspended at FIFA's Annual Congress that June, but the issue was never properly resolved.

Agar wanted more. Hakoah's 1926 tour had been an enormous success, both for the club and for the US owners, but Agar realised he could make even more money if he also controlled the touring party. He commissioned the former BAK half-back Árpád Deutsch, a committed Zionist and evangelist for Muscular Judaism who had moved to Palestine, to put together a team of Central European and Palestinian Jews, to be known as the Maccabees, for a tour of the US.

Deutsch signed up his squad, including his former BAK teammate Ernő Erbstein, who was winding down his career at the second-flight Budapest side Húsos before embarking on a hugely successful coaching career. On 27 May 1927, the Maccabees arrived in New York aboard the *Aquitania* which had set off from Haifa. None, slightly oddly, were registered as footballers on the passenger manifest. Deutsch was described as a 'football trainer', Erbstein was a 'clerk' while there was a butcher, a weaver, a locksmith and numerous merchants. That suggests an element of subterfuge, perhaps because Agar didn't want others getting wind of his wheeze.

The tour was launched at the Hotel Pennsylvania with an event attended by sports writers and various Jewish personalities, including Abe Goldberg, the vice-president of the Zionist Organization of America. 'Fifty per cent of the proceeds of the tour of the invaders,' the *New York Times* reported, 'would go to Palestine to be added to the sum that is expended annually in buying more land for Jews.'[12]

In front of almost 20,000 predominantly Jewish spectators at Ebbets Field, the home of the baseball team the Brooklyn Dodgers, the Maccabees began their tour with a 5–4 win over the New York Stars, a representative side drawn from the Southern New York State Football Association. Shortly after the second game, Deutsch received word from Palestine that his wife had died. As he returned home, most of the organisational duties of the tour seem to have been taken on by Erbstein.

Erbstein was fascinated by what he found, and particularly by how teams had adapted to the 1925 change in the offside law. Before Hakoah's first tour, the vast majority of imports into the ASL had been British and they seem to have managed to institute the W-M within a few months of it being established at home. The tourists struggled at times to deal with the more physical, direct approach and Agar took to lending them players to improve the spectacle. For

[12] Cited in Dominic Bliss, *Erbstein: The Triumph and Tragedy of Football's Forgotten Pioneer* (Blizzard, 2014).

Erbstein, whose tactical acuity was already beginning to emerge, this was a revelation.

Late in the tour, the Maccabees lost 2–1 to Brooklyn Wanderers, for whom Konrád was playing one of his final games. He excelled, scoring twice; if the old star could play like that against a central European defence, Erbstein wondered, why had he so struggled in the ASL? 'The greatest Hungarian player, who also played in New York, Kálmán Konrád, creator of the Viennese School,' he said, 'had serious differences with the manager, because he did not want to adapt his game to the new requirements... I, personally, was not so hostile towards the system which tended to destroy the principles dear to me, because I saw it uncovered new possibilities and new beauties and because, in practice, it could also achieve success.

'Davy Brown, the centre-forward for the Giants, a player equipped with a big shot and a great keenness to shoot, but mediocre in style and mastery of the ball – scored 76 goals in a single season,[13] while Konrád scored two or three. Therefore, it interested me and I studied the system, and when I returned to Europe I already had a decent understanding of it.'[14]

Konrád's technical ability, which had brought almost a goal a game for MTK, he concluded, 'was less significant when he had a centre-half permanently marking him'.

Despite the danger of losing further players, the potential financial rewards were substantial enough that Hakoah also returned for another tour that same summer. It was nowhere near as successful as their first, though, in part because it was no longer a novelty and because there were rival tours, but also because, stripped of so many

---

[13] He scored 52 goals in 38 league games; it's not clear which other matches Erbstein is including.

[14] Cited in Bliss, *Erbstein*.

players, Hakoah simply weren't as good as they had been, even with former players making guest appearances: Guttmann, for instance, played in at least four matches. Hakoah finished the tour having won seven, drawn seven and lost seven of their 21 fixtures, but far more significant was the fact that crowds had been so small that Hakoah made a loss of US$30,000, leading to Körner's resignation as president.

Two more Hakoah players did stay and join the Giants, including the great goalkeeper Alexander Fabian, who had gained legendary status in Hakoah's championship season by carrying on after breaking his arm in the decisive game, leaving his goal to play on the wing and scoring the winner. Vandeweghe also signed the Hungary international inside-forward György Molnár, who had won four league titles with MTK. The New York Giants, meanwhile, picked up the Czechoslovakian half-back Samuel Schillinger, who had joined the Maccabees tour late because he couldn't get out of commitments to the dental practice he ran in Prague, where he played for DFC.

For all the investment, neither the Giants nor the Wanderers really prospered, both finishing mid-table in 1926–27 and 1927–28. Even more damaging, there then came a dispute that threatened to derail the ASL entirely. The ASL wanted to shift the US Open Cup, which made them no money and was regarded as disrupting the schedule, to the end of the season. The USFA refused, at which the ASL announced a boycott. Three clubs, though – the New York Giants, Bethlehem Steel and Newark Skeeters – played in the US Open Cup anyway, for which they were suspended from the ASL. The USFA called for the bans to be lifted and, when they were not, outlawed the ASL and founded their own competition, the Eastern League.

Vandeweghe established a new club to take part in it, New York Hakoah, a team comprised of Central European Jews. He signed, among others, Eisenhoffer and Nemes, while seven Giants players, including Guttmann, switched from one Vandeweghe franchise to the other. They narrowly missed out on the league title in 1929, but did win the US Open Cup, Eisenhoffer's goal giving them a 1–0 win over the Giants in the eastern section final before victory over the winners of the western section, St Louis Madison Kennel, in the first two matches of a scheduled three-game final. The second game, played at Dexter Park in Queens, drew more than 21,000 fans, the largest attendance at a US Open Cup final until Seattle Sounders beat Columbus Crew at their own stadium in 2010.

As had been his habit elsewhere, Guttmann sought money-making opportunities outside football, investing in a speakeasy, which seems to have been extremely profitable. In the autobiography he co-wrote with Jenő Csaknády, Guttmann suggests that by the start of the 1929–30 season, he'd amassed US$55,000, a remarkable sum given his total earnings from football in the US only came to US$13,000 before tax. Everything seemed to be going well. The ASL and the USFA had reached an agreement at the beginning of October to unite their rival competitions as the Atlantic Coast League. New York Hakoah merged with Brooklyn Hakoah of the ASL to create the Hakoah All-Stars. 'I was young, elegant and witty,' Guttmann said. 'My circle of acquaintances raved about me. My mediocre jokes prompted uproarious laughter. The ladies were delighted by my charm. The men admired my brilliant chess moves in business! I was admired and pampered like a star by everyone.'[15]

Then, on 28 October 1929, the Dow Jones Industrial Average fell 13 per cent. The next day, when more shares were traded than on any single day for 40 years, it fell another 12 per cent. Over two days, US$30 billion had been wiped off the value of the stock market.

---

[15] In Jenő Csaknády, *Die Béla Guttmann Story* (Bintz-Dohany, 1964).

By 13 November, the Dow Jones was down 48 per cent on its high of 3 September. The consequences were devastating. Guttmann lost everything. 'I poked holes in the eyes of Abraham Lincoln on my last five-dollar bill,' he said. 'I thought then it wouldn't be able to find its way to the door.'[16]

Hakoah's supporter base was drawn largely from factory workers in industries that were hit first and hardest by the Crash.[17] Crowds fell, and so the Hakoah All-Stars did what Hakoah had always done to try to make money: they arranged a tour and, in the summer of 1930, set off for Brazil and then to Argentina and Uruguay.

---

[16] In *Régi gólok, edzősorsok.*

[17] A point made in more detail by David Horowitz in 'Hakoah in New York (1926–32): A New Dimension for American Jewry', *Judaism* 25, summer 1977.

CHAPTER TEN

FROM SALAMI TO TRIPE

Hakoah's tour was not a success, either for Béla Guttmann or the club. Rather than a flat fee, he had asked for 40 per cent of gate receipts – a proportion that suggests just what a star he remained – but the tour only just broke even. Many who might have attended found themselves distracted by the World Cup being played in Uruguay at the time, and even when crowds were large in Argentina, many of those in the stands were season-ticket holders who added nothing to receipts.

And the truth was that Hakoah by then were an ageing side, nowhere near as good as they had been. They won just two of the 15 games they played. But in São Paulo, Guttmann was approached by another Jew from Budapest, Imre Hirschl. It was a meeting that would have profound consequences, for both men, and for football.

Hirschl is one of the great mysteries of world football. Trying to piece together his back story is far from straightforward; every time you think his life may be coming together, another account or detail emerges that casts everything into doubt. But let us begin with what we do know. He was born in Apostag, a village of around 2,500 inhabitants about 60 miles south of Budapest, on 11 July 1900, the son of Vilmos, a publican, and Cecilia, whose maiden name was Kohn. By

1820, when a fire destroyed a number of buildings including the synagogue, the Jewish community there numbered 176 taxpayers; by 1917, there were only 44 (out of a total Jewish population of 117). That included 20 farmers, 10 traders and a doctor.[1]

By the end of the First World War, Apostag was not a thriving place. The yeshiva had closed in 1905 and religious instruction was led by the cantor. In a directory of 1929, Vilmos Hirschl, Imre's father, is listed as *'gondnok'*. That literally means 'caretaker' or 'guardian', but given he is also described as one of the 'leaders' of the community, it presumably means he was an official with responsibility for buildings.[2]

Hirschl has a daughter, Gabriela, born in 1953, who still lives in Buenos Aires, where she practises as a psychoanalyst. She said that her father rarely spoke about his life before moving to South America, but that when asked about the scars he had around his hip and a bullet wound in his wrist, he told her that he had followed two elder brothers to Palestine during the First World War, where he had lied about his age to sign up with Jewish nationalists to fight the Ottomans, sustaining his injuries in a grenade attack. Corroborating that is very difficult, but a directory of the Apostag area from 1939 says Vilmos had owned his own leather business since 1908, that three of his sons had fought in the war and that one of them, Adolf, Imre's eldest brother, born 1895, had been killed.[3] He was one of seven fatalities among the 26 Jews from Apostag who fought.[4]

---

[1] From *Magyar Zsidó Lexikon*, a 1929 work edited by Péter Újvári that gives details of Jewish settlements throughout Hungary. (http://mek-oszk. uz.ua/04000/04093/html/)

[2] In *Magyar Zsidó Lexikon*.

[3] *Pest–Pilis–Solt–Kiskun vármegye és Kecskemét th. jogu város adattára*, edited István Csatár, Eghia Hovhannesian and György Oláh (1939).

[4] In *Magyar Zsidó Lexikon*.

The White Terror led many from Apostag and the surrounding area to flee in 1920, leaving shops and houses unoccupied.[5] Although it's impossible to be certain whether that influenced Hirschl's thinking, he seems to have moved to Budapest soon after the war. 'I was educated at the University of Budapest, where I played for the first team and discovered I liked coaching,' he said in an interview with the Argentinian newspaper *La Tribuna* in 1939. It's not at all clear, though, whether anything he said in that interview can be trusted. 'I was part of the Budapest Athletic Club,' he went on. 'My debut as a manager, after visiting countries as a player such as Czechoslovakia, India, Africa [*sic*], England, France and Germany, was in Paris, with Racing Club. From there I moved to the United States, where I kept practising football with the Hakoah team.' There is no evidence for any of this.

In 1905, Hirschl's mother's brothers, Lajos, born 1882, and Jenő, born 1888, changed their surname to Kozma[6] and established a butcher's.[7] The first documentary evidence of its existence is an invoice for salami preservatives dated 25 May 1918 (a note on the upper right of the document gives some idea of the difficulties of the time, noting prices rising every day and the difficulty of obtaining goods).[8] The address of the business is given as 1 Király utca, in Terézváros, Budapest. Lajos married a woman called Olga Bleier and, in March 1923, Hirschl married her younger sister, Erzsébet.[9] What Hirschl was doing in the early 1920s isn't clear; it may be true that he was at university. By 1928, though, by which time the Kozma brothers seem to have owned four and possibly five shops in Budapest,[10] he is listed

---

[5] Protocol of 6 June 1920 to PIH's Legal Aid Office. MZSL PIH-I-E, B 10/3. box.

[6] Shown by typed versions of their birth certificates from 1905 and 1906.

[7] Jenő's godfather, József Benedek of Győr, was also a butcher.

[8] In the company records at the Budapest Fővárosi Levéltár.

[9] Confirmed by notices in the newspapers *Az Est* and *Pesti Napló*.

[10] There is, for instance, an advert for a branch of the Kozma butcher's in Óbudai Hajógyár on the front page of *Csillaghegy* on 1 April 1926.

as one of the 23 shareholders of Kozma and Co., while a feature in the newspaper *Magyarság* in November 1928 about new investment in the Kozma brothers' business describes how Hirschl, as factory manager, demonstrated to journalists and dignitaries the passage of meat from pig to plate.

Even with the new investment, though, times were hard. A statement to the company AGM in 1929 described what a tough year 1928 had been. That was explained as being 'in part because the circumstances caused by competition means that cheaper prices than normal have been brought to the market and through this, our business has been forced to lower its prices to continue to bring in custom and keep up with the competition. As well as this, livestock was overpriced in the last year and it is well-known that the costs of the capital city's market cashiers were too high. Finally, due to the bad commercial conditions of the past year, the number of debtors was numerous and despite trying our hardest to collect monies owed, our losses were significant.'[11]

Perhaps related to that, by July 1929, Hirschl was no longer listed among the company shareholders. Trying to determine why he emigrated, leaving behind not only his wife but also a son, Péter, who had been born in 1926, can only be speculation, but with the business struggling it may be that he was seeking import or export opportunities with the meat trade in South America, where it was relatively straightforward to set up a new life.[12] Whatever the reason for his

---

[11] In the company records at the Budapest Fővárosi Levéltár.

[12] Take, for example, the case of Ignaz, Sándor and Jenő Klein, whom I came across because they had a sister Erzsébet who married a Bleier (although, as it turned out, a different family from the Erzsébet Bleier who married Hirschl). They were three brothers who emigrated from Budapest to Uruguay in the 1920s, following a neighbour who had married their sister. Papers were easy to come by in Montevideo, there was plentiful work and a large Hungarian community. The Israeli investigative journalist and presenter Ilana Dayan is the granddaughter of the neighbour.

departure, Hirschl arrived in Santos, the port of São Paulo, on board the *Almanzora* on 20 September 1929 having boarded in Cherbourg, northern France.

Hirschl checked in to an immigrants' hostel, the register of which lists him as a butcher and a Catholic.[13] It also, confusingly, says he was 30 (when he was 29) and, while that is probably nothing more than a slip of a weary Brazilian receptionist, it adds to the sense that with Hirschl nothing is ever quite certain. Gabriela denies her father was ever a butcher, although she accepts that he made excellent sausages. Perhaps in a technical sense she is right, that a factory manager did not get much blood on his hands and so he was not, in the most technical sense, a butcher and he said he was because it was an easy shorthand for his job. But while there are obvious reasons to disguise his Jewishness – and given he was selling pork salami, he seems not to have been devout – it's far less clear why he thought butcher was a less controversial profession than footballer or football coach if that's what he intended to be in South America (then again, given the Maccabees had similarly lied on their immigration documents in 1927, perhaps there was something somehow improper about being a footballer in the Americas in the 1920s).

Hirschl would subsequently, at different points of his career, claim to have played for a variety of clubs. It's commonly believed in Argentina that he was a member of Tóth's Ferencváros tourists of 1929, and a number of Argentinian sources confidently assert he made his debut for them in 1916, before retiring, aged 29, after that tour. There is, though, no reference to him in any document in the Ferencváros club museum. Gabriela has a large collection of cuttings about her father drawn from Argentinian, Brazilian and Uruguayan

---

[13] The register can be accessed at http://www.inci.org.br/acervodigital/upload/livros/pdfs/L107_136.pdf.

newspapers and magazines. They variously suggest that he played for Ferencváros (or perhaps BAK), or maybe Hakoah of Vienna or New York. Others suggest a link with Racing Club of Paris while Gabriela remembers her father saying he had played in Czechoslovakia. In so far as it's possible to prove a negative, sufficient records exist to be almost certain that he never played for Ferencváros, or Hakoah, or any top-flight team in Czechoslovakia, or any side anywhere near the top level in France.

By the time Hirschl approached Guttmann in São Paulo, he seems to have been desperate. 'He introduced himself and told me that he had worked as a butcher in Budapest but he would like to be a masseur for the team as he had strong hands and a firm grasp,' Guttmann said.[14] 'I tested him right away and I'm telling you I was given one hell of a massage! So at my request he got a contract and he came with us to Argentina. But there we were quite short of money so we thanked him for his work and said goodbye to him in Buenos Aires.'

The problem is that the account Guttmann gave the journalist Tibor Hámori is riddled with omissions and errors. It is set out as a gossipy conversation and that is what it is. It's a great story, a rollicking listen, but whether it is true is another matter entirely.

Take what he claims happened next. 'After we left, Hirschl spread the news that he had actually been our trainer – he was often seen running out with the team – so he got a good contract as a coach. But no one knew his real plans! Hirschl had a wife and a child living in Pest, and for a long time he hadn't been able to invite them to join him due to a lack of money.

'Now, he decided to make some atrocious mistakes at the beginning of his coaching career so his contract would be terminated, he would be

---

[14] In Hámori, *Régi gólok, edzősorsok*.

paid the rest of his fee, out of which he would then buy the tickets for his family. But what should he do to make the club leaders angry? Well, he turned the team upside-down in the very first match. He made the goalkeeper play at outside left, he put the centre-half in the goal and so on, the supporters didn't recognise the team. What happened next? They beat the most probable winner! Hirschl was scratching his head, then in the second match he made an even bigger mess of the team. And they won again! And it didn't matter who he put where, they won their matches, one after the other. People started to praise him. He was labelled a great coach. And Hirschl didn't care about the termination of his contract any more, he got carried away with the success.'

The truth, while still extraordinary, is a little more prosaic. Around 18 months after Hakoah had left him in Buenos Aires, Hirschl became the first foreign coach in Argentinian football since the end of British domination in 1912 when he was put in charge of Gimnasia y Esgrima La Plata. It's entirely plausible that he exaggerated his qualifications when lobbying for that job. It was one to which, as a salami salesman, he was perhaps unusually suited: Gimnasia are nicknamed '*los Triperos*' (the Tripe-men) – a reference to the fact that many of Gimnasia's fans worked in the meat-processing plants of nearby Berisso.

The slightest interrogation, though, exposes the holes in the rest of Guttmann's account. Charitably, perhaps it can be said that it as a highly exaggerated version of reality, with Hirschl's attempts to implement a W-M in a culture that was unfamiliar with it and his decision to promote a number of youth team players causing confusion before they clicked, winning six and drawing one of their last seven games of the season to finish a highly creditable seventh. But that is a normal pattern when a new coach makes radical changes; it does not make Hirschl some footballing version of Max Bialystock in *The Producers*, seeking profit through failure.

And while we can be fairly sure what happened at Gimnasia, none of that explains either what Hirschl had been doing before introducing himself to Guttmann in São Paulo or what happened in the months before being appointed at Gimnasia. Or even, really, in his time working for Hakoah.

In the 1939 interview in *La Tribuna*, Hirschl said that, having been a left-winger, he operated in all five forward positions for Hakoah. It's hard to see how that can be true: not only did Guttmann have no knowledge of him, but there is no record of him having played in New York, or of him having entered South America before landing at Santos in 1929. In an interview with the same newspaper the previous year, Hirschl had been asked directly if he had played any games in Argentina. 'Yes,' he replied, 'one time in Rosario. I believe it was against Nacional. What I haven't forgotten is that I was centre-forward of Hakoah and *"el Vasco"* Lecea was the centre-back. It ended 1–1. My teammate Grünfeld scored our goal.'

Hakoah did play three games in Rosario and drew them all 1–1, although none were against sides called Nacional. The match to which Hirschl was referring was presumably the friendly against Newell's Old Boys, for whom Fermín Lecea played before moving to Independiente, and Grünfeld was Joszef Grünfeld, who had played for New York Hakoah. It is just about possible that Hirschl did play in a tour game, stepping in for one of the regulars, and perhaps half a century later, speaking to Hámori, Guttmann did not remember that, but there is no hard evidence.

Hirschl seems to have found a job as assistant to his countryman Jenő Medgyessy at the Paulista club Palestra Italia (now Palmeiras).[15]

---

[15] There is a version of the story that has Hirschl in the US embassy in Paris, seeking a visa, bumping into Palestra Italia's owner Count Materazzo, the richest man in Brazil at the time, and persuading him to give him a job.

According to Fernando Galuppo's history of the club,[16] Medgyessy was dismissed after a 2–2 draw against Portuguesa on 6 October 1929 and replaced by the former Brazil international Amílcar Barbuy. After just one game, though, a 6–0 victory over Ypiranga, he stood aside and Hirschl oversaw the final two games of the season, a 3–2 win at Guarani and a 4–1 home defeat to the champions Corinthians. Medgyessy returned to Palestra Italia in January 1930, and Hirschl found himself out of a job – which perhaps explains his desperation when he approached Guttmann later that year.

A profile of Hirschl in *Nemzeti Sport* published on 29 November 1932, by a correspondent based in Buenos Aires, remembered Hirschl as 'an all-legs, blond lad running up and down the sideline, giving a massage to the injured players'. He then returned to Brazil, where he 'stayed behind as a coach for one of the teams'. Which team this was *Nemzeti Sport* does not say and there is no concrete evidence he returned to Brazil at all.

If Hirschl did go back to Brazil, he soon left and returned to Buenos Aires. There, the feature in *Nemzeti Sport* said, 'he was a day-labourer, an agent and a newspaper boy. He was wretchedly poor, he starved and lived in a refuge but in the meantime he put great effort into learning Spanish to reach his goal, to become a coach for one of the great Argentinian teams.

'When he had learned to speak a little bit of Don Quixote's language, he went from club to club to get a petty $100 job. This is how he ended up in La Plata. Although he wasn't welcomed with open arms they did give him a try, because the champions of 1929 were in 11th place and they had already consumed five or six coaches without being able to improve their position as the team bringing up the rear.

---

[16] *O time do meu coração: Sociedade Esportiva Palmeiras* (Leitura, 2009).

'That happened back in May. And what this lad has done since then, how he has managed to get this undisciplined lot of constantly drinking, almost always half-drunk coffee-house dwellers to lead a sporty lifestyle and to take part in regular training sessions is still considered to be a miracle today. But one thing is sure, today this soft-spoken, tall lad instructs the team with a blink of his eye.'

A certain amount of poetic licence, you suspect, has been taken and Hirschl himself probably had a hand in outlining just what ragtag bunch of ne'er-do-wells he inherited. There does, though, seem to have been some truth to Guttmann's claim that Hirschl's priority on taking the Gimnasia job was to raise sufficient money to get his wife and son over to Buenos Aires. He succeeded.

Immigration records cross-referenced with the passenger manifest for the *Duilio*, a ship that departed from Genoa, show Erzsébet and Péter (and a Henrik Hirschl, who may be Imre's elder brother) arrived in Buenos Aires on 20 January 1933. How long they stayed is far from clear; all we know is that at some point over the six years that followed, Hirschl's wife and son returned to Hungary and by 1939 were living with Erzsébet's niece and her husband György Scheer. It's easy to speculate that Erzsébet was homesick or couldn't settle in Argentina, and that Hirschl, making a name for himself in Argentina and aware that back in Europe he had no reputation as anything other than a seller of processed meat, wanted to stay, but there is no way of being sure.

Péter died in Budapest in 1940 at the age of 14 from pneumonia and deterioration of the kidneys. Erzsébet is listed in the register of Holocaust survivors compiled in Budapest in 1946. She died in 1971 and is buried with her son in an overgrown plot at the back of the Kozma utca cemetery,[17] Keresztúridűlő, to the north-east of Kispest.

---

[17] The name is a coincidence.

Her sister and mother are in a slightly better maintained area of the graveyard, while the Kozma brothers and their wives have well-tended graves much nearer the main gate.

Gimnasia began the 1933 season with five straight victories and, with the forward Arturo Naón in superb form, led the table at its halfway point.[18] The Argentinian press, rarely moved to investigate far beyond the five *grandes* of the capital, began to take notice. 'Los Triperos,' a profile in *El Gráfico* observed in May 1933, 'have never been more than a mid-table side, that usually fought hard against the *grandes*, but at the end of the tournament the result was always disappointment. How did the miracle happen? The truth is almost unquestionable. "It's the Hungarian," people say... The change at Gimnasia is astonishing. The players can't just change so much by chance. His influence is evident.'

Hirschl, the piece notes, had come to Buenos Aires for the first time with Hakoah, which is probably true, even if the claim he was 'part of the team' is not. It also says he was a winger and inside-left, which is entirely plausible, and that he had played football for 26 years, which is an odd detail given he was still only 32.

'After being in Havana[19] and Brazil,' the article continued, 'he returned to Buenos Aires, brought by businessman Adolfo Doce (the organiser of several tours), ready to take over Gimnasia y Esgrima La Plata.' Hirschl spoke 'gently', the interviewer wrote, and was not at all 'dizzy about being so successful'.

'I have no secrets,' Hirschl insisted. 'I will say nothing extraordinary. First things first: I do not teach football,' he said. 'It would be ridiculous to pretend to be teaching football in the country where the

---

[18] For more on Hirschl's impact on Argentinian football, see my book *Angels With Dirty Faces* (Orion, 2016).

[19] This is a detail that doesn't seem to be corroborated anywhere else.

best football is played. Players like the Argentinians cannot be found anywhere else. The *criollos*[20] have potential: everything I do is based on taking advantage of it.'

'Potential', frankly, is a slightly odd term to use, given Argentina had lost in both the 1928 Olympic final and the 1930 World Cup final and were clearly, at the time, one of the world's leading powers. The way Ferencváros had been received in 1929, though, perhaps suggests an underlying sense that the New World still had something to learn from Europe, and certainly the handful of Argentina matches against England in the 1950s and early 1960s were all dressed in the tropes of student against master. It may be Hirschl, a man adept at persuading others of his own worth, recognised that and played on it.

Hirschl, the profile went on, had watched three Gimnasia matches before deciding to take the job, at which he told the club directors that he could put together a side that would challenge for the title without any need of a budget for transfers. Given Gimnasia's status in Argentinian football, that was a significant claim. It must also have come as a relief to directors in the period of frenzied transfer activity that followed the legalisation of professionalism the previous year. The forward Pancho Varallo, for instance, had left Gimnasia for Boca Juniors in 1931 having been offered the seemingly incredible sum of 4,000 pesos when his father, as he put it, 'had never seen a 100-peso note'.

Hirschl began by making significant changes, promoting reserve team players to replace first team regulars – the origins, presumably, of Guttmann's outlandish claims. 'The board,' the profile said,

---

[20] The meaning of '*criollo*' is complicated. It initially meant somebody of Spanish parentage born in Latin America, but in Argentina at least it came to be used of anybody born there of southern European parents and was essentially used in contradistinction to the small but still influential section of society of British descent.

'protested, because they thought that these players would be useless… But his contract said he had carte blanche to make decisions, so these players remained. Today, it's clear that his promise to be among those clubs fighting for the title will be fulfilled.'

Naón remains Gimnasia's all-time leading scorer, but the key player in a side that became known as '*el Expreso*' was the centre-half José María 'Pepe' Minella. He had started out as a centre-forward[21] before being forced into emergency cover as a centre-half on Gimnasia's post-season tour of 1930–31. He never returned to the forward line and, according to the journalist Juvenal, who was widely regarded as Argentina's foremost authority on tactics at the time, he came to redefine the role of the centre-half, forming, with Oscar Montañez and Ángel Miguens a midfield celebrated as '*las tres Ms*'.

'The first months,' Hirschl said, 'were difficult, because the *criollo* footballers needed some discipline to take advantage of their potential and quality so they could perform better.' Gabriela remembers her father telling her that he would trail around bars, sending his players home before they got drunk.

Why did he not sign players? 'If I had already seen that there were players here and the raw material I needed, why would I make them spend to bring new ones?' Or why would a manager seeking an early exit and an easy pay-off risk antagonising the board by demanding new signings?

This is the problem of Guttmann's testimony: it becomes insidious, colouring everything. How much of what Hirschl said is genuine; how much post-hoc rationalisation? At one point, he even

---

[21] He first made a name for himself as a 16-year-old when he was selected for a local league selection in his home city of Mar del Plata as they beat the crew of the HMS *Repulse* 1–0, a game staged to celebrate the visit of the Prince of Wales, later Edward VIII, to Argentina in 1925.

seems to explain the art of the confidence trickster. 'Everything is based on clear explanation,' he said, 'approaching the players with an affectionate attitude. If things are said in a good way, it's easier to do deals.' But maybe that's an unfairly negative way of looking at what happened. After all, Hirschl was a good public speaker. In almost every photograph of him with players, it's clear the respect they have for him, the way they seem to hang on his words. Gabriela, similarly, remembers his charisma, how in banks, shops or stations, he would speak and others would listen. He found a way to inspire his players and, whatever his background, whatever route he took to Gimnasia, once there he was an undeniable success.

He made them fitter, introducing 'Swedish gymnastics and American gymnastics, combined' and insisted on a mix of sprints, long runs, basketball and football in training. When they beat the *grandes* Independiente and San Lorenzo, it was because, *El Gráfico* said, they had outlasted their opponents.

He also made them more pragmatic, encouraging the use of the long pass where necessary. 'I've told my players that the forwards don't have to entertain much with the ball and should make forward passes instead...' he said. 'The heading game is very useful, too. But we had to practise it! The idea is to try to direct the ball with the same accuracy as with the feet. See? There's no secret. The lads could do everything: they only needed someone trying to convince them that they were capable of it. Naón, for example, was very fearful, and we had to convince him almost by suggestion. [Antonio] Palomino was weak: he couldn't handle more than half an hour. The method-ical gymnastics have helped him match the others. As for Minella, I always thought he was a great centre-half.'

The implication again is that Hungarian football was a little more direct than the game in Argentina. The other great innovation

Hirschl introduced, one that suggests he may have been rather more committed to the long term at Gimnasia than Guttmann's version of events would allow, was to put the entire team on the same salary 'so there was a common sense of sacrifice'.

By the end of September, with nine games of the season remaining, Gimnasia were two points clear at the top of the table. Then they played away at Boca, who were second. At half-time they led 2–1 and seemed on the verge of a decisive victory. But in the second half the referee Ángel De Dominicis awarded a highly contentious penalty to Boca. A few minutes later Boca added a third despite Gimnasia claims it had been offside. It's impossible at this remove, of course, to have any level of certainty as to what happened, but the league was concerned enough to suspend the referee while a verse published in the magazine *La Cancha* made clear what the wider public thought:

Por tocar tan bien el pito	For blowing his whistle so well
En aquella tarde loca	On that mad evening
Lo nombraron a Angelito	They nominated little Ángel
Bombero voluntario de la Boca	A volunteer *bombero*[22] for Boca

Gimnasia beat Independiente at home before an even greater outrage the following week at San Lorenzo, who by then were managed by Medgyessy. Trailing 2–1, Gimnasia were awarded a penalty, only for the referee Alberto Rojo Miró to reverse his decision and decide the offence had taken place outside the box. A little later, he gave a goal to San Lorenzo despite the ball seeming not to have crossed the line. Distraught, Gimnasia staged a sit-down protest, allowing San Lorenzo to walk in four further goals before Miró abandoned the

---

[22] *Bombero* literally means 'fireman' but was commonly used in Argentina to refer to referees who had taken a bribe.

game. San Lorenzo went on to win the title with Gimnasia three points back: had they beaten Boca and drawn with San Lorenzo, they would have finished level on points, necessitating a play-off. Or, in a more positive frame of mind, they may not have lost back-to-back games at River Plate and Racing in the fourth- and fifth-last matches of the season and thus have won the title outright.

Either way, Gimnasia were convinced they had been cheated by two referees. That season, they had scored 90 goals, four more than Boca, the next most prolific, while conceding 55, more than anybody else in the top seven. They drew widespread sympathy as well, with a growing sense that the five *grandes* were becoming too powerful and dominating the league, by fair means and foul, to an unhealthy degree.[23]

But just as Gimnasia and Hirschl begin to emerge as victims, there is Guttmann to puncture the bubble. 'He had a famous or infamous trick,' he said. 'Hirschl made his players train with a heavy ball, similar to the ones used in England… Hirschl came up with the idea of giving a barbed ring to his goalkeeper to puncture the ball at the right moment so they could use their special, heavy ball – which the team had already got used to at the training sessions. He was a real hustler, I'm telling you.'[24]

Is the story true? Who knows? A similar story was also told about the River Plate striker Bernabé Ferreyra who supposedly liked to substitute a heavy ball to take advantage of his preternaturally powerful shot. Perhaps the literal truth is less important than the fact

---

[23] The anthropologist Eduardo Archetti notes in *Masculinities* that in 1936 the big five had 105,000 members and assets of 3.56 million pesos, while the other ten clubs from Buenos Aires or Avellaneda had only 56,000 members and assets of 1.35 million pesos between them.

[24] In Hámori, *Régi gólok, edzősorsok*.

that Guttmann regarded Hirschl as the sort of coach who might have got up to such tricks.

Which is not to say they did not get on. Subsequent events show they clearly did (from Guttmann, indeed, 'hustler' may have been intended as a compliment). And that meeting in São Paulo in 1930, when Guttmann was on tour with Hakoah, would go on to shape the whole course of football history, not just in Argentina, but in Uruguay and Brazil as well.

CHAPTER ELEVEN

CRAFTING *CALCIO*

It was supposed to be Luigi Allemandi's redemption but the day of the decisive game of the season, Inter's penultimate fixture, had gone very wrong indeed. The defender had been banned for life in 1927 after accepting an offer of 50,000 lira to ensure Juventus lost their derby to Torino, easing their city rivals' path to a title that was subsequently stripped from them. Only a pardon from Umberto, prince of Savoy, the son of Victor Emmanuel III (later Umberto II, the last king of Italy) allowed him to resume his career a year later. He had joined Inter, but life there was difficult.

They hadn't won the championship since 1920 and there was a clear sense that a club whose name celebrated its international origins had no place in Mussolini's Italy. There was a growing feeling too that, as the league was rationalised and a single national top division implemented, as opposed to the mess of regional competitions funnelling to a single final as had been the case, there was something unseemly about a city boasting multiple clubs. And so in 1928, Inter had merged with Unione Sportiva Milanese, Milan's third team, to 'avoid the dispersion of Milanese soccer forces' to create the Associazione Sportiva Ambrosiana and to free up a space in the league for Fiumana, a club from the symbolically important eastern city of

Fiume (now Rijeka in Croatia).[1] They had a red-and-white badge approved by the fascist authorities and wore an all-white kit.

Under the Hungarian coach József Viola, Inter[2] finished 1928–29 seventh in the eight-team final group, eight points adrift of the champions Torino. Crucially, though, by qualifying for that final group, Inter secured their place in Serie A, the national, professional top division inaugurated in 1929–30. Viola was nonetheless replaced by the man he had succeeded, his energetic young compatriot Árpád Weisz. Weisz was far from the first Hungarian to have a major impact in Italian football, but he would become perhaps the most significant, at least before the Second World War.

Inter regained their blue-and-black colours for the 1929–30 season, although with a black-and-white collar as a nod to US Milanese, but they lost the tactically astute centre-forward Fulvio Bernardini, who had joined Roma after expressing a desire to play in midfield. Weisz was unfazed. 'At last,' he is supposed to have said, 'I can play the kid.'

The kid was Giuseppe Meazza, a 19-year-old forward who had been rejected by AC Milan for being too small. Weisz, though, had recognised his ability, put him on a steak diet to build up his strength and had him kick a ball against a wall with each foot until he became equally comfortable with both. It took him just six minutes of the new season to demonstrate why Weisz had such faith in him, putting Inter ahead in a game they won 2–1 at Livorno.

Inter then lost 1–0 at Pro Vercelli, but a 2–1 victory over a strong Bologna in their first home game suggested that this might be a different Inter to the under-achievers of the previous decade. A win at Milan on the sixth day of the season, Meazza getting the

---

[1] The modern clubs of Napoli, Fiorentina and Roma were formed in the same period by similar mergers.

[2] To avoid confusion, I have continued to refer to the club by its original name.

winner, took them to the top of the table and although back-to-back defeats to Roma and Triestina saw them slip four points back by mid-December, the new year brought a run of six consecutive wins in which they scored 24 goals and beat their title rivals Genoa, Juventus and Torino to go top.

Weisz had introduced the concept of the *ritiro* by which the players stayed together in a hotel the night before a game, which seemed to give them a focus in keeping with the new professional age, while Allemandi thrived in the variant of the W-M the Hungarian had implemented. In terms of tactics and preparation, Inter were outstripping the rest of the division.

On the third-last weekend of the season, they faced Genoa, the team who lay second in the table, four points behind them. Win that game and they were champions. Within 14 minutes, they were 2–0 down. Meazza pulled one back. Genoa scored again. Inter were 3–1 down and facing a defeat that would have cut their lead to two points with two games to go and perhaps induced a decisive jitteriness. But Meazza scored two more to complete his hat-trick, the game was drawn 3–3 and Inter needed a single point from their final two games to seal the title.

They faced Juventus, who were third in the table, but a few minutes before kick-off, Allemandi still hadn't arrived. It had been his temper that had led to him being caught in 1927, as he was overheard remonstrating with a representative of the match-fixers who was reluctant to hand over the second half of his fee, and it got him into trouble again at the decisive moment of the season.

On the way to the stadium, he had been involved in a car accident and as he argued with the driver of the other car, punches had been exchanged. When he did eventually arrive at the ground, he was dishevelled and showing the effects of a fist fight. But he did get there on time, he did play and Inter won 2–0, making Weisz the first foreign coach to win the Italian title. At 34, he remains the youngest coach ever to do so.

* * *

Weisz had been born to a Jewish family in Solt, about 50 miles south of Budapest, on 16 April 1896. The son of Lázár, a vet, he was named after Árpád, the legendary Hungarian chieftain who had played a leading role in the conquest of the Carpathian basin and who is widely regarded as having founded the Hungarian nation in 895. Weisz moved to Budapest to attend law school and joined Törekvés, for whom he played as a left-winger. He volunteered to fight in the First World War, attaining the rank of lance-corporal, leading infantry in the 2nd Battalion. Archives held in Vienna show he was captured by Italian forces on 18 November 1915 on Mrzli Vrh, a mountain on the Isonzo Front in what is now Slovenia, where the Hungarians were entrenched. He remained as a prisoner of war in Trapani, in Sicily, until the end of 1919.[3]

Despite the White Terror, Weisz returned to Hungary and worked in a bank while resuming his career for Törekvés and winning seven international caps. In 1923, he and his teammate and good friend Ferenc Hirzer moved to Makabi Brno in Czechoslovakia. Both were named in the Hungary squad at the 1924 Olympics, although Weisz did not play, and both left Brno straight afterwards, Hirzer joining the Hamburg club SC Union 03 Altona and Weisz heading to Italy where he signed for Padova. He scored on his debut for them but never really settled, making just six appearances that season then moving to Inter, where he soon suffered a serious injury that effectively ended his playing career.

---

[3] I am grateful to Gábor Andreides for alerting me to these documents.

There follows a frustrating lacuna. Although there is a rumour that Weisz, having been impressed by the Uruguay side that won gold at the Olympics in Paris, moved briefly to Montevideo to learn more about how they played the game and ended up coaching the Uruguayan club América, I have found no evidence to support that claim.

What is certain is that if Weisz did leave, he was back in Italy in 1926. He worked briefly as an assistant to the Alessandria coach Augusto Rangone, who had been a member of the technical committee of the Italian Football Federation (FIGC) for four years and was a fan of the Danubian school. After a couple of months he returned to Inter (by then known as Ambrosiana), Italianising the spelling of his own name to Veisz. Bernardini may have left before the championship season but he acknowledged his debt to Weisz after he had become a manager and confirmed his reputation as one of Italy's foremost tactical thinkers by winning the *scudetto* with Fiorentina and Bologna – making him the only man to win the league with two sides from outside Turin and Milan.

For reasons that remain obscure, Weisz in 1928 returned briefly to Hungary, managing Sabaria in the western city of Szombathely, where he married a 19-year-old called Ilona Rechnitzer. Sabaria had won promotion to the top flight for the first time in 1926, finished fourth in each of their first two seasons up and were clearly ambitious, embarking on a four-month tour to South America, Mexico and New York but, within a year, Weisz was back in Italy, taking charge of Inter again.

Weisz's influence went far beyond producing a winning team. Along with Aldo Molinari, Inter's director of sport, he wrote *Il giuoco di calcio* [*The Game of Football*], which for a long time was regarded as a standard reference. The preface, by Vittorio Pozzo, described Ambrosiana/Inter as 'the most technical of Italian teams'. Meazza, who would go on to score 272 goals for the club, win two World Cups and have the stadium named after him, described Weisz as the best coach he ever had. Another of that *scudetto*-winning team, Gipo Viani, went on to lead Salernitana and Roma to promotion from Serie B and win two scudetti with Milan. He is regarded as one of the pioneers of *catenaccio* and was also clear about the role Weisz had played in his education.[4]

The season after the championship win was difficult, as injuries to Valentino Degani and Bonifacio Smerzi led to the premature elevation of the 20-year-old goalkeeper Pietro Miglio. Within the first six games of the season, Inter lost 6–0 to Torino and 5–0 to Triestina. Although they rallied in the second half of the campaign to finish fifth, Weisz left for Bari, and was replaced by another Hungarian, the diminutive former Ferencváros manager, István Tóth.

Tóth spoke fluent Italian and German and could also understand English well enough to translate articles to try to educate himself about tactical developments in what was still widely regarded the motherland of the game. Under Tóth, Inter finished sixth and Weisz, who had augmented his reputation by keeping Bari up in a relegation play-off, returned in 1932–33. Inter came second, but they were eight points adrift of the imposing champions Juventus, who sealed their third successive title. Inter by then had a new president, Ferdinando Pozzani, who would gain a reputation as a meddler and the nickname General Po as he went through seven managers in seven seasons. Tóth had been the first and Weisz in 1934 became the second, quitting after Pozzani tried to bring in another coach to work alongside him.

* * *

---

[4] For a detailed account of Viani and the development of *catenaccio*, see my book *Inverting the Pyramid*.

The Hungarian influence on Italian football was extraordinary, perhaps even greater than it had been in Austria. Between 1920 and 1945, 60 Hungarians coached in Italy. There was, for instance, Géza Kertész, who became a master of the Italian lower leagues. He had been born in Budapest in November 1894, the youngest of three children. There are suggestions that he was illegitimate and that he was brought up by his grandparents but his grandson Lajos Péczely, the son of Kertész's daughter Kató, is unsure and there seems to be no documentary evidence.

As a footballer, Kertész was regarded as intelligent and versatile, although so lacking in pace that he was nicknamed 'Lajhár' [Sloth]. It was not a moniker he relished. 'He never belonged to those people with a childlike spirit who were overjoyed by having a nickname,' *Nemzeti Sport* noted.[5]

Kertész joined BTC in 1911, fought in the First World War, returned to Budapest and then moved to Ferencváros in 1920, where he was mainly used as an inside-forward with István Tóth as the central striker. Kertész played once, in a 2–0 defeat to Austria in 1914, for the Hungary national side and, in 1925, he moved to Italy where he became player-manager of Spezia.

He led them to promotion from the Seconda Divisione (the third flight) and, after retiring from playing, moved to Carrarese as manager. He took them to immediate promotion as well, and then kept them up in the Prima Divisione. His career then was one of constant wandering around Italy's lower leagues. He won promotions from the third flight to Serie B with Salernitana, Catanzarese, Catania and Taranto and, in 1938–39, he missed out on promotion to Serie A with Atalanta only after a defeat on the final day of the season to Venezia.

---

[5] *Nemzeti Sport*, 11 April 1925.

'My father always remembered Géza as somebody with a good heart,' said Péczely. 'He was a calm, balanced man. He didn't look for conflict, or shout at his players as a coach. He loved dry red wine and was a great fan of opera. He and my father loved the Italian tenor Beniamino Gigli.'

* * *

Then there was the half-back Ernő Erbstein, who had joined Olimpia in Fiume (Rijeka) in 1924, and soon found the Italian game to his liking. A little over two decades later, as manager, Erbstein would create one of the greatest sides Italy has ever known, Il Grande Torino. He had been born in Oradea (then Nagyvárad; the city is now in Romania) in May 1898 and his family moved to Budapest in the first decade of the 20th century. He joined MTK as a youth player but wasn't good enough to progress to the senior side so signed for BAK, essentially a mid-table side although they did reach the Hungarian Cup final in 1913.

In 1916, Erbstein earned his school-leaving certificate, made his debut in the Hungarian league in a 7–1 defeat to Törekvés and began his military service. Because of his education he only had to serve one year rather than three and had the right to apply to a training school for reserve officers. He was sent to the front as a corporal in November and by the time he returned to Budapest in September 1917 he had been promoted to sergeant. Erbstein and his men joined the Aster Revolution, seeking a reformist government and the dissolution of the monarchy and, to that end, on 31 October 1918 they stormed and occupied the Budapest post office.

When the war and the subsequent upheavals were over, Erbstein rejoined BAK while continuing to work as a stockbroker. He was noted for his tough tackling and, as Dominic Bliss points out in his biography, Erbstein seems to have been mentioned in the newspapers a disproportionate amount for somebody at such an unfashionable club.

BAK were relegated in 1921 and, in March the following season, an article in *Nemzeti Sport* referred to Erbstein as 'infamous' after a league game against BEAC:[6] 'Erbstein jumped with both feet into the stomach of the BEAC centre-half Sághy.'[7] The referee decided the offence was unintentional but Sághy's brother, a police officer who happened to be present, intervened and recommended that charges be filed against Erbstein and that the MLSZ take action against Szeiff, the referee, but nothing seems to have come of it.

In April 1922, Erbstein moved to Arad, part of the Transylvanian territory that had been ceded to Romania at Trianon. He remained on the books of BAK but joined Hakoah Arad, who were part of the local league, seemingly playing more as a forward than as a half. The MLSZ was unhappy with his shuttling back and forth and his registration with BAK was briefly suspended. He remained a tenacious player, *Nemzeti Sport* wearily reporting a series of disciplinary hearings, noting that he had broken an opponent's leg 'in the usual style'.

In September 1923, a month after being called into the Romania squad for a game against Poland but not selected for the starting XI, Erbstein returned to Budapest, began playing for BAK again and was sent off in his first game back. At around that time, he met Jolán Huterer; they married the following year.

One game into the 1924–25 season came Erbstein's big break as he was offered a professional contract by Olympia. Fiume had been declared a neutral city at Versailles, placing it under the control of the League of Nations but, in 1919, Italian nationalists led by Gabriele D'Annunzio, a romantic poet, seized the town. The Italian government

---

[6] Budapesti Egyetemi Atlétikai Club, the Budapest University Athletics Club.

[7] Cited in Bliss, *Erbstein*.

wanted nothing to do with D'Annunzio and he ruled Fiume as his personal fiefdom for 15 months before international neutrality was reimposed. But in October 1922, fascist brigades marched on Rome, forcing the resignation of the liberal regime. The king, Vittorio Emanuele III, allowed Mussolini to form a government and he, recognising the symbolic potency of what D'Annunzio had done, annexed the city in March 1924. In hindsight, it may look odd that Erbstein should move to an overtly fascist state but at the time there was no direct relationship between Italian fascism and anti-Semitism.

Erbstein settled quickly, seemingly a more mature player than he had been in Budapest. Certainly the references to his rough play in match reports became far less regular, although it may be that says more about Italian football at the time than it does about Erbstein. According to Luca Dibenedetto's history of football in the region, *El balon fiuman*, Erbstein became 'an undisputed leader who assumed responsibility on the pitch... He managed central midfield with methodological intelligence, setting the tempo of the team like a true organiser of the game.'[8] He was sent off for retaliating against Arnaldo Novello in an away game at Venezia but the local press, far from condemning him, praised him for defending the honour of the team.

Late in the season, Erbstein missed a penalty in a derby against Gloria. It proved costly as Olympia drew a game they should have won. The dropped point meant they finished the season joint top with Vicenza and Udinese, necessitating a three-team play-off. Olympia lost both their games; Vicenza won both of theirs. With Vicenza apparently promoted, Erbstein agreed to join them, only for it to emerge that the two Hungarian players Vicenza had signed a few months earlier, Ferenc Molnár and István Horváth, had already turned out

---

[8] Cited in Bliss, *Erbstein*.

for Italian clubs earlier that season, which was against the regulations. They remained in the same division and Udinese were promoted in their place. Vicenza's manager was another Hungarian, János Béky, who had been a centre-half for Törekvés the previous decade. That season, Erbstein and Jolán had their first child, Susanna.[9]

Changes were coming in Italian football, though, as the authorities sought to reduce the reliance on foreign talent. At the end of 1925–26, journalists and senior figures from the Italian game met in the Tuscan resort of Viareggio to discuss the future of the Italian game. One of the aims, said Landro Ferretti, the fascist president of the Italian National Olympic Committee (Coni), was to 'find a point of harmony between the superior rights of the sport as a racial gymnasium – gymnasia of discipline, courage and solidarity – and the rights of the club to affirm and consolidate their sporting apprenticeships in the long term.'

They decided to begin work on establishing a national league and to ban foreign signings, with a one-year amnesty for those who had already agreed deals for 1926–27. That was at least 80 players, the majority of them from Austria or Hungary. His one-year contract up, Erbstein returned to Budapest and joined Húsos.

There was no legislation, though, against foreign coaches and, after his trip to the US with the Maccabees, Erbstein returned to Italy as manager of US Bari, a club formed by the merger of three local clubs as the municipality sought to create a force that could compete on a national level. Erbstein's start in management was not auspicious. He tried to implement the variant of the W-M he had learned in the US, but Bari didn't win a single away game and finished 13th of 16 in

[9] In Hungarian this would be spelled Zsuzsanna, but I have stuck with the Italian spelling by which she is better known. For her younger sister, similarly, I have preferred 'Marta' to the Hungarian 'Márta'.

their division, meaning they failed to qualify for the inaugural Serie A season. Erbstein was replaced as manager by the great Austrian centre-forward Josef Uridil.

Erbstein moved to Nocera Inferiore in Campania to coach AG Nocerina in the Southern Division, from which one team would be promoted to Serie B. Nocerina finished joint-second behind Palermo, who had inflicted their only home defeat of the season, a game awarded to the champions following a 1–1 draw after fans reacted furiously to the sending off of their captain Rescigno for punching the centre-forward Carlo Radice. That might, perhaps, have been the basis for another promotion challenge the following season, but Nocerina were struggling financially and applied for voluntary relegation. Erbstein moved on to Cagliari, who had finished a place behind Nocerina.

As Jolán, eight months pregnant, returned to Budapest so Marta, their second daughter, could be born a Hungarian citizen, Erbstein enjoyed his first meaningful success as a coach. He had a gift for identifying previously unsung talent and began to have his players practise preset moves. Cagliari won promotion with ease in that 1930–31 season and then finished 13th of 18 sides in Serie B in 1931–32. They too, though, then embarked on a policy of retrenchment and Erbstein was effectively forced out.

He returned to Bari but he lasted just six games before being sacked following a 5–1 defeat to their relegation rivals Casale and replaced by another Hungarian, János Baár. Erbstein may have been in charge for little more than a month, but it had been enough to attract another suitor. Lucchese's owner, Giuseppe Della Santina, a major figure in the burgeoning Italian construction industry, had seen one of those six games (probably the win over Fiorentina) and, liking what he had seen, appointed Erbstein in 1933.

Lucchese were a club with ambition and completed a new stadium, built to blend in with the famous city walls, in 1934–35. Erbstein signed Bruno Scher, who had scored three times for Triestina against Erbstein's Bari in 1928–29 and had been his second signing in his second stint at Bari. In terms of ability, he probably should have been playing in Serie A but he was a Communist from Istria, one of the 'reclaimed' territories, had expressed anti-fascist sentiment and was perceived as unreliable.

Erbstein's abilities as a manager were finally becoming clear. 'He could understand better than anyone the nature, character and feelings of his boys,' wrote Luca Tronchetti, the sports correspondent of the local newspaper *Il Tirreno*.[10] He was strict, with very clear ideas about what he needed. On one occasion he is said to have refused to sign a player because 'his hair is too long; he cannot be a great player.' He demanded effort and commitment: 'Courage and sweat,' he would say, 'are the ingredients with which we must prepare the cake of victory.'

Erbstein's approach was rooted in counter-attacking, as was the case for many who employed the W-M, but where many other exponents of the system were concerned primarily with pace and physical conditioning, he prioritised technique, striving to make his players two-footed. One favoured drill was to take them to a patch of rough ground behind the training field – known as the '*Campaccio*' ('bad pitch') – and have them kick a ball against a brick wall alternately with one foot then the other – deliberately perhaps, recreating the conditions of the *grunds*.

Lucchese won First Division group F with some ease, scoring 80 goals in 28 games to finish seven points clear of Pisa and qualify for a play-off group for promotion to Serie B. They cruised through that

---

[10] Cited in Bliss, *Erbstein*.

as well, winning five and drawing one of their six games. It may still have been at a relatively low level, but there was a sense of Erbstein maturing as a coach.

On promotion, Erbstein signed the goalkeeper Aldo Olivieri. He was 24 and would go on to be one of the heroes of Italy's victory at the 1938 World Cup, but at the time he was without a club having been released by Padova after suffering serious head injuries in a game in Fiume seven months earlier.

Lucchese finished seventh in 1934–35. They had the second-best defensive record in the league but had found goals hard to come by. Crucially, though, they finished in the top half and so took their place in the newly unified national Serie B the following season. Erbstein resolved their goalscoring problems by signing the forward Vinicio Viani from Fiorentina that summer; the forward scored 34 goals in 1935–36.

Lucchese's main strength, though, remained the inventiveness of their manager. In a game at home to Pro Vercelli near the end of the season, Erbstein found himself without either recognised full-back because of injury. His solution was to play Viani at full-back and introduce the 17-year-old Danilo Michelini at centre-forward. Michelini got both Lucchese goals in a 2–1 win, helping them to promotion to Serie A.

His performance emboldened Erbstein, who let Viani return to Fiorentina at the end of the season, with the *oriundo*[11] left-winger Carlos Gringa and the left-half Bruno Neri moving the other way. An extremely cultured and proud liberal, Neri was just as controversial a figure as Scher and had refused to give the fascist salute at the

---

[11] The *'oriundi'* – literally 'returners' – were South American players who claimed Italian heritage and so were able to circumvent the ban on foreign players.

inauguration of Fiorentina's Stadio Giovanni Berta in 1931.[12] At the time, the swap was widely seen as an example of Fiorentina flexing their authority as the biggest team in Tuscany but as the season developed it began to be suggested that Erbstein had taken the ruthless decision that Viani, despite his goals, was too predictable for the style he wanted to play. If that was his reasoning, Erbstein was thoroughly vindicated: Lucchese finished their first Serie A season seventh in the table, unbeaten at home, and while Michelini scored 13 goals, Viani managed only ten.

* * *

After leaving Inter, Weisz took charge at Novara in Serie B, leading them to fourth and then, in the spring of 1935, he moved on to Bologna, replacing another Hungarian, the former MTK defender Lajos Kovács. He moved into a house on via Valeriani, about half a mile from the Stadio Littoriale and quarter of a mile from the training ground. Not far away was the Café del Corso, where the Austrian coach Hermann Felsner, wearing his trademark bowler hat and a monocle, had announced himself in 1920 after Bologna officials had forgotten to meet him at the station. It would become a meeting point for the city's fascists before being destroyed by a US bomb in 1945.

---

[12] In October 1936, Neri was called up to the national side for a game against Switzerland. He refused to give the fascist salute and although, slightly surprisingly, he was picked twice more, unease was growing about his dissidence. In September 1943, after the German occupation of Italy, Neri joined the Partisans, becoming a battalion vice-commander with the codename Berni. He was still playing for Faenza while gathering information to pass on to the Allies. In July 1944, Neri and his commander, carrying sensitive documents, were surrounded by a German patrol while sheltering in a hermitage between Faenza and Florence. Knowing the situation was hopeless, they came out firing and were gunned down by the side of the road. Two years later, Faenza renamed their stadium after him.

Bologna finished sixth that season as Juventus won a fifth straight title. Although the previous summer the captain Eraldo Monzeglio had moved to Rome – where he taught Mussolini's children tennis – Weisz's squad was packed with gifted players and big personalities. There was Angelo Schiavio, who'd scored the winner for Italy in the 1934 World Cup final, while in midfield there were a pair of Uruguayan *oriundi*, Raffaele Sansone and Francisco Fedullo, who switched positions so much that they became known as Fedone and Sansullo. That flexibility and inter-movement was key to the passing game Weisz demanded. Monzeglio had been replaced at the back by the agile Dino Fiorini, who would join the National Republican Guard and be killed by partisans in 1944. The centre-half and leader of the side was Michele Andreolo, another Uruguayan, who was notorious for his love of late-night drinking and cards, and for taking his teammates to the brothels around via Indipendenza.

Weisz was a tolerant and well-liked boss. If he had a point he wanted to make to a player, he would invite him to his house for dinner. His family settled well. Sansone's wife Olga described Weisz's wife Ilona as 'beautiful and elegant'. School reports show his son Roberto was the best in his class in both 1936 and 1937, considered 'praiseworthy' in arithmetic and accounting, spelling, various notions, religion (Catholicism), physical education and conduct.[13]

Again Weisz introduced various modernisations, subcontracting a company to maintain the pitch to his satisfaction and installing a heated dressing room and treatment facility at the stadium. As what would now be called a conditioning coach, a concept that was all but unknown at the time, he brought in Filippo Pascucci, who'd coached Argentina at the 1934 World Cup before becoming a gymnastics

---

[13] As revealed by Matteo Marani's research, detailed in his book, *Dallo scudetto ad Auschwitz* (Imprimatur, 2014).

instructor on a cruise liner. In that first full season, Weisz led Bologna to the title. That August, he and his team were granted an audience with Mussolini.

Schiavio, Bologna's all-time top scorer, retired that summer, but Weisz was prepared, having groomed the winger Carlo Reguzzoni to replace him. Bologna retained their title, something only Juve had managed previously, and Reguzzoni went on to become the second-highest scorer in the club's history.

Even greater success followed. In the summer of 1937, Bologna went to France to play in the Tournoi International de l'Exposition Universelle de Paris. Also competing were the French champions Marseille, the French Cup winners Sochaux, the 1936 Mitropa Cup[14] winners Austria Wien, the Czechoslovak champions Slavia Prague, the German Cup winners VfB Leipzig, Phőbus Budapest, who had just finished fourth in Hungary, and Chelsea, 13th in England that season. Bologna beat Sochaux and Slavia Prague to reach the final, in which they hammered Chelsea 4–1, Reguzzoni scoring a hat-trick. They became the first Italian side to beat an English club in a competitive match, being described back home as 'the team that shook the world'.

There was no reason to think Bologna would not continue to prosper, but history was catching up with Weisz.

---

[14] The Mitropa Cup was an early international tournament for clubs from central Europe.

CHAPTER TWELVE

THE GERMAN REFORMATION

When the full-time whistle blew in Berlin, Nürnberg and Hamburg were level at 2–2, sending the final of the 1922 German championship into extra time. It had been a thrilling game and a brutal one. Numerous Hamburg players had been carried off on stretchers – to be dismissed as 'actors' when they recovered sufficiently to carry on – while the Nürnberg defender Anton Kugler lost five teeth. On and on the game went, beyond the usual 30 minutes of extra time and into sudden death. 'They were staggering across the pitch, near a complete breakdown,' one contemporary report said.[1] 'Nobody had any strength left for a shot on goal, but nobody was willing to give up either.' Finally, darkness forced the referee, Dr Peco Bauwens, to bring the game to an end.

A replay was arranged for Leipzig seven weeks later. The ill-feeling of the first game fermented. Around 60,000 packed into a stadium designed for 40,000 and witnessed a match of shocking violence. Nürnberg's Willi Böß was sent off after 17 minutes for kicking Albert

---

[1] Cited in Uli Hesse, *Tor!* (WSC, 2002).

Beier in the stomach, something that earned him a 12-month suspension. Heinrich Träg, who had also scored the opener in the first game, put Nürnberg ahead three minutes after half-time, but Karl Schneider levelled with 21 minutes remaining. Again, the game went into extra time. Kugler was injured after 100 minutes and forced off; Nürnberg were down to nine. Then Träg was sent off. 'His act was so mean,' Bauwens said, 'that I came close to ending the game right then.'[2]

At half-time in extra time, it was still level. But then Luitpold Popp collapsed, and Nürnberg were down to seven. The Eternal Final, as history would remember it, could not, Bauwens decided, go on. Nürnberg protested and, after months of wrangling, the German Football Federation (DFB) came upon a solution. They awarded the title to Hamburg but urged them not to accept on grounds of sportsmanship. Hamburg acquiesced, and the trophy has both clubs' names engraved on it for that season.

Hamburg's manager was AW Turner, a mysterious figure who was probably but not necessarily English. Nürnberg's was the great former MTK centre-half Dori Kürschner.

After leaving MTK's 1919 tour in Stuttgart, Kürschner's ascent in Germany was rapid. He won the Württemberg championship with Stuttgarter Kickers in 1921, which qualified them for the South Group of the Süddeutsche Meisterschaft. They went out of that having drawn three of their four games, but Kürschner's management had caught the eye of Nürnberg, who appointed him for the national play-offs. He led them to success in the final, in which they beat Vorwärts 90 Berlin 5–0. Kürschner left for Bayern Munich, had a brief stint at Eintracht Frankfurt and was back at Nürnberg by the end of the following season for the Eternal Final.

---

[2] Cited in Uli Hesse, *Tor!*

Kürschner moved on in 1923 to Switzerland, where he became Nordstern Basel's first full-time coach and led them to promotion to the top flight. So impressive were his achievements that he was placed in charge of one of three regional selections to prepare the Switzerland national team for the 1924 Olympics; the other two were overseen by Jimmy Hogan and another Englishman, Teddy Duckworth, a former Blackpool outside-right who was coaching Servette in Geneva. Duckworth was named head coach for the Games, to which Switzerland travelled with such low expectations that they'd booked their return rail ticket for ten days after their arrival. A pre-tournament friendly victory over Hungary was largely overlooked at the time, but it came to seem increasingly significant as Switzerland, inspired by the goalscoring feats of Max Abegglen,[3] beat Lithuania, Czechoslovakia, Italy and Sweden to reach the final, where they were beaten by a Uruguay side beginning a period of global domination that would bring them another Olympic gold and, in 1930, the inaugural World Cup.

Kürschner returned to Germany, becoming the first full-time coach of Schwarz-Weiß Essen – with whom he beat MTK in a friendly – before he went back to Switzerland and, after all the years of travel, settled down in Zurich as manager of Grasshoppers, who had by then signed Abegglen. In nine years there, he married a woman called Alice Widmer and won three league titles and four Swiss Cups.

Kürschner was a hugely popular figure, the creases around his eyes in contemporary photographs suggesting a man used to smiling. When outside, he was rarely without a hat to cover the thinning hair

---

[3] The Swiss team Neuchâtel Xamax derives its name from him. It was founded in 1970 by a merger of Cantonal and Xamax, a team of which Abegglen, nicknamed 'Xam', had been a founder member.

that became increasingly sparse as time went by. 'He is a great person, all over Switzerland they know and love him,' said 'a respectable citizen' quoted in a profile in *Ujság*.[4] He was good friends with both Hugo Meisl and Walther Bensemann, a pioneer of German football who founded the magazine *Kicker* in 1920 and was its editor before being ousted for being a Jew in 1933; Bensemann subsequently moved to Montreux, where he died in November 1934. Kürschner's home in a leafy suburb of Zurich, a profile in *Pécsi Napló* noted, was 'a meeting place for Swiss and foreign football politicians'.[5] Some indication of his sense of a wider responsibility to football is perhaps offered by the fact that, in 1931, he loaned money to save Austria Vienna, who had fallen into financial difficulty, for which he was awarded a gold medal by the Austrian football federation.

Kürschner left Grasshoppers in 1934 after a year with Young Boys in Bern, before making the move that would revolutionise global football.[6]

* * *

After injury forced his retirement as a player, Kálmán Konrád needed a job. As Gertrud, his fiancée, invested in a second cinema in Berlin, he found one at Bayern Munich, where he succeeded another former MTK player, albeit somebody who had been largely a reserve, Leó Weisz.[7] Since MTK's 1919 tour, Bayern had been determined to find a way of playing the Danubian way.

---

[4] *Ujság*, 21 May 1931.

[5] *Pécsi Napló*, 28 February 1937.

[6] I am grateful to Gunnar Persson for his help in piecing together Kürschner's career.

[7] There is a certain amount of confusion over this, in part because Weisz in various accounts is referred to as Konrad Weiss, which appears to be a conflation of the two Hungarians.

After Jim McPherson, a Scot who had tried to instil a short-passing style, had been sacked having led Bayern to fourth in the regional league in 1925, the Bayern chairman Kurt Landauer tried to appoint another former MTK player, Imre Pozsonyi, who was about to leave Barcelona. Pozsonyi, though, opted instead to accept an offer from DFC Prag. Bensemann expressed his regret because Pozsonyi was not only a great coach but also 'a consummate chef'.[8] Landauer turned instead to Weisz, on whose culinary abilities Bensemann was silent.

Weisz took Bayern to the Süddeutsche Meisterschaft, earning a spot in the play-offs for the German championship in which they lost in the semi-final to Hamburg, leading to his replacement by Konrád. In Konrád's first season in charge, 1928–29, Bayern got through the regional leagues and progressed to the national quarter-final by beating Jimmy Hogan's Dresden but then lost in extra time against Breslau. The following season they finished third and didn't even make the national play-offs. Konrád's contract was not renewed and he was replaced by the Austrian Richard 'Dombi' Kohn, who finally led Bayern to their first national championship in 1931–32.

Konrád moved on to FC Zurich in 1930–31 and finished fifth in the eastern group as Grasshoppers, under Dori Kürschner, won the title. When his contract wasn't renewed, Konrád went to Berlin and began working in the cinema he owned, selling tickets and working as a projectionist. He had married Gertrud in 1929 and it was in Berlin in 1932 that his son Peter was born. Perhaps, given his managerial career hadn't really taken off, Konrád would have been happy there working in his cinema, but the option was soon closed to him.

---

[8] Cited in Schulze-Marmeling, *Der FC Bayern, seine Juden und die Nazis*.

His brother Jenő, meanwhile, after a brief stint as coach of Hakoah, had worked in Timişoara (Temesvár) and again in Vienna when, in August 1930, he was appointed coach of Nürnberg. With five national titles, they were at the time the most successful club in Germany – so successful, in fact, that they were nicknamed simply 'the Club'. In 1932 his side reached the semi-final of the southern division before being beaten by Kohn's Bayern.

Generally, though, things were good. 'We had a pleasant and comfortable life,' Evelyn Konrád said – although the political situation meant it could never be entirely pleasant or comfortable. 'My parents played tennis and bridge but to get to the club you had to walk past the Nazi HQ,' she recalled. 'My mother would close her eyes when they got near and my father would have to lead her past.'

They socialised with the former Germany international Hans Kalb and the pencil magnate Baron Faber. 'My main memory of my mother in those days was of her leaning over my crib before she went out for the night,' Evelyn said. 'She always smelled good. She was a very beautiful woman. I was always looking out for my father and I was always thinking men swarmed around my mother – well, they did!'

But she enjoyed life in Nuremberg as well. 'I always liked boys, I liked attention, and they would tease me,' she said. 'On Sundays I would always have time with my father. He would tell me stories from literature and history. My mother would tell my father not to take a fiacre but we always would and there would be boys chasing after us for his autograph while I sat there proud like a *Hahn auf dem Mist* [literally "a rooster on a pile of dirt" – a German (and Hungarian) idiom meaning somebody very pleased with themselves].'

But, like Weisz and Kohn, the Konráds were Jewish and in Germany in the early 1930s, that was an increasingly dangerous thing to be. In August 1932, the Nazi propaganda paper *Der Stürmer* launched an attack on Konrád. 'Nürnberg football club is being destroyed by the Jews,' it said. 'A Jew is unthinkable as a true sportsman. He is not built for it, with his abnormal and deformed figure ... Club! Come to your senses and wake up. Give your coach a ticket to Jerusalem.'[9]

Konrád decided he had no future in Germany. 'I have been insulted in my person,' he said. 'After careful consideration, I decided to go immediately For me, the two years at the club were not a small episode that you forget on the train between Nuremberg and Vienna, but an experience that will live on with me, even when I've lived elsewhere for a long, long time.'[10]

A few days later, Konrád, Greta and Evelyn left Nuremberg, taking an overnight train to Vienna. 'The club didn't want him to go,' said Evelyn, 'and officials all came to the railway station to see us off.'

'With emotion,' said the vice-president Karl Müller, 'those present saw an irreproachable person leave, to whom bitter injustice has been done.'[11]

The rise of the Nazis as a political force in Germany had been rapid. They had been involved in a series of violent clashes with Communists through the 1920s, but in the presidential election of March 1929, the Nazi candidate Erich Ludendorff polled only 1.1 per cent of the vote. A referendum that December, though, a failed attempt by nationalists to renounce the Treaty of Versailles, brought the Nazis credibility and popularity. A month later Horst Wessel,

---

[9] *Der Stürmer*, 3 August 1932.

[10] Cited in Werner Skrentny's article '*Von Serbien nach New York, von Budapest nach Stockholm: die Odysee der Konrad-Zwillinge*,' in *Davidstern und Lederball*, ed. Dieter Schulze-Marmeling (Werkstatt, 2003).

[11] Cited in Skrentny.

one of the leaders of the Sturmabteilung, the SA – the Nazis' 'storm-troopers' or Brownshirts – was shot and killed by two Communists in Berlin. A song he had written the previous year, the 'Horst-Wessel-Lied', became a Nazi anthem while Wessel was portrayed as a martyr.

An unprecedented propaganda campaign fed on the global economic collapse that had followed the Wall Street Crash and, in elections in September 1930, the Nazis gained 107 seats in the Reichstag, making them the second largest party. The following month, the SA launched its first major anti-Semitic attack, smashing the windows of shops owned by Jews on Potsdamer Platz.

The Nazis made further gains at elections in July 1932, becoming the largest single party but without a majority. Hitler withdrew support from the chancellor, Franz von Papen, and demanded the post for himself. Papen dissolved parliament and called another election for that November. It was no more conclusive, though, and the German parliament remained hopelessly divided. Papen proposed ruling by decree while a new electoral system was devised and an upper house introduced, but the ambitious Major-General Kurt von Schleicher convinced the president, Paul von Hindenburg, to sack Papen and install him instead. Papen, having nearly defeated Hitler, began negotiating with him to overthrow Schleicher.

The result was that Hitler was made chancellor of a short-lived coalition between the Nazis and the German National People's Party, with a new cabinet sworn in on 23 January 1933. Following the Reichstag fire the following month, which was blamed on the Dutch communist Marinus van der Lubbe, the Nazis began to suspend civil liberties. The Communist Party was banned and, after further elections again failed to produce an overall majority, Hitler, with the SA surrounding the Reichstag, persuaded the other parties to pass the

Enabling Act on 24 March 1933, giving him notionally temporary emergency powers to act without parliamentary consent. Non-Nazi parties were banned in July and, after the death of Hindenburg in August 1934, Hitler combined the positions of president and chancellor, achieving full dictatorial power.

Almost as soon as the Enabling Act had been passed, a programme of systematic anti-Semitism began. On 1 April 1933, a boycott on Jewish shops and businesses was announced. Six days later, Jews were banned from government positions, the first of a series of laws designed to encourage emigration. In May 1935, Jews were banned from serving in the army. That autumn, sexual relations between Germans and Jews (later extended to include other 'non-Aryan races') were prohibited, and Jews were stripped of their citizenship – the so-called Nuremberg Laws. In 1936, Jews were banned from all professional jobs and over the following two years, further measures were taken effectively to segregate Jews from the rest of the population. When, on 7 November 1938, a young Polish Jew called Herschel Grynszpan shot and killed the German diplomat Ernst vom Rath in Paris, the Nazi propaganda minister Joseph Goebbels ordered retaliation. On 9 November, the SS and SA perpetrated *Kristallnacht*, a night of attacks on synagogues and Jewish property in which 91 Jews were killed and a further 30,000 taken to concentration camps.

In total, an estimated 35,000 Jews fled Germany and Austria in the 1930s. By 1945, three-quarters of the Jewish population of 140,000 were dead.

As the 1930s went on, the number of countries in which Jewish coaches could be employed became increasingly small. After Bayern, Leo Weisz had gone to Breslau (Wrocław), then Würzburger Kickers and Alemannia Aachen. He was forced out in 1932 and went to Switzerland with Biel/Bienne. Landauer was forced to stand down as president of Bayern in March 1933 and, on 9 April, in Stuttgart, the biggest clubs in southern Germany signed a declaration that they would co-operate with the Nazi regime 'in particular with regard to the removal of Jews from sports clubs'. Bayern were among them; Dombi Kohn, having led them to the championship the previous season, was expelled and, after a stint working with Kürschner at Grasshoppers, became coach of Barcelona.

Under threat in Berlin, Kálmán Konrád moved to Prague in 1933 where he was named coach of Slavia. They won the league under him in 1934–35 and forced a play-off against FK Austria in the Mitropa Cup quarter-final in July 1935. The depression, though, had hit Slavia hard and they struggled to pay their staff. Never shy of taking legal action, Konrád sued for 23,500 krone (£200 when the maximum wage for players in England was £8/week). A court settled the case in November 1935.

In February 1936, Konrád moved on to CFR Bucharest (the fore-runner of Rapid), finishing runners-up in the league and winning the Romanian Cup in his second season. Konrád also assisted the Romania national team manager Costel Rădulescu in five matches between May 1936 and June 1937. He left Romania in the summer of 1937 to go to Brno where he took charge of SK Židenice. They came third in 1937–38, equalling their previous best finish, which had been achieved under his brother. His managerial career was picking up.

Having left Nürnberg, Jenő Konrád had found work in Romania, leading Ripensia Timişoara to the league title in 1933. 'We lived in a villa on the river,' Evelyn remembered. 'I had two yellow ducklings as pets, but one morning I went out and… they tried to shield it from me, but the river rats had got them. They were a bloody mess. I never wanted pets after that.'

Then it was on, via Vienna, to Brno, where Jenő took Židenice to third in 1934–35 and fourth in 1935–36. Evelyn's main memory of her time there was of a ferocious ballet teacher who corrected her pupils' posture with a silver-tipped black cane. The Konráds returned, briefly, to Vienna, where they stayed with Greta's mother. 'My grandmother,' Evelyn said, 'had a movie theatre. She was a remarkable woman. The hairdresser came every day at 10am. Otto Preminger[12] was a protégé of hers. My grandfather had owned a haberdasher's on Mariahilfer Straße,[13] but he had gone missing during the First World War. For a time, the police came nearly every week to show my grandmother a suicide and see if she could identify him. She then married a man who produced combs and then a very distinguished gentleman with a grey moustache called Breitner. It was only when I was 14 that I learned he wasn't my real grandfather.'

But then it was on again, as Jenő was offered the Triestina job. 'My mother never wanted to leave Vienna,' Evelyn said. 'She would cry when she heard *Wienerlieder*.[14] I remember her locking herself in the bathroom, shouting through the door that she would divorce my father if we left. But she went ahead of us to Trieste to find a suitable school. She found a convent school and they asked if I'd be wearing a cross – all the girls at the convent wore an ivory cross on a ribbon

---

[12] Preminger emigrated to the US where he became a major film director. He was nominated for the Academy Award for Best Director for *Laura* (1944) and *The Cardinal* (1963), while his film *Anatomy of a Murder* (1960) was nominated for Best Picture. He also directed Jean Seberg in *Saint Joan* (1957) and the George Gershwin-scored *Porgy and Bess* (1959), as well as playing Mr Freeze in the 1966 *Batman* TV series with Adam West.

[13] One of the most exclusive shopping streets in Vienna.

[14] Traditional Viennese songs that typically combine humour and melancholy.

whose colour designated their house. "If all the other pupils do, then she will," my mother said.'

Evelyn was a good student and enjoyed her time there. Trieste, generally, was good to the Konráds, but Europe was becoming increasingly volatile and increasingly dangerous.

CHAPTER THIRTEEN

SOUTH AMERICAN REVOLUTIONARIES

Brazil in 1937 were not the footballing power they are now. They had won the Campeonato Sudamericano in 1919 and 1922, both on home soil, but that was all, and there was a clear sense that they lagged behind Uruguay and Argentina. The potential was manifestly there, given the size of the country and the love for football, but it remained largely untapped.

José Bastos Padilha had made his fortune in printing, producing adverts for newspapers, and had become president of Flamengo in 1933. He was ambitious, determined to make Flamengo the most successful club in Rio de Janeiro. He developed the stadium, signed the hugely gifted trio of Fausto dos Santos, Domingos da Guia and Leônidas da Silva in 1936 and, the following year, appointed Dori Kürschner as manager. Quite why he turned to him remains unclear. He perhaps remembered Jenő Medgyessy's time at Botafogo and Fluminense a decade earlier; perhaps he recognised that central European expertise could help Brazil catch up tactically.

It was an appointment that was not without difficulties. Kürschner, whose name would soon be transmuted into 'Kruschner', leading to decades of confusion as Brazilian historians tried to track the origins of this mysterious prophet from a distant land, did not speak Portuguese. As an interpreter, he used his assistant Flávio Costa. Unfortunately, Costa had been pushed aside to let Kürschner take over as coach, and he had not taken the demotion well.

Kürschner's football was very different to the Brazilian game. He may have grown up in the cerebral MTK style, but he, like so many Hungarians, had recognised that after the 1925 change in the offside law, the 2–3–5 needed reform. The centre-half had to drop deeper and, while the tendency by the Danube was for him to function just in front of the full-backs as a deep-lying creator with some defensive responsibility, in Switzerland the interpretation tended more to the British style, with the centre-half, if not quite a pure stopper, then certainly more a back with some characteristics of a half than a half with some characteristics of a back.

There had been some recognition in Brazil of developments in Europe. Gentil Cardoso was an extrovert and a great teller of tales and he may have revolutionised Brazilian football before Kürschner's arrival had it not been for two major issues: he had next to no background as a player and he was black, which in the Brazil of the time made managerial positions extremely hard to come by.

Cardoso had been a bootblack, a waiter, a tram driver and a baker before joining the merchant navy. He travelled regularly to Europe, where he seems to have spent most of his free time watching football. English football, in particular, fascinated him and he later claimed to have watched first hand Herbert Chapman's development of the W-M at Arsenal. He recognised the possibilities of the new system, different as it was to Brazilian football, and sought to introduce it back at home. He was given his chance at the Carioca side Sírio Libanês, where he oversaw the emergence of the great centre-forward Leônidas da Silva, but that was too small a club for his ideas to resonate and even after he'd moved to Bonsucesso, a slightly larger club, taking Leônidas with him, he found it hard to find an audience for his ideas. 'When Kruschner [*sic*] arrived in Brazil, Gentil was talking a lot about the W-M,' Flávio Costa said, 'but he never had the prestige to apply it. Kruschner was the one who tried to apply *futebol sistema*.'[1]

It didn't work. One of Flamengo's great stars when Kürschner took over was the centre-half Fausto dos Santos, 'the Black Wonder'. He was an elegant player used to dominating games, a living example of the hierarchy of positions that existed in Brazilian football at the time, placing centre-half at the top and full-back at the bottom: everybody wanted to control the game and create from the centre; nobody wanted their primary job to be stopping others.

Kürschner insisted Fausto had to play deeper, as his formation demanded. Fausto refused: he was not a full-back, he insisted, not a defender. Fans and journalists were split and argued enthusiastically before the issue was resolved by the intervention of Padilha, who fined Fausto and effectively told him to get on with what he was paid to do and do what the coach told him. Or, at least, that's one version of the story. The great historian of Flamengo, Roberto Assaf, has another variant, in which Kürschner was appalled by the medical facilities he found at the club and insisted all players undergo a health check. Fausto's revealed the early stages of the tuberculosis that would kill him two years later and his deeper positioning was the result of his declining fitness. Perhaps both are true and Kürschner pushed Fausto back when he might otherwise have asked him to play as a wing-half.

Either way, Flamengo amended their shape. Results were disappointing and Flávio Costa, taking advantage of Kürschner's lack of

---

[1] In Aidan Hamilton, *An Entirely Different Game* (Mainstream, 1998).

Portuguese, undermined him at every turn, pouring scorn on the W-M. Kürschner and his methods were widely derided in the local press and, despite scoring 83 goals in 22 games, Flamengo finished second in the Carioca championship behind their arch-rivals Fluminense. When Flamengo lost 2–0 to Vasco da Gama in the opening game of the 1938 season, the first match played at their new stadium, Kürschner was sacked.

His ideas had been widely misunderstood, but Kürschner did not return to Europe. His cachet was still sufficient that he was asked to work as an advisor to the national coach, Adhemar Pimenta, at the 1938 World Cup in France. There Brazil used Martim Silveira as an attacking centre-half, but did withdraw the two inside-forwards to bolster the midfield. Brazil reached the semi-final, the best result they had achieved at a World Cup, but João Saldanha, the journalist who became national coach in 1969, was critical, and concluded they would have gone further had they deployed a third back. Brazil let in ten goals in their five games, three of them from penalties – an indication of an outnumbered defence being forced into risky challenges.

Kürschner was named coach of Botafogo in 1939. They finished as top scorers, but were second behind Flávio Costa's Flamengo. Kürschner left the club the following year and, in 1941, contracted a virus and died. His legacy, though, lived on. Flávio Costa may have mocked him in public, but he had realised how effective the W-M was. Unable to use the new formation directly given how he had dismissed it, he tweaked it, devising what he called the *diagonal*.

At the heart of the W-M, a 3–2–2–3, are the four midfielders who form a square. Flávio Costa nudged that, pushing one of the wing-halves deeper and the opposite inside-forward higher, so the shape in the midfield became a rhombus. How radical that was in global terms is difficult to say. According to the former Portugal coach Cândido de Oliveira, when Flávio Costa was later taken to Europe by a director of Vasco da Gama to explain his revolutionary formation, it was dismissed as a simple repackaging of the W-M. Perhaps, though, it is fairer to say that he formalised a process that was always inherent in the W-M, so that one wing-half was always more defensive than the other, one inside-forward more attacking. Certainly it was radical for Brazil and it led to an even greater innovation. Once that square has been tipped into a rhombus, it doesn't take much for the deeper-lying wing-half to become a second central defender, or for the more advanced inside-forward to become a second striker: a 4–2–4.

Eventually, even Flávio Costa acknowledged Kürschner's significance in that development. After his Flamengo side had beaten Ferencváros 5–0 at the Népstadion in 1954, he said, 'Our knowledge of what is good came from your teacher, Dori Kürschner.'

* * *

River Plate had won the Argentinian championship in 1932 under Víctor Caamaño, but he had always regarded himself primarily as an athletics coach. As their programme of investment continued, it became increasingly apparent that they needed a football specialist. They tried the Italian Felipe Pascucci (later Weisz's conditioning coach at Bologna) and Medgyessy before in 1934 persuading Imre Hirschl to leave Gimnasia.

As in La Plata, Hirschl began slowly as, he suggested, his players took time to grasp the principles of the style he was trying to introduce with a deep-lying centre-half. After a year, taking advantage of River's wealth, he signed Pepe Minella from Gimnasia to fulfil the role. He did, though, continue his policy of promoting youth, giving Adolfo Pedernera, one of River's all-time greats, his debut at

16 in 1935 and making the 18-year-old José Manuel Moreno, another legend of the club, a regular that same season.

Success followed a year later as River won both the Copa Campeonato and the Copa de Oro.[2] They retained the Campeonato in 1937, as Argentinian football reverted to a more straightforward structure. 'No other team managed to walk on a pitch with the preparation that distinguished River,' said *El Gráfico*. 'No other team could match their fitness training. That was one of the biggest advantages, the stamina shown in second halves was much better than the opposition. They had a clear tactical plan both in attack and defence, and so it was that the harmony that was vital for their victories could be seen.'

Harmonious it may have been, but Hirschl's style was more direct than the traditional *criollo* way of playing, exaggerated by the presence at centre-forward of the mountainous Bernabé Ferreyra. 'He had the virtue (or the flaw) of changing the subtle *rioplatense* style that had so surprised the Old World,' an analysis in *El Gráfico* in January 1938 observed. 'Short combinations and sly dribbling were avoided, the idea being they had to get close to the goalkeeper to score, so the goal was sought in two or three passes, with his potent shot. Our public … established Bernabé as the new idol and the clubs started looking for players like him. Football lost much of its attractiveness: it became quicker, more intense, rougher and more positive, but it never offered again the great displays of spectacle and subtlety that had characterised the era before that of professionalism.'

---

[2] Trying to keep track of the various formats of the Argentinian season is only marginally less trying than getting to grips with the Schleswig-Holstein Question but, for what it's worth, the Copa Campeonato was a short-lived variant of the league, but with each team playing each other only once, while the Copa de Oro was a play-off against the winner of the Copa de Honor, which in every previous season had been a knockout competition but that year was played on a round-robin basis.

Argentinian football has been lamenting a lost golden age since its infancy, so that criticism should perhaps not be taken too seriously: more pertinent is the consensus that Hirschl's style was more robust than the typical football of Argentina. British observers in the 1930s, judging largely on a series of tight games between England and Austria, tended to see Danubian football as overly mannered, more concerned with beauty and attractive patterns of passing than putting the ball in the net, yet Argentinians consistently diagnosed the reverse issue. That suggests a spectrum with Hirschl, even when the influence of Ferreyra is taken into account, occupying a middle ground.

Whether it was a matter of style or Ferreyra's power, River's football under Hirschl produced goals. They scored 49 in 17 games in winning the Copa Campeonato in 1936 and 106 in 34 in winning the league in 1937. They scored 105 in 34 the following year as well, but that was only enough to finish second behind Independiente, and Hirschl left the club. It was only the year after that that his tactical innovations were really appreciated.

In January 1939, Argentina faced Brazil in the Copa Julio Roca, a tournament hastily arranged after the two sides had pulled out of that year's Campeonato Sudamericano following a dispute with Conmebol.

Argentina won the first of four scheduled games 5–1, a result that seemed to confirm the pre-existing South American hierarchy. But in the second fixture, a week later, the scores were level at 2–2 when Brazil were awarded a late penalty. Arcadio López, who had set up both Argentina goals, was sent off for dissent and after police had finally persuaded him to leave the pitch his teammates stormed off in solidarity. The penalty was knocked into an empty net and the game awarded to Brazil.

The Argentinian delegation took their team home, and the competition was concluded only the following year with a 2–2 draw and a

3–0 win for Argentina. But more significant was the question that was asked of how Brazil had improved so rapidly from the 5–1 defeat to the 3–2 win. The answer was that they'd imported wholesale Dori Kürschner's three-man Botafogo defence and adopted a W-M. That, it was realised, was precisely what Hirschl had been doing at River. That was the future for Brazilian football and, it was soon accepted, for Argentinian football as well.

The Hungarian influence was spreading.

CHAPTER FOURTEEN

DARKENING SKIES

The tour to South America could not save Hakoah All-Stars. As the financial situation in the US worsened, Béla Guttmann took to giving dancing lessons once again to get by. When the club folded in 1932 with the ASL in major financial difficulty, he returned to Europe. Along with József Eisenhoffer and the Austrian Leopold Drucker, Guttmann joined up with Hakoah as they toured France.[1]

He went back to Vienna. 'I must admit,' he later said, 'I was happier to breathe the air here. I never really liked America. I'm the type that is not too interested in money, and a guy like that is as good as dead there.'[2] Given his constant haggling, business ventures and love of luxury, that's a remarkable claim but, even leaving that chutzpah aside, neither Austria nor Guttmann were what they had been when he had left six years earlier.

In September 1931, there had been an attempted coup in the southeastern province of Styria by radical members of the Heimwehr, which had developed from being loosely organised militia established from

---

[1] In *The Greatest Comeback*, David Bolchover suggests he may have also played one league game for Metz; a 'Guttmann' is listed on a team sheet, but no forename is offered.

[2] In Hámori, *Régi gólok, edzősorsok*.

demobbed soldiers at the end of the First World War to become an increasingly militant right-wing group. Although a number of towns were taken and Graz surrounded, the coup was badly organised, easily suppressed and widely regarded as a fiasco. The coup's leader, Walter Pfrimer, fat, bald and a poor public speaker, was ridiculed, but when he was put on trial he was acquitted by a jury that demonstrated its solidarity with his ideals by raising their arms in the fascist salute. The Heimwehr's leadership had largely opposed Pfrimer's action, but found themselves losing the support of those who wanted more direct action against Marxism and, in Landtag elections in April 1932, the Nazis gained significant support. As the Social Democrats withdrew their backing for the governing coalition, the Christian Socialist chancellor Karl Buresch resigned a month later and was replaced by Engelbert Dollfuß.

Dollfuß was also a Christian Socialist and headed a coalition with the Heimatsblock, the parliamentary wing of the Heimwehr, that had a majority of a single seat. In March 1933, after two presidents of the lower chamber of the Austrian house resigned to be able to cast a vote in parliament, Dollfuß persuaded the president Wilhelm Miklas that the chamber was unworkable and needed to be adjourned indefinitely. From then on, he ruled as a dictator, banning both the Communist Party and the National Socialists and creating a one-party state.

In February 1934, following a crackdown on their members, the Social Democrats called for nationwide resistance against Dollfuß, resulting in a 16-day civil war. There was fierce fighting in the east of the country, while the government shelled workers' accommodation blocks in the suburbs of Vienna and northern parts of Styria. Having put down the uprising and outlawed the Social Democrats, Dollfuß proclaimed a new constitution in April 1934. Three months later, he was assassinated by ten Austrian Nazis as part of a failed putsch that led Mussolini, who blamed Hitler, to mass his troops on the border in defence of Austrian sovereignty.

However turbulent the political situation, Guttmann's concerns on arriving back in Vienna were more immediate and more personal. Austria was in chaos and age was beginning to catch up with him. On 6 November 1932, Hakoah lost 5–2 to Rapid at the Praterstadion. 'There were two big clocks by the pitch,' Guttmann said. 'I looked at the hands. There were 15 minutes left. But just as if I had been given a tiring injection, my legs became like lead and everything got blurry and I felt I was completely helpless. And a voice whispered to me, "Béla, it's time to finish it!" It was a horrible quarter of an hour. But after that I was relieved.'[3] He retired immediately after the match and, although the directors tried to dissuade him, Guttmann, strong-willed as ever, never played another game.

Hakoah themselves were a very different side. The departure of so many players to the US and the financial losses incurred on the 1927 tour had a major impact. They were relegated in 1930 and although they came straight back up, they finished tenth in a 12-team league in 1932. The coach then was Vinzenz Dittrich. He became joint-manager for the 1932–33 season with Artur Kolisch, who had joined Hakoah from the Cricket Club shortly before the war and would become, as Baar had been, one of those eternal figures in the background, always ready to step in as manager when required. Hakoah lost five games in a row before the winter break and, with relegation a serious possibility, a change was required. Dittrich left for Marseille and was soon followed by Drucker and Eisenhoffer, Kolisch stepped back into an administrative role and Guttmann was put in charge. His impact was immediate: Hakoah won six of 11

---

[3] In *Régi gólok, edzősorsok.*

games in the spring part of the season to finish eighth, comfortably clear of the drop.

The improvement, though, was short-lived. Hakoah narrowly avoided relegation the following year and they were struggling again the season after that when Guttmann left the club during the winter break.

In 1935, Hugo Meisl helped secure Guttmann a job as coach of SC Enschede in the Netherlands. He negotiated for himself a huge bonus if he won the national championship, to which the directors gladly agreed, assuming such a feat was impossible and seeing nothing in Guttmann's previous managerial career to suggest he was a miracle worker. Enschede, though, won all but three of their 18 games that season to top the Eastern group and go into a five-team play-off for the title. His directors knew that the club faced bankruptcy if Enschede won and they had to pay Guttmann his bonus, but they lost twice to a Feyenoord side managed by the former Bayern coach Dombi Kohn and finished two points behind them.

Eisenhoffer, meanwhile, was enjoying managerial success of his own. He reached the French Cup final as a player with Marseille in 1934 and won it the following year, by which time he was player-manager. Apart from a brief stint at Lens in 1938, he held the post until 1940–41, and in 1937 led them to the first league title in their history with a polyglot team that included the eccentric Brazilian goalkeeper Jaguaré, noted for playing in a mariner's cap, the great Moroccan forward Larbi Ben Barek, the French-Algerian defender Abdelkader Ben Bouali and the Hungarian former Ferencváros forward Vilmos Kohut.

* * *

Guttmann was always an impact coach, not that the term existed in the 1930s. He would arrive at a club, have a rapid galvanising effect, and then form would slowly subside. So it was at Enschede and, in 1937, as results fell away, he returned to Vienna. He was reappointed at Hakoah, who were by then in the second flight, and by spring they seemed to be heading for promotion. The political environment, though, was rapidly worsening and on 12 March, Austria was annexed by Germany.

The unification of Austria and Germany had been mooted from the end of the Holy Roman Empire in 1806, but was opposed by Prussia, which preferred a smaller confederation of northern German states and defeated Austria in the Austro-Prussian War of 1866. Political union of Austria and Germany was expressly prohibited by the Treaties of Versailles and Saint-Germain but, shortly after Hitler had become leader of the German Nazi party in 1920, the National Socialist Programme set out as the first of 25 aims 'the unification of all Germans in the Greater Germany on the basis of the people's right to self-determination'. The Christian Socialists in Austria were, broadly speaking, not in favour, while the Heimwehr vehemently opposed absorption into a greater Germany, but the disintegration of the first Austrian Republic following the Civil War into a right-wing one-party state from 1934, combined with the rise of Hitler in Germany, gave the idea fresh impetus.

Austria, though, was still opposed – at least at government level, although unification certainly wasn't an ambition only of the Nazis, drawing support from across the political spectrum. After his assassination, Dollfuß had been succeeded as president by Kurt Schuschnigg, another Christian Socialist opposed to the Anschluss. He deployed police to suppress the Nazis, who pursued a terrorist campaign that killed at least 800 people between 1934 and 1938. The violence was almost certainly counter-productive: the US journalist John Gunther wrote in 1936 that public opinion had swung from, by his estimation, around 80 per cent pro-unification in 1932 to 60 per cent against by the end of the following year.[4]

German rearmament prompted a demand for Austrian raw materials and labour, while Austria's economy had not recovered from the Great Depression, exacerbated by a German boycott. In July 1936, the pressure had mounted to the point that Schuschnigg reached an agreement with the German ambassador Franz von Papen to release Nazi prisoners in return for a recognition of Austrian sovereignty and an end to the Nazi campaign of terror. Austria, though, had to declare itself 'a German state', following Germany's lead on foreign policy while admitting members of the 'National Opposition' to the cabinet.

Mussolini's opposition to unification, seen in his deployment of troops on the Austrian border after Dollfuß's murder, was rooted in his fear that an expanding Germany would claim territory in Italy that had once been part of Austria. His need for German help in his Abyssinian campaigns, though, and the personal assurance of Hitler that he would not seek Italian land, removed that obstacle, an agreement formalised in the Berlin–Rome Axis of 1937.

By the end of 1937, as Germany's Four-Year Plan to increase military output fell behind schedule with the budget spiralling, the need to secure access to Austria's iron ore had become acute. Hitler had already discussed the prospect of taking Austria by force when he met with Schuschnigg at Berchtesgaden on 12 February 1938, demanding the placement of Nazis in key government positions, notably the appointment of Arthur Seyss-Inquart as Minister for Public Security, in return for a confirmation of the 1936 treaty. Eight days later, he gave a radio address in which he announced that 'the

---

[4] In *Inside Europe* (Hamish Hamilton, 1936).

German Reich is no longer willing to tolerate the suppression of 10 million Germans across its borders.'

Austrian Nazis responded by rioting, leading Schuschnigg on 9 March to declare a referendum on absorption into Germany to be held four days later, promising to re-legalise the Social Democrats if they supported him, and restricting the vote to those aged over 24 as the young were perceived as being the group most supportive of the Anschluss. Hitler's propaganda machine immediately began spreading stories of electoral fraud and falsely reporting that Austrians were calling for the arrival of German troops to restore order following (non-existent) rioting across the country. Austria was issued with an ultimatum: surrender power to Austrian Nazis by noon on 11 March or Germany would invade. Schuschnigg resigned as chancellor, but the president Wilhelm Miklas initially refused to appoint Seyss-Inquart to replace him. At 8:45pm, Hitler gave the order for the invasion to begin at dawn the following day. At 10pm, a forged telegram was sent, purporting to be from Chancellor Seyss-Inquart, begging for German troops to enter the country and restore order. At midnight, Miklas accepted his position was hopeless, appointed Seyss-Inquart and resigned in order, he said, to avoid the shedding of *Bruderblut* – fraternal blood.

The Wehrmacht crossed the border unopposed the following morning, greeted by cheering crowds waving flags bearing swastikas. Hitler visited his birthplace of Braunau am Inn that afternoon, the beginning of a triumphal three-day tour to Vienna. Leading representatives of the Austrian republic were arrested, and around 70,000 potential dissenters rounded up and held at a makeshift concentration camp in a disused railway station. By and large, though, the reception the troops and Hitler received was so overwhelmingly positive that he changed his plan to run Austria as a puppet through Seyss-Inquart and instead absorbed Austria fully into the Reich. On 13 March, Seyss-Inquart announced the revocation of Article 88 of the Treaty of Saint-Germain, which prohibited a union of Austria and Germany. The Anschluss was confirmed by a plebiscite the following month.

There were attacks on Jews immediately and the Nuremberg Laws were applied from May 1938. Within three years, more than 130,000 Austrian Jews had emigrated.

Hakoah were forcibly dissolved on 14 March. At least 37 members of the Hakoah club were killed in Nazi camps, including the co-founder Fritz Löhner-Beda. He was arrested after the Anschluss in 1938 and sent to Dachau, then moved later that year to Buchenwald, where, with the composer and cabaret star Hermann Leopoldi, he wrote the anthem of the camp, 'Das Buchenwaldlied'.[5] His wife and two teenage daughters were gassed in converted vans in Minsk in September 1942. A month later he was moved to Monowitz, one of the three main camps in the Auschwitz complex, and on 4 December, struggling with illness, he was beaten to death after being singled out for supposed laziness during a visit by a party of executives from the chemical conglomerate IG Farben.

Guttmann was lucky. When German troops invaded, he was in the US. He had been granted a visa on 18 January 1938 and sailed from Cherbourg to New York on 2 March.[6] He was one of 869 Hungarians that year granted the right to permanent residence in the

---

[5] *O Buchenwald, ich kann dich nicht vergessen,*   O Buchenwald, I cannot forget you,
weil du mein Schicksal bist.   because you are my fate.
Wer dich verließ, der kann es erst ermessen,   Only he who leaves you can appreciate
wie wundervoll die Freiheit ist!   how wonderful freedom is!
O Buchenwald, wir jammern nicht und klagen,   O Buchenwald, we don't cry and complain;
und was auch unser Schicksal sei,   and whatever our destiny may be,
wir wollen trotzdem Ja zum Leben sagen,   we nevertheless shall say 'yes' to life:
denn einmal kommt der Tag, dann sind wir frei!   for once the day comes, we shall be free!

[6] As shown by David Bolchover's research presented in *The Greatest Comeback*.

USA and yet he returned to Europe, arriving in Vienna on 6 August. Eight days later, he travelled to Budapest. The reason for his return from safety is unclear – he may simply, as so many did, have underestimated the risk – but it appears he may have been trying to establish an all-European team in a reformed ASL, an idea that was reported in *Nemzeti Sport* the following summer. The plan seems to have been thwarted by the difficulty of securing visas but the US economy, anyway, had dipped again and unemployment was running at 20 per cent, making it extremely unlikely that the successes of the mid- to late-1920s could have been repeated.

* * *

No World Cup has ever been played out against a backdrop of such unease as that of 1938. Uruguay and Argentina refused to travel, short on cash and angered that a second World Cup in a row was being staged in Europe. The British nations continued their boycott of FIFA, supposedly still making a point of principle in a decade-long row over definitions of amateurism, although almost certainly motivated largely by xenophobia. Brazil hadn't played for more than a year before the tournament. Czechoslovakia looked anxiously at German military spending and Hitler's aggressive noises over the Sudetenland and decided not to compete, while Austria, after the Anschluss, had been subsumed into Germany, handing Sweden a bye in the first round.

Hungary went to France for the tournament unconvinced of their own status. Although their clubs had won three of the first 11 Mitropa Cups, their influence over Austrian football was clear and they had lost only four of 17 games against Austria since 1930, international tournaments had tended to go badly for Hungary. They hadn't gone to the inaugural World Cup in Uruguay in 1930, and in Italy four years later, although they had beaten Egypt to achieve a measure of catharsis for their Olympic defeat in 1924, they had gone out to Austria in the quarter-final.

Károly Dietz, short, round-faced and bespectacled, had taken over as manager after that tournament. He was not an obvious choice. He had been a player before the First World War with Magyar AC and during it with Műegyetemi AFC, all the while serving as the head of the State Police Department of Budapest. He became chief of police after the Aster Revolution and was jailed under Béla Kun's Soviet Republic. After it had collapsed, he briefly became head of the Budapest police again, before working as a bookkeeper for a private company through the 1920s. He took a law degree at the University of Szeged in 1930 and the following year opened a law firm in Budapest.

That lack of obvious managerial experience perhaps explains why, in 1937, he brought in Alfréd Schaffer to work alongside him. Schaffer's return to Budapest with MTK in 1933 had been brief. He was an inveterate wanderer, always seeking a better deal, another club, another bar, another woman. He had returned to Nürnberg in 1933, then came back to MTK for two seasons before accepting Dietz's offer.

Their collaboration went well. Hungary won four and drew one of six games in 1937–38 before hammering Greece 11–1 in their sole World Cup qualifier. Their first opponents, the Dutch East Indies, were not, it's fair to say, the most testing opposition. They had qualified only because Japan withdrew, nine of their team were making their international debuts, while their captain, Achmad Nawir, a qualified doctor, played in glasses.[7]

---

[7] Hungary's captain in that game, György Sárosy, was nicknamed 'Doktor' for his academic prowess, but although he was a qualified lawyer, he did not have a doctorate. The Dutch East Indies' best player was probably their goalkeeper, Mo Heng Tan, the only man to play for both the Dutch East Indies and Indonesia. He gained notoriety for the large doll he would carry as a mascot.

That set up a quarter-final against a tough Switzerland side, who had beaten England earlier in the year and eliminated Germany (incorporating Austria) after a replay in the first round. Three days before that game, Hungary's hotel in Lille was shaken by an earthquake. 'The management was in the hallway of the hotel when the ground shook a few minutes before 12,' *Nemzeti Sport* reported. 'Plates and glass jars were smashed, plaster fell from the walls and even the armchairs seemed to move away from them. It was over in a few seconds, but it was enough to frighten the whole city. Tiles and bricks fell from the rooftops, the streets were covered with puddles, rushing women ran and fell, full of confusion. Chimneys were particularly badly affected by the movement of the earth, dropping from houses ... some of the weaker buildings collapsed.'[8]

The game, though, went ahead as scheduled and Switzerland were despatched 2–0. 'We did it!' exulted the front page of *Nemzeti Sport*, but inside doubts were expressed about the quality of the performance. 'The team has two excuses,' the report said: 'the bumpy, uneven pitch was the main opponent. It's hard to play football on such a poor surface. The fine blade of the Hungarian style of attack is not suited to such soil.'

There were also numerous complaints about the voracious mosquitoes in Lille, and the goalkeeper Antal Szabó played with a large iodine stain on his face where he had been bitten. The major positive from the game was the form of the MTK midfielder József Turay, the player Tóth had pinched from the sleeping Feldmann when they'd shared a house 12 years earlier. 'We did not expect so much,' said *Nemzeti Sport*. 'He ... cleared up many unpleasant situations. He played right across the line. Whether he had to defend or help the attack, he did very well.'[9]

---

[8] *Nemzeti Sport*, 12 June 1938.
[9] *Nemzeti Sport*, 13 June 1938.

On a better surface at the Parc des Princes in Paris, Hungary were brilliant in the semi-final, hammering Sweden 5–1. In the months leading up to the World Cup, much had been made of the 'Think Tank' of the two inside-forwards György Sárosi and László Cseh and the centre-forward Gyula Zsengellér, a fluid and deadly front three. In September 1937, in a game against Czechoslovakia, Dietz had swapped over Sárosi and Zsengellér so the former played at centre-forward and the latter at inside-left. Cseh, unhappy at the change, suggested to Zsengellér that they should make their point by not passing to Sárosi, but the striker needed the win bonus and refused. Sárosi ended up scoring seven in an 8–3 win and cementing his place at centre-forward.

Cseh, though, was injured shortly before the tournament and so missed out, with the abrasive Géza Toldi taking his place. His effectiveness seemed clear as Hungary reached the final having scored 13 goals in the tournament and conceded just one, but in the immediate aftermath of the semi-final, Dietz talked about bringing back Vilmos Kohut, the 31-year-old Marseille and former Ferencváros forward, for the final against the defending champions Italy, who had beaten Brazil in their semi-final. Toldi, logically, would have been the player to miss out.

On the morning of the final, *Nemzeti Sport* printed the team as revealed to them the day before by Dietz: Szabó; Polgár, Bíró; Szalay, Turay, Lázár; Sas, Vincze, Sárosi, Zsengellér, Titkos. That meant Gyula Polgár, who had not played for the national team for a year, coming in at full-back for his Ferencváros teammate Lajos Korányi and Toldi being replaced not by Kohut but by the Újpest forward Jenő Vincze. As it turned out, Turay missed out as well, with the Újpest centre-half György Szűcs replacing him.

Italy took an early lead and although Pál Titkos levelled, they were 3–1 up by half-time and went on to win 4–2. *Nemzeti Sport's* response the following day was measured, preferring to see the positives in Hungary having reached the final rather than analyse too closely the reasons for the defeat. 'We were a very serious opponent for the Italians,' the report said, 'but it cannot be disputed: the right side won. Our direct defence did everything but the game of our forward line could not succeed against the tough Italian defence. The Italians did not always play the game cleanly but they did it very cleverly; our men were powerless against them, but the referee did not even notice the clever tricks.'[10]

A cartoon in the newspaper three days later, though, did raise the issue of Toldi's absence, depicting the Italy manager Vittorio Pozzo as a knight in a besieged castle gratefully throwing a bucket of boiling water over Dietz, as he sits astride a donkey marked 'Vincze' armed with just a slingshot while a huge battering ram marked 'Toldi' stands unused behind him. Even the initial report acknowledged that Hungary had felt the absence of Korányi, Cseh, Turay, Toldi, János Dudás and István Balogh.

Some of them were missing through injury, but there has been no suggestion that Toldi was unfit. Turay, it's true, had been struggling with an ankle problem throughout the tournament and was said to be 'tired' but, really, who feels too tired to play in a World Cup final? Gyula Zsengellér told his son Zsolt that Toldi was dropped following a half-hour meeting between Dietz and Pozzo and other Italian officials, seemingly because it was felt his aggressive style would not be in keeping with the 'continuing spirit of friendship between the two countries'. Korányi and Turay supposedly pulled out in protest. Oddly, Toldi barely mentions the World Cup in his 1962 memoir *Fodboldnavn paa flygtningepas*.

---

[10] *Nemzeti Sport*, 20 June 1938.

So, was it a fix? Péter Szegedi, who co-wrote the definitive work on the tournament *Az 1938-as magyar vb-ezüst*[11] [*The Hungarian Silver at the 1938 World* Cup] with Tamás Dénes, is sceptical. 'An Italian political order can be ruled out since Hungary was not dependent on Italy,' he said. 'However, the idea has come up that maybe the Hungarian coach got an order from Budapest to throw the match, so that the Hungarian political powers could be assured of Italy's goodwill towards their desire to revise Trianon. No proof of that has been presented so far and it is not likely that politics would have interfered with the events in such a direct way. And we haven't even mentioned the question that rightfully arises: if the Italians had to be made to win the match, why didn't the coach leave out the best Hungarian forward, Sárosi, or Zsengellér, who had scored five goals in the tournament?'

Something strange, though, was clearly going on. As Szegedi points out, Brazil had made two bizarre selection decisions before their semi-final against Italy, leaving out the forwards Leônidas da Silva and Tim. Italy had provocatively worn all black in their quarter-final win over France when they had twice, to the fury of the home crowd, given the fascist salute; whatever Pozzo and various players may subsequently have said, there was a clear political edge to their campaign. They also managed to ensure that the final was refereed by the Frenchman Georges Capdeville, rather than by the pre-eminent referee of the age, the Belgian John Langenus. 'It's easier,' Szegedi said, 'to accept this version than the idea of direct political influence, but it's strange that the coach would have met such a request without making any conditions and asking for an Italian player to be left out in return.'

---

[11] Akadémiai, 2018.

Bringing Polgár back makes even less sense; it's hard to imagine the Italians being especially troubled by Korányi, for any reason. Szegedi wonders whether Dietz, perhaps, 'wanted to offer evidence of his own genius with unexpected moves'. It is, simply, impossible to know anything for sure, other than that the team Hungary selected for the final did not help their cause.

* * *

Immediately after the tournament, Hungary's right-winger Ferenc Sas left for Argentina where he had been offered a deal by Boca Juniors. According to Sas's granddaughter Debora Sohn[12] who still lives in Buenos Aires, the Boca manager had seen him playing in France. It is just about possible that Juan José Tramutola, the Boca manager of the time,[13] attended some Hungary games at the tournament, but it seems improbable, in part because foreign transfers of that type simply didn't happen then and in part because he would have had Boca games in the Argentinian championship to oversee at the same time. More likely is that some other Boca employee, or perhaps some intermediary, heard Sas was open to the prospect of emigration and found a club willing to take on a forward who had just played in the World Cup final.

'For some reasons I don't know,' Debora went on, 'he was asked to remain in Rio de Janeiro, but he said that he had already accepted the offer from Boca Juniors and had committed to them.' Again, this is only speculation, but Dori Kürschner was in Rio at the time managing Flamengo, and perhaps saw an opportunity to hijack a

---

[12] Sohn was Sas's original surname; 'Sas' the Magyarised variant.

[13] He had been Argentina's manager at the 1930 World Cup and remains the youngest man ever to coach at the World Cup, although the job was very different then and carried far less responsibility.

deal for his fellow Hungarian, a player who could help his Brazilian charges understand his conception of the game.

When he arrived in Buenos Aires, Sas stayed with a friend, another Hungarian, and became friendly with Imre Hirschl. As he moved into his own place, he began to bring his family over from Europe. That was a far from straightforward process. Sas was in a relationship with a woman who had two children from her first marriage. Although she was able to travel to Argentina, her husband (it's not clear whether they were ever formally divorced) prevented her children from leaving and sent them to live in an orphanage until their grandmother rescued them and brought them up. One of them, Ivan, became a distinguished historian. Family legend has it that, because of restrictions on divorced women travelling alone, Sas's partner was not allowed to disembark the ship in Buenos Aires until he had boarded and married her.

Tough and single-minded, Sas won a league title with Boca but at one point refused to play for the club for two years after they decided against honouring a deal to improve his contract. He ended his career with Argentinos Juniors and later worked in a cinema, a jeweller's and the Raitor clothing store. He never, though, lost his love of football and Debora remembers Sundays at his house with her two brothers, kicking a ball about in the garden while listening to commentary of league games on the radio.

* * *

While others fled, Guttmann came home. That summer, a vacancy had opened up at Újpest when their coach László Sternberg, who had played alongside Guttmann when New York Hakoah had won the US Open Cup, secured his own visa for the US. The job represented a great opportunity for Guttmann: Újpest had won four league titles in the 1930s as well as the Mitropa Cup in 1929; they were essentially Hungary's third team. 'Two years ago, when I was on a holiday in Pest, I saw Újpest play and I said that I would be happy to coach them, because you could get this team to produce great things At Újpest there is real class in every line and if one of them happens to play poorly, the others can still play in a way that the team can bear the poor performance from, say, Zsengellér, Vincze or another player...'[14]

But Budapest had also changed. István Bethlen had been prime minister for a decade, but a fall in living standards following the Depression led to a general shift to the right, and he was replaced in 1931 by Gyula Károlyi, a moderate and the cousin of Mihály Károlyi, the hapless pacifist who had briefly assumed power after the Aster Revolution. Károlyi lasted less than a year, though, before Horthy deposed him for Gyula Gömbös, a nationalist who had led the purges against Communists after the collapse of Kun's government in 1920 and had euphemistically blamed foreign influences for Hungary's embarrassment at the 1924 Olympics.

Gömbös instituted a programme of Magyarisation for Hungary's remaining ethnic minorities, agreed a treaty with Italy and, as part of a more general policy of closer co-operation with Germany, signed a trade agreement that drew Hungary out of depression but at the cost of making it reliant on Germany for both raw materials and markets. Gömbös had publicly disavowed anti-Semitism on taking office and had the broad support of Jewish leaders, leading to friction with Hitler, who agreed to support Hungary in territorial disputes with Czechoslovakia but not with Romania or Yugoslavia.

Gömbös died from cancer in 1936 and was succeeded by Kálmán Darányi who initially sought to improve relations with France and the

---

[14] *Nemzeti Sport*, 13 November 1938.

UK, as well as banning the fascistic Party of National Will. But after the Anschluss and the tepid response of the Western powers, Darányi accepted that Hungary had little option but to follow the course set by Germany and Italy. He drafted the First Jewish Law, restricting Jewish involvement in the economy by the implementation of quotas, although by the time it was passed, wider dissatisfaction on the right with his willingness to deal with the fascists had led to him being deposed for Béla Imrédy.

Imrédy was an ambitious pragmatist, keen to cement his own power on the right of Hungarian politics. As he became increasingly extreme, he drafted a Second Jewish Law, further restricting the involvement of Jews in society and defining them by race rather than religion – meaning that conversion to Christianity was no longer a way of evading the regulations. The law was passed in 1939, but by then Imrédy had been forced from office after it was revealed that he himself had a Jewish great-grandmother. He was replaced by the former prime minister Pál Teleki, who had rejoined the government in 1938 as Minister of Education.

Yet for all the turmoil, Guttmann enjoyed his return to Budapest, regularly going to the Újpest Theatre. There was a salon there, one of two owned by a hairdresser called Pál Moldován, who would occasionally take on small acting roles. So too would the middle of his three daughters, Mariann. 'The Moldován girls were pretty, striking and elegant, always having the latest haircuts,' said their nephew, Pál Moldoványi. 'Males circled around the house: footballers, actors, comedians and a coach, of course. In the end, it was Béla who won the cup, but he had to fight for Mariann.'[15] Their relationship would soon become extremely complicated, though:

---

[15] In Claussen, *Béla Guttmann*. Mariann's nephew adopted an older form of the family name, so her brother was Pál Moldován and his son Pál Moldoványi.

Moldován was a Catholic and the Third Jewish Law of August 1941 made extramarital sex between a Jewish man and a Gentile woman punishable by five years in jail.

Guttmann broke a rib in a training ground collision with the forward Géza Kocsis in November 1938, but his stint at Újpest generally went well. 'At the time I was introduced to them, I was able to win them over,' he said, explaining how he made an immediate impact. 'I just said to them, "Lads, just see me as an older companion who has travelled the world, has a lot of experience and wants to give some of that to you ... I lived with them, supported them, worked with them. If they won I claimed no part in the triumph; if they lost, I didn't blame them for taking the bread from my hand.'[16]

Újpest were far from a team of stars; Guttmann inherited a side that had finished second the previous season, three points behind Ferencváros. 'The president said, "Let's cook this with the ingredients we have,"' he explained, 'and I said OK.' He did, though, as he always would, insist upon complete autonomy. 'Because it's important to have a full freedom of action for the coach, as too many cooks spoil the broth.'

He spoke of the team spirit and the absence of cliques, but Guttmann also had to modify his approach. 'Essentially,' he said, 'I am an English tactician.' He had learned that at MTK, where the lessons of Robertson and Hogan remained guiding principles, and then played under Billy Hunter at Hakoah before his years in the US where British influence was strong. By the late 1930s, that meant a W-M with a recognition of the value of direct play if well targeted, filtered through an appreciation of the importance of a good first touch and ball possession, an area in which Robertson, Hogan and

---

[16] In an interview in *Nemzeti Sport* on 3 August 1939.

Hunter were far more aligned with traditional Danubian values than most in the English game.[17]

This was a fraught issue in Hungary at the time. The journalist László Feleki, later the editor of *Nemzeti Sport*, spent the 1938–39 season in London, studying Arsenal's use of the W-M, and became a passionate advocate for it. He became an unpaid coach at Törekves in 1939 and implemented the system there with initial success, although they were relegated in 1940–41.

While *Nemzeti Sport* argued for the 'English system', which was presumably why Guttmann was given such space to expound upon it, *Képes Sport* argued against. For months, the debate went back and forth. György Sárosi, the national captain, wrote a passionate open letter against the W-M. As a result, when his form dipped in 1939, *Nemzeti Sport* was forthright in its criticism of him. Most vociferous was a journalist called Béla Mattanovich, who was outspoken in his right-wing beliefs and as a result was effectively silenced after the war, working as a page-setter. Eventually, after the 1956 Uprising, he was allowed to publish again, writing for *Labdarúgás* where he loved to regale younger colleagues with stories of the old days.

One of his favourite anecdotes concerned Sárosi, Hungary's captain at the 1938 World Cup, who once responded to a particularly critical article by storming into the offices of *Nemzeti Sport*, grabbing a bottle of ink from the table and tipping it over Mattanovich. Mattanovich, startled but aware such an outrage demanded a reaction, challenged Sárosi to a duel. Neither had much experience of fencing but both turned up at the allotted hour and agreed to fight only until

---

[17] The Scottish game at the time was still regarded as being far more focused on close passing than the more physical approach of England. Whether Guttmann was precise in his use of 'English' rather than 'British' is impossible to say, but the two were often used in the Hungary of the time as though synonymous.

first blood. For a few minutes they ineptly prodded at each other until one – Mattanovich would never say who – received a scratch bad enough to declare the whole thing over and honour satisfied. Sárosi, though, never reconciled himself to the W-M.

Guttmann, for all he favoured English tactics, did not impose them at Újpest. 'If a player has a tactical system in his blood,' he explained, 'if he has played it for years, he cannot go the next day to another system.' He was specifically concerned with marking structures and whether the full-back picked up the opposing winger – as in the W-M – or started narrower and dealt with the opposing inside-forward, leaving the opposing winger to the wing-half, as had been common (if not universal) in the 2–3–5. 'I cannot make a 27- or 28-year-old full-back, who has been taught to cover the inside-forward since he was a child, track a winger as he is going to drift inside anyway.'

He was also concerned about whether his Újpest players had the range of passing to play in the English style. Guttmann did, though, introduce English elements to Újpest's game: 'a lot of crosses, preferably basic moves with a ball over the top, overmanning and no overlapping. It was a simple game to give the ball to the best-placed player in the shortest period... If we were defending a lead we would defend with three backs and four covering.'

An early 6–1 defeat to MTK – the result of 'a lack of confidence', Guttmann insisted – could have derailed the season, but they rallied and developed a reputation for second-half comebacks as they lost only one further game all season to finish a point above Ferencváros at the top of the table. Even better followed in the Mitropa Cup. Having beaten Inter and the Yugoslav champions Beogradski SK,[18] who were

---

[18] BSK were disbanded during the war, then refounded as Metalac by former members in 1945. In 1957, they took on the name by which they are known today: OFK (Omladinski fudbalski klub – Youth Football Club).

managed by Guttmann's former Hakoah and Hakoah All-Stars teammate Sándor Nemes, they faced Ferencváros in the final, beating them 6–3 on aggregate.

Guttmann later claimed that the following day he met with Lipót Aschner, the Jewish club president and industrialist, and asked for a pay rise. When he was turned down, he quit. That would certainly have been characteristic, but it might not be the full story. On 1 August, *Sporthírlap* reported that Guttmann had decided to leave before the final, having received 'a very lucrative foreign offer' but that he had kept it from the players so as not to unsettle them. It's not clear who that could have been from.

Moldoványi suggests that the issue may have been anti-Semitism – which would make the conflicting accounts an attempt to hide an embarrassing truth: 'Even though Béla didn't have much money back then, people still envied him because of his success as a coach, and they started "Jew-bashing" him. The team loved him, most of them supported him, but the political pressure was too strong.'[19]

Whatever the reason for Guttmann leaving the job, he and Aschner remained on good terms, and Guttmann appears to have continued to work for Újpest in an unofficial capacity after being replaced as manager by István Mészáros. Soon, finding work would be the least of his problems.

War was coming.

---

[19] In Claussen, *Béla Guttmann.*

above and left: In an overgrown plot at the back of the Kozma utca cemetery stands the grave of Péter and Erzsébet, the son and wife of the pioneering coach Imre Hirschl.

below: Dori Kürschner (back row, centre) was a well-respected centre-half for MTK before becoming a coach and revolutionising the Brazilian game.

right: Jimmy Hogan's arrival in Budapest in 1916 was the catalyst for Hungarian football's first golden age.

© HUNGARIAN SPORTS MUSEUM

© HUNGARIAN SPORTS MUSEUM

right: Hungary went to the 1924 Olympics with high hopes but suffered a humiliating defeat to Egypt. From left to right: Károly Fogl, Ferenc Hirzer, Rudolf Jeny, József Eisenhoffer, Béla Guttmann, Gyula Mándi, Gábor Obitz, József Braun, György Orth, Gyula Tóth, János Biri.

© HUNGARIAN SPORTS MUSEUM

© HUNGARIAN SPORTS MUSEUM

above: A capacity crowd of more than 10,000 turned out in Munich to see Bayern lose 7–1 to the MTK tourists in 1919.

left: István Tóth (Potya), a prolific centre-forward, successful coach, *bon viveur* and war hero, killed by the SS, February 1945.

right: Márton Bukovi (hooped shirt, far right), perhaps the most tactically astute of all the Hungarian coaches, was brought to Ferencváros by Tóth.

above: The MTK players Béla Révész, Alfréd Schaffer, Imre Schlosser and Vilmos Kertész relax in a Budapest coffee house.

right: The last photograph of Árpád Weisz, the youngest coach to win Serie A, before his death at Auschwitz.

© ULLSTEIN BILD DTL/CONTRIBUTOR/GETTY

© ROGER VIOLLET/CONTRIBUTOR/GETTY

© KEYSTONE/STRINGER/GE

© TASS/CONTRIBUTOR/GETTY

© SVF2/CONTRIBUTOR/GETTY

After it had been occupied by the Germans, Budapest was besieged and then taken by the Soviets.

© ULLSTEIN BILD DTL./CONTRIBUTOR/GETTY

© KEYSTONE/STRINGER/GETTY

© HUNGARIAN SPORTS MUSEUMC

top and above: Ernő Erbstein (back row, far right) with his all-conquering Torino side, which was destroyed by the air-crash at Superga in which 18 players, five club officials including Erbstein, three journalists, four crew and a tour organiser were killed.

right: Erbstein in his days as a tough-tackling centre-half at Cagliari.

© KEYSTONE/STRINGER/GETTY

left: Béla Guttmann, the most successful of the Hungarian coaches, talks to the British media before his Benfica side faced Tottenham in the 1962 European Cup semi-final.

© HUNGARIAN SPORTS MUSEUM

right: Guttmann was a wanderer who travelled the globe; Gusztáv Sebes, an astute political operator, stayed at home and managed the great Hungary national team of the early fifties.

below: Ferenc Puskás and Billy Wright lead out the sides at Wembley before Hungary's 6–3 victory over England in November 1953.

© POPPERFOTO/CONTRIBUTOR/GETTY

© POPPERFOTO/CONTRIBUTOR/GETTY
© ULLSTEIN BILD DTL./CONTRIBUTOR/GETTY

above: Unbeaten in almost four years, Hungary lost the one that mattered, 3–2 against West Germany in the 1954 World Cup final.

left: The moment the golden age came to an end: an injured Puskás is carried from the field in the rebel Honvéd side's 2–1 win over AC Milan in December 1956. The team didn't return home after the uprising, in which 4,000 Hungarians were killed.

II

Success at times can be a curse. Ernő Erbstein's achievement in leading Lucchese to seventh in Serie A in 1936–37 came at a cost familiar to smaller clubs. That summer, Danilo Michelini, Libero Marchini and Bruno Neri were all lured away by wealthier sides. Erbstein, though, had much more serious concerns than replenishing his squad.

The political climate was becoming notably more tense. In 1932, Mussolini had insisted that 'anti-Semitism does not exist in Italy', which was probably broadly true, if only because the Jewish population there was very small and largely assimilated. Closer ties with Nazi Germany and the acquisition of an African empire, though, meant that race increasingly became a feature of Mussolini's fascism. Late in 1937, Italy withdrew from the League of Nations. To make matters worse, Lucca was a fascist stronghold. Carlo Sforza, the chief provincial party officer in the region, was a member of the Fascist Grand Council while also living there was Costanzo Ciano, the president of the Italian Chamber of Deputies and the father of Mussolini's son-in-law.

Erbstein fell ill with pneumonia and went to Sanremo on the Ligurian coast to recuperate. In February 1938, he persuaded Jolán and his doctor that a trip to the hillside spa of Montecatini would do him good. Unbeknown to them, though, he had arranged to meet his players there. The centre-half Umberto Caligaris, signed the previous year, had taken over as caretaker coach, but the team were struggling.

Lucchese won only five games that season and picked up only two points away from home, but they avoided relegation by a point.

Lucchese's form, though, was only one aspect of a general sense of unease at the club. Bruno Scher was asked by local fascists to change his name to something more overtly Italian and, when he refused, he was sold to Ampelea, a third-flight club in his native Istria.[1] Erbstein's contract was terminated, the club blaming his failing health, although other factors were clearly at play.

In summer 1938, Mussolini's government published the Manifesto of Race, which instituted a legally binding racial hierarchy. They began to enact it in the autumn, conducting a census of foreign Jews living in Italy.

Erbstein's dismissal may have come as a relief, albeit a short-term one. He left fascist Lucca and, after being turned down for the Lazio job seemingly because he was Jewish, moved to liberal Turin as coach of Torino, succeeding the former MTK manager Gyula Feldmann, István Tóth's former housemate. The club's president was Ferruccio Novo, who had been a full-back in the youth ranks at the club before accepting he had no future as a professional player. He had made his money in agricultural equipment while working his way through the club hierarchy in a series of administrative roles.

Pre-season training consisted of a lot of games, many of them seemingly quite frivolous – photographs, for instance, show grinning players running three-legged races – all part of Erbstein's developing theory of learning through fun. There is a poignancy to those shots now, young men smiling and laughing in the sun as they lark about on tree-lined fields. It's impossible, of course, to know what tensions there may have been behind the grins, but knowledge of what was to

---

[1] Ampelea Dopolavoro Isola are now known as Mladinski Nogometni Klub Izola and, as of 2019, played in the Slovenian third division.

come cast the photographs as reflective of a time of innocence whose end was drawing close.

Torino's squad included not only Bruno Neri, who had left Lucchese the previous summer, but Raf Vallone, a graduate in law and philosophy who gave up football after the war to become the film and drama critic for *La Stampa* and cultural editor of *L'Unità*, the official newspaper of the Italian Communist Party. He then became an actor, playing Altabani, the mafia boss, in *The Italian Job* and Cardinal Lamberto in *The Godfather III*.

Erbstein was given a sizeable budget but, as was his wont, he didn't go after stars, focusing rather on young players and those from the lower leagues. He picked up Walter Petron, a 20-year-old inside-left from Padova in Serie B, spending 250,000 lira (£2,700) despite scepticism about his capacity to cope in the top flight. Petron was nicknamed Farfallino – the Little Butterfly – because he was slight and graceful but Erbstein recognised he had a hard edge and an eye for goal. The centre-forward Giovanni Gaddoni came in from Piacenza in Serie C while the goalkeeper Aldo Olivieri followed his manager from Lucchese.

For the first time, Erbstein had a genuinely top-class side to work with, and he took full advantage. Before every game, he would outline tactics on a blackboard in what his players came to know as the 'killer hour' because they found it so boring. But it worked. In the 1970s, as Ajax and the Dutch dazzled with their own development of the Scottish tradition, Vallone said they reminded him of Erbstein's Torino. 'As long ago as that,' he said, '[Erbstein] exploited the wide areas, making use of every corner of the pitch – we were playing some sort of Total Football. Every time one of us had the ball, his teammates were on the move in order to give him not one but three different options.'[2] Which is natural, of course, for Bob McColl

---

[2] Cited by Bliss, *Erbstein*.

and Peter McWilliam had carried that ideal to England where it had inspired Jimmy Hogan, whose work on the foundations laid by John Tait Robertson had inspired the school of Hungarian football. It is that same basic principle that lies behind Pep Guardiola's *juego de posición*, his division of the pitch into 20 zones so players, by avoiding the creation of straight lines, offer multiple angles and possibilities for the man in possession.[3]

Torino started the season superbly. They won six, drew two and lost one of their first nine games, a 3–0 victory over Napoli on 27 November leaving them level at the top of the table with Bologna. But on 3 December 1938, Erbstein was gone, forced out of his job by anti-Semitic legislation.

* * *

Six weeks before Torino's win against Napoli, Bologna had beaten Lazio 2–0 thanks to first-half goals from two Uruguayan *oriundi*, Ettore Puricelli and Michele Andreolo. After two successive defeats, it left Bologna fifth in the table, three points behind the early leaders Liguria and Torino. 'The match has dealt justice to the too hasty voices, which said that Bologna were in a precarious condition of sporting health,' said the report in *La Gazzetta dello Sport*. 'The team, in fact, played well and proved its traditional gifts of initiative and combativeness almost unchanged.'[4]

But it was Árpád Weisz's last competitive match as coach of Bologna. A week later, during a break in the league programme, he led his side in a friendly away to Milan, but soon after, he resigned. The newspapers were largely silent on the reasons for his departure. *Calcio Illustrato* devoted just three lines to the story, and two of them

---

[3] For much more on this evolution see my book *The Barcelona Legacy* (Blink, 2018).

[4] *La Gazzetta dello Sport*, 19 October 1938.

focused on the return of the monocled Hermann Felsner to replace him. 'As for Veisz,' the report went on, 'it seems that he will leave Italy at the end of the year.'[5]

Weisz and his wife were listed on the census of foreign Jews conducted that August, although their children were not, perhaps because they had effectively lived as Catholics. Initially it was decided that only those who had moved there after 1933 had to leave, but that threshold was later amended to 1919. Weisz's son Roberto was unable to enrol in the third grade at school and on 7 September the family was given six months to leave Italy.

Weisz, Ilona and their two children left Bologna on 10 January 1939[6] and made for France. For a long time their story was a mystery, but the journalist Matteo Marani went through a list of Roberto Weisz's classmates and eventually found one, Bruno Savigni, who not merely remembered him but had been close friends. They had corresponded after the family's departure. From those letters, detailed in Marani's book *Della scudetto ad Auschwitz*, it is clear the Weiszs had stayed at the Bachaumont Hotel in Paris before moving on to the Netherlands, where Weisz had been offered a job as coach of Dordrecht. He was the tenth foreign coach of the club; the first had been Jimmy Hogan. A couple of months earlier, the Bologna team Weisz had built had won the league for the third time in four years.

In truth, the Dordrecht job was beneath Weisz. They were an amateur side playing in a 5,000-capacity stadium in a town with a population of 50,000, but he was in no position to be choosy. Immediately, Weisz began to professionalise the club. 'We boys were used to

---

[5] *Calcio Illustrato*, 29 October 1938.

[6] This is confirmed by files of Foreign Surveillance A16, part of the General and Private Affairs Division of the Ministry of the Interior, held at the Central State Archives.

warming up, in winter, running with a scarf on,' recalled the defender Nico Zwaan. 'The first thing that Weisz did, as soon as he arrived, was to stop that. He was a human person, generous, but firm when it came to work on the pitch.'[7]

Weisz insisted on three training sessions a week and, although there could be no *ritiro*, the players would meet on a Sunday morning at the Hotel Ponsen to talk through his plans for the game. 'He made us work in rain or snow,' Zwaan went on. 'He insisted everybody remained physically fit. But the thing that amazed us most, at least at first, was his knowledge of athletic training.'

He may have been more demanding than they were used to, but players remember Weisz's general decency. 'He was a shy person, but very courteous to all of us,' said the Dordrecht defender Dick Bergeijk. 'He was scared and tried to avoid being in photographs. When he spoke of Italy he was still sad.'[8]

Wim Verzijl, a fan who went on to be president of the club, remembers Weisz being shy, eschewing a social life and expressing fear about a number of issues, not least the fact he couldn't speak Dutch. And yet he clearly loved his work. 'He always talked about sport,' said Verzijl. 'Every moment. And he read the newspaper continuously. I have an image of him walking on the street immersed in the sheets of the newspaper, to the point of stumbling or bumping into people on the pavement. I remember him as an excellent man, a great professional, very strong in tactics. He brought many young people to the first team.'[9]

* * *

---

[7] Quoted in Mariani, *Della scudetto ad Auschwitz*.
[8] Quoted in Mariani, *Della scudetto ad Auschwitz*.
[9] Quoted in Mariani, *Della scudetto ad Auschwitz*.

Late in the autumn of 1938, Kálmán Konrád, still managing SK Židenice in Brno, had received a letter from an old friend Peter Brie, a German-Jewish sportswriter who had left Berlin for Prague in 1934. Brie had recognised the dangers of Germany's expansionism early and had travelled north through the Baltic states and Finland to Sweden where he had settled in Stockholm. Brie was convinced Jews had to get out of Germany's reach but was unable to persuade his family of the seriousness of the danger they faced. Although one sister, Lili, left for Shanghai in 1939 and the youngest, Edith, hid in Paris for the duration of the war, his eldest sibling Elsa died in Warsaw in 1942, his father Alfréd in Theresienstadt in 1942 and his mother Margarete in Auschwitz in 1944.

Others, though, were much more ready to listen. Through his work with the sports paper *Idrottsbladet*, Brie had learned that Örebro Sportklubb were looking for a manager and might be prepared to pay a significant salary. He suggested Konrád and the club agreed. His letter containing the job offer arrived, Kálmán's son Peter said, like 'a gold piece'; by then Brno was under German rule.

After the Anschluss, Hitler's attention had turned to Czechoslovakia. On 28 March 1938, he met with Konrad Heinlein, the pro-Nazi leader of the Sudeten Germans, and instructed him to raise demands unacceptable to the Czechoslovakian government. On 24 April, the Sudeten German Party (SdP) issued the Karlsbader Programm, calling for autonomy for the Sudetenland so Germans there would be free to pursue National Socialist ideology. With Britain and France desperate to avoid war, they advised the Czechoslovakian president Edvard Beneš to accede to the SdP's demands. He did not, and began to mobilise, believing a German invasion was imminent.

A British mediator, Lord Runciman, was appointed and by 2 September 1938, Beneš was willing to accept most of the Karlsbader

Programm. That, though, was not part of Hitler's plan. Sudeten Germans protested, provoking clashes with police in Ostrava on 7 September. The SdP withdrew from negotiations on 13 September and, two days later, after Heinlein had flown to Germany, called for Germany to take over the Sudetenland. Hitler met with Chamberlain, claiming the Czechoslovak government intended to slaughter their German population and insisting Germany had to be granted the Sudetenland. The British and French government agreed and issued Czechoslovakia with an ultimatum that it accepted on 21 September. Hitler promptly made new demands, insisting Poland and Hungary must also be granted territory to which they had a historical claim.

At a series of rallies across the country, Czechoslovakians called for Germany to be resisted. Czechoslovakia had a modern army and significant border defences, while the Soviets had suggested they would support Czechoslovakia if it came to military conflict. Beneš, though, was unwilling to go to war without the backing of the Western powers. On 29 September, Hitler met with the leaders of Britain, France and Italy in Munich. Chamberlain returned to London claiming to have reached an agreement that secured 'peace for our time'. It was illusory, and came at the cost of 38 per cent of Czechoslovak territory. Moreover, Czechoslovakia, having lost its natural western border and its frontier fortifications, became essentially indefensible. By March 1939, it had fallen entirely into German hands.

Germany's annexation of the Sudetenland had benefited Hungary, as the Vienna Awards of 1938 and 1940 restored to it territory that had been lost at Trianon. The dissolution of Czechoslovakia brought further conflict as Hungary occupied Carpatho-Ukraine and, briefly, fought the remnants of the Czechoslovakian army. But Hungary's prime minister Pál Teleki was wary of becoming too involved in Germany's military campaigns and on 24 July 1939 wrote to Hitler to advise him that Hungary would not support an invasion of Poland.

After receiving Örebro's offer through Brie, Konrád, his son said, left 'as soon as possible'. His plan was to establish himself then bring over his wife, son and widowed mother-in-law. For the Konráds to make the move required both a Swedish visa and a permit to leave Germany, a process complicated by a lack of communication between the German and Swedish authorities. Finally, in February 1939, at the third attempt, Konrád's family acquired the documents they needed and set off for Sweden.

Leaving their furniture behind, they packed up their other belongings in wooden crates. Regulations against taking cash out of the country meant they had only 10 Reichmarks with them. By the time they got to Sassnitz, from where they took the ferry to Trelleborg, they were down to their last 10 Pfennigs – 'not even enough for a glass of milk,' as Peter Konrád put it. They just had to hope Kálmán had received their message and was waiting to meet them at the port.

He was. They went to a hotel in Malmö and then to Örebro, where their crates were waiting. But they'd been opened and not all their belongings were there. 'My father's stamp collection was missing,' said Peter, 'as well as our best bed linen and my Märklin train set.' His mother-in-law, meanwhile, was held up by bureaucracy and didn't arrive for a further three weeks.

Örebro finished third that season. The following campaign they won 14 and drew four of 18 games, with a goal difference of 93–13, then won a promotion play-off to make it into the second flight. So popular was Konrád and so revered for his tactical nous that he was asked to be an advisor for their bandy[10] team, even though he couldn't skate and had only ever seen a handful of games.

* * *

[10] An 11-a-side game played on ice with bowed sticks and a small ball.

Kálmán Konrád's elder brother Jenő was a success at Triestina, taking an improving team to 12th in Serie A in 1936–37. 'I only rarely got to go to games on a Sunday,' his daughter Evelyn said. 'I would get too excited. And I knew when my father was in trouble because he'd reach over his head with his right hand and scratch his left ear.'

Once she saw a boy playing with a ball in a square. She asked to join in but he said football wasn't for girls. Her father was sitting nearby so she pointed to him and asked if the boy knew who the man was. Of course he did, he said. She told him that she could go over and sit on his lap any time she wanted. The boy scoffed, at which she approached her father and sat on his lap. The boy let her play after that.

Triestina finished sixth in 1937–38. Jenő Konrád was popular and well respected but that was no protection from Mussolini's newly adopted anti-Semitism. One morning in the last week of October, Evelyn was in the garden of their house in the hills overlooking the city when the post arrived. There was a letter from the convent school. 'I always got good grades and praise,' Evelyn said, 'so my mother let me open it, but this was a letter saying I had to leave the school.

'That was the first thing. Then they wanted all alien Jews to leave Italy. The Triestina president asked for special permission for me to stay – so we were the first who had to go.'

The family returned to Budapest, living with Jenő's parents and his sister Ilona, who owned a factory manufacturing silk flowers with her husband. 'I didn't much like my father's parents,' Evelyn said. 'They had a huge cook who was always stuffing me with food, and when I was playing dominoes against my grandmother, my grandfather always wanted her to win, which didn't seem right.'

As Jenő had been an officer in the First World War and was under 49 years of age, he was still part of the Hungarian army reserve and, as the political situation across Europe became increasingly tense, he was concerned he would be called up. In 1938, he went to Paris in the guise of a representative for the silk-flower company, but with the intention of securing visitors' visas for his wife and daughter. 'I was terrified there was going to be a war so we would be cut off from my father,' said Evelyn. 'I was so relieved after Chamberlain reached a deal at Munich.'

Metz offered Jenő a job, but he turned it down, worried the city was too close to Germany, and went instead to Lille, leading them to the 1939 French Cup final, in which they were beaten 3–1 by Racing.

Their permits secured, the family went to join him. 'In May 1939 we travelled to Vienna,' said Evelyn. Anti-Semitic legislation had cost her grandmother the cinema, though, and her mother's home had changed almost beyond recognition. 'I remember the sound of jackboots on the cobbles,' she said. 'The projectionist from the movie theatre, who used to bow and scrape, walked up to us and turned away. Two washerwomen pushed my mother off the sidewalk. I wanted to go for them, but my mother dug her nails into my arm and probably saved our lives – who knows what they'd have done if I had attacked them?

'The concierge – nobody had a lower bow than him – practically slammed the door in my grandmother's face. They'd moved other people into my grandmother's apartment so when my mother bought some bread for the train my grandmother locked it in the cupboard. That was the last time I saw my grandmother alive.'

She died three years later on a transport to Treblinka.

* * *

'We took a train to France,' Evelyn went on. 'I didn't start breathing properly till we were past the Maginot Line. The French were so proud of that. "Oh, the Germans will never get through," they said – and of course they didn't. They went round.'

Even after getting to France, Jenő was haunted by the fear he and his family might be interned as enemy aliens and so looked to move on even further. 'We were living out of a trunk,' said Evelyn, 'never sure if they might come for us. There were air raids, planes unloading their bombs after returning from reconnaissance missions over England. We were provided with gas-masks, which said "Made in Germany", which didn't give you much confidence. They made air-raid shelters out of wood – they were so screwed up it was unbelievable. We used to hide in a neighbour's cellar.'

Lisbon offered a possible route to the US, and so Jenő secured visitors' visas for Portugal. Two weeks before the German invasion of France, Greta and Evelyn sewed gold dollars into the lining of Jenő's dressing gown and the three took the train south, across France and Spain. At the border town of Villa Formosa, though, they had to wait. For three days, the Konráds stayed with the family of a border guard and their goats before the Portuguese government, apparently persuaded by leading football figures, allowed them to continue their journey.

Jenő found work with Sporting, but the fear that, as foreign nationals, they might be sent to a camp in Tangiers never went away. 'I still can't stand pineapples because we ate them every day,' said Evelyn. 'The whole place seemed to stink of *bacalhau*. I remember the spies on the Rossio. You could always tell which country they were from. The French held their cigarettes between thumb and forefinger and smoked them down to the toothpick. The Americans held them between two fingers. The Germans wore short jackets above their big bulbous behinds.'

On visiting the US embassy, Jenő was told that the quota for Hungarian immigrants was filled. 'The US consulate was selling them,' Evelyn said. 'It was as corrupt as could be.' Finally, in May

1940, after Jenő had pointed out that his birthplace in Vojvodina had not been part of Hungary since Trianon, he was registered as a Yugoslav and visas issued for him and his family. Jenő was offered work in Montevideo, but by then Greta's heart was set on the US.

There was still, though, the matter of getting across the Atlantic. With no passenger ships available, Jenő booked on to the first-ever voyage of the cargo ship *San Miguel*, exporting cork to the US. There were no other passengers. 'We got the captain's cabin for my mother and me,' said Evelyn, 'and the first mate's cabin for my father. It was smaller than the Staten Island ferry. We were carrying cork, and I thought, "Thank God – if a U-boat gets us, we'll still be able to float."'

It took 15 days to cross the Atlantic and a further two for the fog outside New York to lift sufficiently for Evelyn to see the Statue of Liberty and for the ship to make its way into harbour.

Jenő initially tried to work as a masseur in New Jersey, then found employment in a factory manufacturing Singer sewing machines, while Greta worked in a textile factory making blouses and later, with the help of some cousins who had emigrated a few years earlier, opened a curtain shop in Elizabeth, New Jersey – 'the toilet seat of the country', according to Evelyn, 'an awful place'.

Hers, in a sense, is the perfect immigrant story. She escaped peril, became a journalist for NBC, wrote a novel[11] and, at the age of 73, graduated from law school. At the age of 89 she was still practising in Manhattan and preparing for a skiing holiday in Vermont to celebrate her 90th birthday.

But Jenő's career in football was over. 'My father had a very hard life,' Evelyn said. 'He could speak every language but all of them with a heavy Hungarian accent. He gave me my love of literature, history

---

[11] *Indiscretions*, published by HarperCollins for a $20,000 advance in 1979.

and learning. I'd write to him from college and he would always have read not only the book I was studying but every other book by that author as well. He had an iron will. My father always taught me you shouldn't look left or right at what others were doing but should go your own way.'

He died in New York in 1978, at the age of 83.

* * *

Ernő Erbstein remained in Turin for two months after being forced out of the Torino job but the situation was intolerable and he knew he and his family had to leave. Erbstein let it be known he was seeking work and received a reply from his former BAK teammate Ignác Molnár, who was coaching Xerxes in Rotterdam but was keen to test himself in Italy.[12] Effectively they swapped jobs. Xerxes were a significantly smaller club than Torino, but Erbstein was grateful for any opportunity: he had to get out of Italy.

He arranged a flat in the Netherlands, sent his luggage on ahead and sorted out a work permit. In February 1939, the family took the train north from Turin. On the way, Erbstein read to his daughters from a book about the Netherlands, telling them about the exciting new life on which they were about to embark. But they never got there. At Cleves, a small border town on the Rhine, Dutch guards examined their papers and invalidated their visas with a stroke of a red pen – probably because of a secret arrangement between the Dutch and German governments not to permit refugees across the border.

The Erbsteins couldn't go on, but they couldn't go back and most of their belongings were already in the Netherlands. They had only the clothes they wore and the few possessions they carried with them.

---

[12] Molnár subsequently was a success in Turkey, where he led Fenerbahçe to the league title in 1959 and 1968 and had two stints as national coach.

In despair, they asked at the station where they could go and were told of the Judenhause – Jew House – on Klosterstrasse; it had previously been the Clever Hof hotel. All Jews in Cleves had been forced to live there and were under a curfew but the Erbsteins, as Hungarian citizens, were at least theoretically free to come and go as they pleased.

Susanna recalls the family finding a bleak, unoccupied room on the first floor, the windows shattered by stones thrown by anti-Jewish mobs, probably on *Kristallnacht* when the local synagogue had been burned down. They stayed there, waiting for new Dutch visas to be sent from Italy, hoping the next time the border guards would let them across. Erbstein rang the Torino president Ferruccio Novo, the Hungarian embassy and the FIGC and begged for help. The secretary general of the FIGC, Ottorino Barassi, sent a letter vouching for Erbstein's character and listing the clubs for whom he'd worked.[13] The new visas arrived after around a month but the Dutch authorities again refused the Erbsteins entry. At that, they did the only thing they could and set off back to Hungary.

Jolán was ill with the stress while Marta fell silent during their ordeal, forgot everything that had happened before they got on the train, including her Italian, and didn't speak for several weeks afterwards.

* * *

Snow had fallen over Debrecen in the east of Hungary, so much that the pitch for Bocskai's league game against MTK on 12 March 1940 was covered by three or four inches and the lines had to be marked with loose earth. When the captains tossed for choice of ends, the coin sank through the snow and the referee sheepishly had to borrow another one.

---

[13] This letter is published in the Hungarian edition of Bliss, *Erbstein*.

The MTK coach Gyula Feldmann was desperate for the game to go ahead. His side was three points clear of Ferencváros at the top of the table and with his team in form he wanted to keep up the pressure. Feldmann's first stint at MTK had ended after a year as Ferencváros had claimed the title. He had briefly managed Juventus Bucharest[14] before a successful career in Italy, during which he led both Fiorentina and Palermo to promotion out of Serie B, and also managed Inter and Torino. There was a season in Belgrade with SK Jugoslavija, before he returned to his former club in 1939. With just ten games of the season remaining, this was his big chance of a first-ever title as a manager.

József Turay, the centre-half Feldmann had had stolen from him while he slept, had been an important figure that season, but he was largely marked out of the game by his younger brother András. It didn't matter, though. Two early goals from the veteran forward Jenő Kalmár, who had played for MTK between 1928 and 1933 and, after five years in France, had returned home the previous season, were enough to give MTK a 2–1 win and maintain their lead over Ferencváros.

Back in Budapest two days later, the snow had gone and the kit man had left eight balls out on the training pitch to dry. As the players emerged onto the track, though, it became apparent something was wrong. Feldmann had been calmly talking to his squad when he abruptly turned to one of his assistants, Béla Mandik.

---

[14] Trying to stay on top of the various mergers, changes of name and location of Romanian clubs is an almost impossible task, but this is not the same Juventus Bucharest that played in the Romanian top flight in 2017–18 and was subsequently forced to change its name to Daco-Getica following legal action by the Italian club Juventus. Rather this was the side formed in Bucharest in 1924 by the merger of Romcomit and Triumf that from 1947 went through a series of name changes – to Distribuția, Petrolul, Competrol, Partizanul and Flacăra – before moving to Ploiești in 1952, eventually settling in 1957 on the name by which it is known today, Petrolul Ploiești.

'"Come here," he said. "I feel really bad,"' Mandik recalled.[15] He took Feldmann off to seek medical help, leaving the players in the hands of the captain, Gusztáv Sebes. 'At first,' Mandik went on, 'we didn't think too much of it but when we got to the dressing room, my brother Gyula began to lose consciousness. Before he did, he said to me in a frustrated voice, "Tell Sebes to run two laps with the boys." Then he collapsed completely.'

A stroke was diagnosed and while MTK waited for Feldmann to recover, it was decided that Sebes and the fitness coach Béla Takács should lead training sessions while Mandik took over Feldmann's managerial role. This was Sebes's first taste of coaching; within a decade, he would be manager of the national side.

But Feldmann did not recover. According to Géza Werling, István Tóth's grandson's half-brother, the ambulance men who came to take Feldmann to hospital let him slide off the stretcher, causing a serious injury to his leg, which later became infected leading to erysipelas. Because he did not receive proper treatment, Feldmann had to have his leg amputated just above the knee, probably late in 1940. That meant he was exempt from the labour service for which Jewish men had to report, but he spent the final months of the war in hiding.

Feldmann was fitted with an artificial leg and worked with MTK when they were re-formed after the war. By the 1950s, though, he barely left the house on Telepes utca he and Tóth had bought two decades earlier. 'He was an endlessly nice, kind man,' Werling remembered. 'He talked a lot and I played Marokko[16] with him a lot.' He died in 1955.

---

[15] In *Nemzeti Sport*, 14 March 1940.

[16] A game, also known as Mikado or Pick-up Sticks, that comprises 41 sticks of varying points values. They are tossed onto a flat surface and players then take it in turns to remove sticks without disturbing the others.

Without Feldmann, MTK's form dipped. The three-point lead was overhauled, not only by Ferencváros, but also by Újpest, who went on to win the title. In normal times, that would have been a major frustration, but these were not normal times.

For years MTK had found itself under attack. When Gyula Gömbös had been prime minister he had seen MTK as a threat, a 'cosmopolitan' – those anti-Semitic dog whistles again – body antithetical to his nationalist vision. Ferenc Kossuth, who became head of the National Federation of Hungarian Wrestlers in 1933, said that Gömbös had told him to ostracise MTK, leading to the wrestling section being gradually disbanded in the early 1930s, while others claimed to have heard Gömbös vow he would erase the club 'with a stroke of the pen'.[17]

Gömbös did not live long enough to carry out his threat, but as more and more anti-Semitic legislation was enacted in the late 1930s, circumstances became harder and harder for MTK and the wrestling, cycling, fencing and water polo sections of the club were all wound up. Jewish directors were forced to stand down in the autumn of 1940, when Alfréd Brüll fled to Switzerland, but, despite talk of dissolution, the football, athletics, tennis and table tennis sections went on. In the spring of 1941, though, there came a concerted attack. The Hungarian Athletics Association accused MTK of insufficient activity and allowed athletes at the club to make immediate transfers. And then the MLSZ decided that Jan Burko, a Polish Jewish refugee who had been playing for the club, was ineligible, and suspended MTK's playing licence. At the same time, they assigned the stadium on Hungária út to the Hungarian National Defence Association. Ferencváros and Újpest protested on MTK's behalf, but the MLSZ refused even to meet their delegates.

---

[17] In Sándor Barcs (ed), *Száz éves az MTK-VM sportklub* [MTK-VM Sport Club is 100 years old] (MTK, 1988).

The legal *coup de grâce* came on 29 November 1941 as the National Sports Committee announced that 'only such sports clubs as have their fundamental rules acknowledged by state authorities can be members of the sports association which, according to par. 9 of Article 14. 1941, do not have a member who is defined as a Jew, or a member who has a spouse who can be defined as a Jew.' MTK refused to comply with demands to submit an amended version of their rules of association including a list of members and in the spring of 1942 the club was officially disbanded, its assets confiscated and its archives destroyed.

* * *

The Hungarian prime minister Pál Teleki had only been able to resist Germany for so long and, in November 1940, he affiliated to the Tripartite Pact. The following year, Hitler asked Hungary to join Germany's invasion of Yugoslavia, after a coup had deposed the pro-German Prince Paul and replaced him with the pro-British King Peter, something that threatened Germany's invasion of the USSR.

Teleki, having failed in his efforts to keep Hungary out of the war, committed suicide. He was succeeded as prime minister by the radical right-winger László Bárdossy, who oversaw the annexation of small parts of what are now Serbia, Croatia and Slovenia. The Second Vienna Award of August 1940 had secured for Hungary the northern, majority-Hungarian part of Transylvania, which had been ceded to Romania at Trianon. Drawn by the prospect of reclaiming the southern part as well, and facing the threat of Romanian retaliation, Hungary formally joined the war on the German side on 1 July 1941, committing troops to support the German push east.

Later that month, responsibility for 18,000 Jews from Carpatho-Ruthenian Hungary, who did not have Hungarian citizenship, was passed to German armed forces. They were sent to Kamenets-Podolski in what is now Ukraine, where around 16,000 of them were shot by Nazi killing units, one of the first massacres perpetrated against Jews during the war. In August 1941, Bárdossy passed the Third Jewish Law, which prohibited both marriage and sexual relations between Jews and non-Jewish Hungarians.

The president Miklós Horthy was uneasy about Hungary's dependency on Germany and forced out Bárdossy, replacing him with Miklós Kállay, a conservative who had served in Bethlen's government in the 1920s. Hungary continued to fight the Soviets, but at the same time Horthy tried to negotiate with the Western Allies.

An obligation for Jews to perform forced labour had first been set out on 11 March 1939. In Hungary, the labour details were overseen by the Ministry of Defence: they were essentially military units and, until 1941, in contrast to the practice in Germany, Italy and Romania, they were used on active service, as in, for instance, the invasions of Transylvania and Transcarpathia.

On 17 March 1942, the General Staff issued an instruction that Jewish men performing labour service should be sent to war zones. According to a secret Ministry of Defence instruction of 22 April, 10 to 15 per cent of labour servicemen had to be 'prominent Jews'. From the spring onwards, labour units were deployed with the Second Army in Ukraine.

One of those prominent Jews was József 'Csibi' Braun, the rapid winger Jimmy Hogan had signed in 1917 after seeing him playing in Városliget with György Orth. He had been one of the most popular players in that great MTK side of the immediate post-war years, so much so that at the height of his fame it was said that old men would give up their seats on the tram for him to spare 'the golden legs'.

Those legs took a fearful battering. He suffered his first serious injury in 1921 and by 1925 he was forced to contemplate the end of his career. In March 1926, he took a director's job at Erzsébeti TC, a club from Pesterzsébet in the south of Budapest that would be relegated that season. In the summer of 1927, he had a third operation on his injured leg and needed further surgery three months later, at which MTK made him a free agent. He continued to train with Ferencváros, though, and played in some friendlies for MTK. By 1929, he was desperately hunting for a club and played a couple of matches for Hakoah in Vienna (seemingly illegally) before heading to the US for a year in which he played for Brooklyn Wanderers and Brooklyn Hakoah. He returned to Hungary early in 1930 and rejoined his first club, VAC, playing his final match in June that year against Vasas.

Braun became a coach, managing the Norway national side and having stints with various Hungarian and Czechoslovakian clubs before being appointed manager of Basel in August 1938. Within a month, the war had brought an end to his career there. 'For now, every kid in Switzerland has been called up as a soldier and all football has been terminated,' he said on his return to Budapest.[18] 'They don't even play friendly or youth matches.' He worked briefly with Gloria in Arad, before returning once again to Budapest.

Braun was sent first to the camp at Nagykáta about 40 miles east of Budapest, where Jews were trained and arranged into units to be sent east. As soon as they arrived, they were subject to ill treatment and abuse, and no attempt was made to disguise the fact that their lives were considered expendable. The camp was run by Lieutenant-Colonel Lipót Murai-Metzl, who would be executed for war crimes on 1 May 1945.

---

[18] *Nemzeti Sport*, 20 September 1939.

In June 1942, the Braun family appealed for József to be released from Nagykáta given that, as an Olympian, he was theoretically exempt from labour service. But the authorities refused to issue the necessary document.[19] Braun was drafted into company number 101/5 and sent to Ukraine. In company 101/4 was Attila Petschauer, the double Olympic fencing gold medallist who had helped György Orth in the street fight in 1926 before his duel. In January 1943, amid intense cold, guards acting on the orders of a Hungarian officer who was also an Olympian, made him strip naked and climb a tree. They taunted him, forcing him to crow like a cockerel, then sprayed him with water. Frozen, he died soon after.[20]

Braun was stationed nearby. Precisely what happened to him remains unclear. The writer András Kepes, the grandson of Róna Braun, József's cousin, can say merely that nothing of him is left, not a personal possession, not a photograph. He died somewhere in a Ukrainian labour camp in February 1943.

* * *

The news came as a surprise. Was Alfréd Schaffer, the great woman-iser, the great pursuer of dreams and cash, finally settling down? After the 1938 World Cup, he had left his job with the Hungary national team to take charge of Wacker Munich for the third time, to marry a German woman and to manage the restaurant that she owned.

The answer came soon enough: he was not.

After a year, Schaffer took a job with Rapid Bucharest, and references to his wife vanished. In May 1940, he became manager of Roma, taking over a side that a month later would finish the

---

[19] More details are given in *Felvilágosodás*, 12 October 1945.
[20] A fictionalised version of his life and death form the basis of the 1999 film *Sunshine*, directed by István Szabó and starring Ralph Fiennes and Rachel Weisz.

season sixth, 15 points behind the champions Inter. They came tenth the following season and lost to Venezia after a replay in the Coppa Italia final, but the arrival of a new president with money to spend, Edgardo Bazzini, changed everything. 'Give me a wing-half and an inside-forward and I'll win you the league,' Schaffer said and, presented with Edmondo Mornese, Renato Cappellini, Fosco Risorti, Cesare Benedetti and Sergio Andreoli – everything he had wanted and more – he made good on his promise, leading Roma to the first *scudetto* in their history.

They suffered a poor start the following season, though, and after a draw at Bari at the beginning of December extended a poor run to one win in seven games, he was replaced by Géza Kértész, who was slowly emerging from his pigeonhole as a promotion specialist.

Schaffer returned home to a deteriorating situation in Budapest. For a long time, Hungary's was a tentative war. Trianon had forbidden them from having an army and so involvement on the Eastern Front was limited. Jews in Hungary, meanwhile, although far from comfortable and deprived of many freedoms, were not in the same immediate danger as they would have been in other Axis power countries and Horthy actively sought to repress the fascistic Arrow Cross, which was effectively the successor to the outlawed Party of National Will. By 1942, though, there were tens of thousands of Hungarians fighting on the Eastern Front, many at Stalingrad, where they sustained around 100,000 casualties. Through 1943, Kállay stepped up his attempts to negotiate a separate peace with the Allies.

Too old for military service, Schaffer got on with the business of finding work, suggesting to the MLSZ that he could take over as national coach. They, though, were quite happy with the job being done by the former MTK forward Jenő Kalmár, who had ended his playing career in 1940, and so Schaffer was without a club till June

1943, when he was appointed manager of Ferencváros. Almost immediately, he led them to victory in the Cup final. The following season they finished second in the league and won the Cup again.

* * *

For Árpád Weisz, it turned out, moving to Dordrecht had been a dreadful mistake. On 10 May 1940, German paratroopers had landed in the Netherlands and four days later, the Netherlands had surrendered.

Slowly the bureaucracy of genocide cranked into action. On 14 December, Árpád's son Roberto sent his last letter to his old school friend Bruno Savigni, wishing him a merry Christmas.

On 10 January 1941, the Commissioner of the Reich in the Netherlands ordered a census of the Jews in the country. There were an estimated 140,000, 80,000 in Amsterdam alone.

Four months later, with a side featuring seven players who had played for Weisz, Bologna won the league again. They have won it only once since; Weisz was in charge for two of their seven scudetti and could be said to have built the side that won two more.

For all his popularity, Weisz could not escape. On 1 September 1941, Roberto and Clara were forced to leave their school in Dordrecht. On 29 September, the Police Commission wrote to the directors of Dordrecht banning Weisz from setting foot on any land 'where games accessible to the public are organised'. It concluded with a chilling directness: 'I strongly advise you not to take or keep in the service of your association any Jews, because in the present circumstances it could have very harmful consequences.'

The Dordrecht president Rinus Scheepbouwer, who had replaced Van Twist, reluctantly complied. Weisz was replaced by the man he had succeeded, Ferry Triebel. A photograph taken in August 1941 shows the two of them in Scheepbouwer's garden. Weisz is notably thinner than the round-faced young coach who had won the league with Inter 11 years earlier, the strain clear behind his smile. There would be no more pictures of Weisz. For months, Van Twist supported Weisz and his family as they waited in terrible limbo, unable to work, unable to leave, unable to live.

Events further east had made the situation of Jews even more perilous. The Nazis' initial plan appears to have been forcible expulsion of Jews from conquered territories to create *Lebensraum*. After the invasion of Poland, though, Jews were forced into makeshift ghettoes, and after the failure of the air war against Britain and the invasion of the Soviet Union in 1941, leading Nazis decided that extermination was a more practical alternative than expulsion. As the Wehrmacht pursued the retreating Red Army, Himmler, operating on the warped logic that Bolshevism was 'the most recent and most nefarious manifestation of the eternal Jewish threat'[21] ordered that any Jew behind the Soviet-German line should be regarded as a partisan and killed. From August 1941, captured Jews were sent to camps to be murdered. Hundreds of thousands had been killed even before the conference at Wannsee near Berlin in January 1942 formalised plans to kill all of Europe's Jews. Death camps were constructed, with permanent gas chambers.

On 1 May 1942, it was made law that Jews in the Netherlands had to wear a yellow star. They were banned from shops between two and five in the afternoon, banned from public transport and the houses of Gentiles altogether. A curfew was imposed, prohibiting them from being outside between ten in the evening and six in the morning.

On 26 June, two trains packed with 4,000 Dutch Jews departed for Auschwitz. They were forced to pay for their tickets. On 14 July, as

---

[21] Christopher R Browning, *The Origins of the Final Solution: The Evolution of Nazi Jewish Policy, September 1939 – March 1942* (Random House, 2004).

prohibitions on mixed marriage and ritual slaughter were introduced, 700 more Jews were picked up in Amsterdam. On 2 August 1942, Jewish women were banned from hair salons and it became illegal for Jews to have telephones in their homes.

At 7am that morning, the Gestapo arrived in Bethlehemplein, mounted the 15 steps to the Weiszs' door and knocked. In retrospect, Erbstein had been very fortunate he had never made it to the Netherlands.

Weisz and his family were taken first to Westerbork, a camp in the north-east of the Netherlands where Anne Frank would later be detained. It was large and well established, with beds for 1,725, shops, a hospital, a bookshop and a football pitch. From seven in the morning till noon and then from two till seven, the inmates worked, but Westerbork was primarily a transit camp. On 15 July 1942 the first train had left, carrying 1,020 deportees to labour and extermination camps. The last would not depart until 13 September 1944.

Twice a week, the trains went east. On Friday 2 October, Clara's eighth birthday, two days before the start of a new Serie A season, Weisz's name was called with those of his family. They walked the couple of miles to the station at Hooghalen and, with 1,010 other Jews, boarded a train. Its destination was marked on the front: 'Auschwitz'.

There was no light in the carriages, no space, no privacy, no food, no water. Three days after it had set off, the train stopped at Cosel in Upper Silesia. Around 300 men were taken off to work in the labour camp at Monowitz (Auschwitz III). It is almost certain Weisz was among them. His family carried on to the dreadful process of selection. To the right, the camp at Auschwitz I; to the left, the gas chambers of Birkenau. Ilona, Roberto and Clara, and 649 others on that train, were sent left. They were murdered later that day.

Árpád Weisz was sent to work in an armaments factory. Physically fit, he survived longer than most, for 13 horrendous months, but exhaustion eventually overcame him. He died on 31 January 1944.

One Saturday in March 1944, Susanna Erbstein faced what felt like the biggest day of her life. She had reached the third and final round of a major dance contest. Win this, and her dreams of becoming a professional dancer would be close to fruition.

On returning to Budapest, she had begun classes at the Ballet Institute, opposite the Opera House, but things had taken a major step forward during a summer holiday on Lake Balaton. There, Susanna had met Éva Kovács, a 20-year-old who would go on to become well known in the world of modern dance. Kovács had been trained at the Orkesztikai Intézet (the Institute of Movement Art) by its founder, Valéria Dienes, and introduced Susanna to Valéria's son Gedeon, a comparative linguist.

Most days in Budapest, Susanna would visit Gedeon, learning English as she taught him Italian, and so got to know Valéria. 'She liked me,' Susanna said, 'approached me with sympathy from the very first moment despite the fact that I was learning dance at a totally different place and in a totally different manner and style.'

To describe Dienes as a dance teacher is inadequate. 'Valéria Dienes,' Susanna said, 'was one of the most important personalities in Hungarian culture in the 20th century in sciences and human sciences, and in the arts as well. She was active in the fields of mathematics, philosophy, aesthetics and worked a lot as a translator. For example, she was the Hungarian translator of the works of [Henri] Bergson authorised by the philosopher himself.

'And it was she who brought to Hungary the new ideas of modern dance. Her starting point was the oeuvre of Isadora Duncan,[1] who wanted to destroy the centuries' old tradition of classical ballet. Valéria had stayed for many years in France as a student of Bergson, and in France during this period she met Isadora Duncan. She enthusiastically accepted her ideas, and readily entered the Duncan community, where they wanted to reconstruct not only dance based on the ancient Greek culture but the whole way of life... Her difference to Isadora Duncan was that Isadora based her dancing on the instinctive approach, while Valéria based hers on scientific principles.'

It was Dienes who had organised the contest and Susanna was desperate to impress. Life had been surprisingly good since escaping Cleves and returning to Budapest. Erbstein had set up a firm importing textiles with his brother Károly, who had been sacked from the bank where he worked. It prospered and the family leased an apartment on Andrássy út, a smart thoroughfare noted for its boutiques, galleries and coffee houses. Six doors up the road, the Arrow Cross would establish their House of Loyalty where many thousands were tortured and killed. After the war it was taken over by the Stalinist state police, the ÁVH, and is now the House of Terror, a museum detailing the atrocities of both the Fascists and the Communists.

Marta was enrolled at the Calvinist Scottish Mission under a British headmistress, Miss Jenny, who ignored the anti-Semitic legislation limiting the number of Jewish children in each school. Marta was still mute and was learning Hungarian, English, German and Hebrew. Finally, in June 1939, when her father pointed at a window and asked what it was, she spoke again. '*Ablak*,' she said, '*Fenster*, window.'

---

[1] Duncan was born in California, but emigrated to Europe at the age of 22. She rejected the rigidity of traditional ballet, promoting a free or natural style she claimed to be able to trace back to ancient Greece.

Erbstein remained in regular contact with the Torino president Ferruccio Novo and his assistant Roberto Copernico, who was himself in textiles, trading contacts and advice about football and business. On at least one occasion after in 1939, Erbstein left Hungary on a false passport and travelled through northern Yugoslavia to Venice to meet up with Novo and Copernico.

Susanna's books were sent from Turin and, for a couple of years, life returned to something approaching normality. Susanna kept dancing, Marta kept studying and Erbstein kept dealing in textiles. At some point, he changed his surname to Egri, and it is under that name that Susanna is listed on the programme of the dance contest.

In 1941 they moved to a modern Bauhaus apartment block on Petőfi Sándor utca, close to the river. They took holidays. Sometimes at the weekend they would stay at Gellért Hotel, not far from their apartment on the riverbank, using the baths while their household staff cleaned their apartment. The atmosphere was threatening, there were restrictions on Jews, and Hungary suffered terrible losses on the Eastern Front, but life in Budapest in many ways went on as before. Susanna suggests that the quality of life was better in those years than it had been even in Turin before the war.

Then, on that spring day at the Orkesztikai Intézet on Krisztina körút, on the west side of the river, not far from the Chain Bridge, Susanna took on six other finalists in Dienes's dance contest. There were four styles of dance competing: a school of classical ballet, Dienes's school, the school of Sára Berczik and the School of Olga Szentpál. Susanna belonged to two schools simultaneously: classical ballet and Sára Berczik's modern school of 'movement art'.

Each dancer danced two pieces. Susanna's first was to music by the French composer Jacques Ibert and the second a Spanish dance to music by Pascual Marquina.

There was a professional panel of judges and the audience also voted. On both counts, Susanna won. A career in ballet that would lead to global fame was under way. She celebrated and spent that night at Éva Kovács's apartment on Mészáros utca, just a couple of minutes' walk from the Orkesztikai Intézet.

The following morning, she woke to a terrible noise. She drew back the curtains and saw the German army driving along Alagút utca having crossed the Chain Bridge. She phoned her family and returned home soon after. Nothing, she knew, could ever be the same again.

* * *

Alarmed by Miklós Kállay's attempts to negotiate a separate peace with the Allies, Hitler invited Miklós Horthy to Klessheim, a palace just outside Salzburg, for talks on 15 March 1944. Three days earlier, he had already given the order for the occupation of Hungary, and negotiations were essentially a ruse to keep Horthy out of the country. By the time Horthy returned home on 18 March, Hungary was already in German hands. With little option, he removed Kállay and appointed the German preference Döme Sztójay as prime minister. New armies were mustered and the battle to prevent Hungary being occupied by Soviet forces taken up with renewed urgency.

Sztójay legalised the Arrow Cross, although at that stage they lacked real influence, and appointed a series of hard-line right-wingers to key positions. On 9 April, the 300,000 Hungarian Jews in labour details were placed at the disposal of Germany. Five days later, Adolf Eichmann took the decision to exterminate all Hungarian Jews, beginning with those in the countryside. He estimated that would take around two months, after which deportations from the ghetto in Budapest would begin.

This was the most efficient phase of the Holocaust. Deportations to the camps began on 15 May and in the 54 days that followed, 435,000 Jews were transported to their deaths; or, to put it another way, during that period one Hungarian Jew was murdered every 11 seconds. Roughly 90 per cent of Jews from the Hungarian country-side were slaughtered; roughly one in two from within Budapest.

What's perhaps most extraordinary is that the death camps were no secret by then. There had been Jewish refugees fleeing to Hungary from Poland for months, as well as the testimony of those who had escaped the camps, some of which were only a few dozen miles from the Hungarian border. The country, though, seems to have been in collective denial. The attitude, as summed up by Götz Aly, the German holocaust historian, seemed to have been, 'This is Hungary. This might be happening in Galicia to Polish Jews, but this can't happen in our very cultivated Hungarian state... I think part of the problem of the Holocaust was that potential victims couldn't believe the information. The idea that something so atrocious would come from Germany and from the civilised European environment was so unimaginable that they didn't take it for real, even when they received overwhelming reports from the death camps.'[2]

Among the first to be deported was Lipót Aschner, the president of Újpest, who was taken to the camp at Mauthausen. He, though, was lucky. Tungsram, the electronics company of which he had been a director, bought his freedom and he saw out the war in Geneva, returning home in 1947. While he was away, Adolf Eichmann moved into his house.

Alfréd Brüll, the long-time president of MTK, was not so fortu-nate. He had escaped to Switzerland after the Second Jewish Law had

---

[2] Interview with Kathryn Berman and Asaf Tal, 'The Uneasy Closeness to Ourselves', Yad Vashem, International School for Holocaust Studies.

been passed, but returned to Hungary in 1943, under the mistaken impression that there would be no escalation of the persecution. It's not clear precisely what happened to him, but it's likely he died either at Auschwitz or in the transit camp at Kecskemét.

* * *

'We set out from Budaliget late one evening,' wrote Gitta Mallász, 'making our way through the dark forests embracing the western part of Budapest. I take the lead, with Hanna and Joseph following a short distance behind.'[3] They were terrified of running into one of the Nazi patrols that guarded the roads into the capital. But they were lucky. 'We emerge safely at a large tram station, Hűvösvölgy, where we are able to mingle unobtrusively among the throngs of the city.' They weren't safe, but they were safer than they would have been in the provinces where the round-up of Jews had begun.

Mallász had been a national swimming champion in both free-style and backstroke. In 1931, she took bronze in the 4x100m freestyle relay at the European Aquatics Championships in Paris. But sport left her unsatisfied; something, she felt, was missing. She sought out an old friend, Hanna Dallos, with whom she had studied at the School of Applied Arts in Budapest a decade earlier. Dallos had left to study in Munich and had married Joseph Kreutzer, a furniture restorer. She encouraged Mallász to resume her artistic career and together the three established a graphic arts studio.

Dallos and Kreutzer were both Jewish and so, with anti-Semitism on the rise, Mallász, who had been born in Ljubljana to a Hungarian army officer and his Austrian wife, took charge of the commercial side of the operation. Gradually, the three became disillusioned with the

---

[3] All quotes from Gitta Mallász drawn from *Talking with Angels*, her memoir, first published in French in 1976.

'collective blindness' of society in the face of political lies and moved to the village of Budaliget just outside Budapest 'for the purpose of starting a new and simple way of life'. At weekends they were joined by another Jewish friend, Lili Strausz, a callisthenics instructor whom Mallász had met when she was giving courses in movement therapy. 'We felt ourselves,' Mallász said, 'to be standing before a world of lies, brutality and all-pervading evil.' She still was not wholly content, but had a sense of waiting for 'something' that would offer purpose.

It was clearly a highly charged environment. On Friday 25 June 1943, Mallász was discussing this feeling of aimlessness with her friends when Dallos interrupted. 'It is not I who will speak to you,' she said in an unusually deep voice. 'Enough of your shadow questions! It is time for you to assume responsibility for yourself.' They came to believe an angel was speaking to Mallász through Dallos. Kreutzer and Strausz were sceptical but as the voice returned every Friday, they too became convinced that Mallász was receiving instruction from the heavens.

Having made their escape into the city, Mallász, Dallos and Kreutzer stayed at an apartment in Pest belonging to Dallos's parents, who were visiting their son, her brother, in Britain. In her notebooks, Mallász observed on 21 April that the confiscation of Jewish apartments and the ghettoisation of the homeless had begun. In the days that followed, Jews were forced to wear the yellow star and Budapest was subjected to its first air raids.

On 3 June 1944, obeying an order from the Hungarian Minister of Defence, Lajos Csatay, that every Jewish male aged between 18 and 44 should report for labour service, Kreutzer gave himself up. He said goodbye to his wife in the apartment but Mallász walked with him to Keleti station where she saw him packed into a cattle truck. 'The train,' she wrote, 'slowly moves off towards its unknown destination.' Kreutzer never came home.

But for the women came a chance of salvation. 'A politically influential friend' told Mallász that the Apostolic Nunciature and 'certain high-ranking officers in the War Ministry', recognising that the war was lost and seeking to avoid facing trial for genocide, had conspired to establish a military sewing factory to protect Jewish women in the Katalin Convent on Budakeszi út. It was run by a priest called Father Pál Klinda, but they needed a volunteer commander. Mallász believed this was the purpose for which the angel had been preparing her and recognised it was a way to save Dallos and Strausz.

Also under her care were Jolán Erbstein and her two daughters. After the occupation Susanna had refused an order that all women of Jewish descent between the ages of 18 and 25 sign up to labour service and had hidden in apartments belonging to her Italian fiancé and various friends, all the while terrified she would be betrayed by one of the caretakers who looked after the big old apartment blocks. She was directed to the convent by Gedeon Dienes, and later arranged for her mother and Marta, who by then was 12, to join her, although they pretended not to know each other. Jolán worked as a cook, while Marta's job was to look after the Angora rabbits farmed by the convent. Éva Kovács also stayed there.

The convent was crowded. Mallász spoke of 'mattresses, cots and whatever the inhabitants have been able to save of their possessions … piled everywhere from the cellar to the attic'. But it was possible to leave. On at least two occasions, Susanna, Éva and their friend Maca Bethlen, the younger sister of Iván Boldizsár who would go on to become a well-known journalist, all of whom were blond-haired and blue-eyed and so not conspicuously Jewish, walked out of the front door of the convent and took a series of trams and buses to cross the Danube to go to the renowned Gerbeaud patisserie in Pest.

To maintain the cover that it was a factory, the refuge had to produce the requisite number of uniforms. The pressure Mallász felt and her frustration at her workforce are clear from her diary. 'Far too many of the women,' she wrote, 'are simply useless as seamstresses, and even more are just plain irresponsible.' You wonder if she was referring to Susanna and her friends' jaunts out to eat cake.

When his family was taken in by the convent, Ernő Erbstein, deciding it was impossible to remain hidden any longer, reported for labour duty and was set to work repairing railway lines that were constantly being damaged by Allied air raids.

* * *

Even after leaving the job of manager of Újpest, Guttmann continued to work for the club as a 'secret advisor'.[4] In that capacity he was watching Újpest lose 2–1 away to the eventual champions Nagyvárad (now Oradea in western Romania) when the Germans invaded. Taking the train back to Budapest, he got off in Újpest and made his way to the hairdressing salon between Virág utca and Petöfi utca on Árpád út in Újpest, where he seems to have spent most of the war.

Mariann's brother Pál inherited the hairdressing business from their father and continued to run two salons, the one in the theatre and another on Árpád út, on the edge of the ghetto. It backed on to the beer garden of a pub on the triangular corner of the block, and had an adjoining flat in which Mariann's brother lived with his wife[5] and young daughter. 'You could go through the flat and end up in the open air at the back of it,' Pál Moldoványi explained. 'And in the salon there was a door to the pantry; through that you could enter the flat.

---

[4] In Hámori, *Régi gólok, edzősorsok*.
[5] This was his second wife; his first, who was of Jewish descent, had died of cancer in 1940.

It wasn't a suspicious thing to go to the barber's; that was always a busy place. Anti-fascists, socialists and communists from the workers' home often turned up there and were keen to use this escape route if they had to get out of sight quickly.'[6]

There was also an attic running the whole length of the building, roughly 50 yards long, that could only be accessed by means of a ladder. It was there that Guttmann lived. 'There was a little corner at the back,' said Moldoványi, 'above the kitchen and ventilation grille of the pub that could hardly be seen. When you looked in through the attic door, you could only see this long room; you couldn't make out the little corner at the back. The Nazis were lazy, they didn't climb 50 yards on the dusty beams to reach the back.'[7] To avoid leaving footprints in the dust, Guttmann or anybody visiting him would walk around on planks.

During bombing raids, the family would take cover in the two-storey cellar, taking Guttmann down only when they were sure they knew everybody in there; people from that block could be trusted, but any outsider might be an informer. On one occasion the salon and apartment were raided by the Gestapo, but Moldoványi's mother was Swabian, spoke German and was able to persuade the officers that they were a good Catholic family. The incident so scared her, though, that she fled with her daughter to the small town of Nagykovácsi, nine miles to the north-west of the centre of Budapest.

Her fear was well-founded. One day on the way to the shops, Moldován was arrested by the Arrow Cross, presumably having been informed upon. The gendarmes called him a 'filthy Jew-lover' and when he swore back at them, they hung him up by his feet and beat him into unconsciousness. When he came to, he had been dumped in the street, but there was no further raid on the salon.

---

[6] In Claussen, *Guttmann Béla*.
[7] In Claussen, *Guttmann Béla*.

Guttmann didn't make the family's life easy. He was a restless fugitive, easily bored, and would often sneak out of the attic. Once, Guttmann failed to return before curfew and so telephoned home from a friend's. Moldován smuggled him back under some sheets. Another time, he was stopped by the police during an air raid but fortunately one of the officers knew Moldován's wife and vouched for Guttmann as a Christian.

Slowly, the worst of the threat was coming to a close. Transports were stopped on 9 July and, in August 1944, with Germany in retreat, Horthy deposed Sztójay, replaced him with Géza Lakatos, an anti-fascist general, and gave orders that no Hungarian citizen should be deported, effectively ending the grim traffic to Auschwitz.

That autumn, though, Moldován was taken into a forced labour unit. Mariann briefly arranged for Guttmann to stay at the Tungsram factory but within a week or so he was back at the salon. It's not clear exactly when, but at some point soon after, probably late September or early October, Guttmann himself reported for labour duty, presumably reasoning that, after the deportations had stopped, it was safer to do so than continuing to hide when discovery would have meant almost certain death. He was sent first to Vác and then to Erdőváros before arriving at the barracks on Timót utca in the south of the Ferencváros district.

He found himself sharing a room with another coach, a man he had played against in the US 15 years earlier, Ernő Erbstein. Given there is a possibility Guttmann worked for Erbstein's textile business in some capacity, that might not be quite the coincidence it appears.[8]

---

[8] I am grateful to Zsolt Gyulás for alerting me to this idea and the newspaper article referring to Guttmann's work for an unnamed textiles company during the war. Certainly the two must have known each other to an extent. Even if they hadn't met on the football circuit in Budapest they must have done in New York.

There was, though, an astonishing stroke of luck: the prisoner in charge of their work detail had served as Erbstein's orderly when he fought on the Italian Front during the First World War. Without him, and his willingness to allow Erbstein to sneak away to use the telephone, the situation would have been far worse.

* * *

Sándor Schwarcz, by his own admission, 'wasn't a very successful footballer', but he was 'persistent'. Born in 1911, the son of a shoemaker, he had gone to primary school on Csapó út, in the same building that his father had his workshop. He remembered dashing out of school after the last lesson, throwing his schoolbag into his father's workshop, then running out to play in the square.

He and his friends played games on Hatvan utca. 'It was such a joy to play football with cloth balls we had made!' he said. 'I just wish I hadn't always been told off by my mother for stuffing the best stockings...'[9]

When Schwarcz was 12, his parents could no longer afford to pay for his schooling. He became the runner for a leather and shoe accessories shop on Csapó út, delivering leather to tanners and boot makers. Two years later he got a job at a haberdashery and began playing for the Debrecen Workers' Athletic Association (DMTE). Only when he was 25 and secured a job at Zerkowitz Textiles did he begin earning a significant income. He joined the factory football club and found training far harder than it had been at DMTE. 'Yes, we had to run more there,' he said. 'Stamina, that's the most important, that comes first...'[10]

---

[9] In Gábor L Kelemen, *Gól a halál kapujában* [*A Strike in the Goal of Death*] (Sportpropaganda, 1981).

[10] In Kelemen.

Neither DMTE nor Zerkowitz Textiles, though, were anything close to being a top-flight side. There was never any possibility of Schwarcz playing for the leading local club Bocskai, who had won the Hungarian Cup in 1930, and he spent his weekends going to the theatre and dances, and playing chess and dominoes at the Margit Workers' Home. But then came the war.

As a Jew, he was called up to a labour detail drilling wells in Hajdúnánás. Then he was moved to Püspökladány, where he was set to work clearing an area of grass. Cruelty was institutionalised: the prisoners were allowed to pick blades of grass only one by one, were not allowed to bend their knees and were not given water, being beaten if they slowed down. A number of the Jews there were formed into a battalion to be sent to Ukraine, but Schwarcz, reasoning he had nothing to lose, protested he had a problem with his knee that meant it would swell if he were forced on a long march. He was sent instead to Szolnok, where he worked on the railways before being demobilised and returned to the ghetto in Debrecen.

It wasn't long, though, before he was called up again and sent to Gyoma, where three companies were drawn up for the Soviet front. Schwarcz again cited his knee, and again he was spared. His brother was not so fortunate. 'I wasn't allowed to say goodbye,' Schwarcz said. 'But he did shout after me, that now it was easier for him to set off on the long journey as there was somebody around to look after our old parents. That was the last time I saw him. He sleeps with God, buried somewhere in Russian soil.'[11]

Then it was back to Debrecen, the barracks in Püspökladány, and Szolnok again, where he worked in a factory making railway carriages. At a medical examination, he complained again about his knee and

---

[11] From an interview with Judit Marsó published on pointernet.pds.hu as part of a wider project entitled 'The Jewry after 1945'.

was briefly demobilised once more. It was winter when Schwarcz was sent to another labour camp. Before he went, his father sewed a pillow into the lining of a short woollen coat. 'It warmed me fine,' Schwarcz said, 'it protected me from the cold, but it gave me a lot of trouble too, because the feathers in the pillow came out one by one on the outside of the wool. My mates often laughed at me when I put on that coat.'[12] At the camp, he cut the hair of other inmates, shaved them and washed clothes in his free time, earning a little money he could send back to his ailing parents. Finally, on 29 June 1944, he was deported to Auschwitz.

Schwarcz arrived on 1 July and with around 40 others was taken to barrack number nine. 'Our bodies,' he said, 'were shaved, then we had the petroleum bath. Later two German officers entered, followed by a modestly dressed man who spoke Hungarian very well. While one of the SS soldiers was selecting men fit for work, the other one was waiting in silence. Then he made a very strange request... "Are there any professional footballers among you?"

'There were [four][13] of us who dared to put up our hands. The man standing next to me just said quietly: "Schwarcz, don't go, you may get into trouble! We're going to work, we're going to be fine, come with us." I didn't listen to him, I stepped forward. The others were led out. They were taken to a nearby mine to work. They were brought back to the camp a couple of months later totally exhausted, then their lives were put to an end in the gas chambers.'[14]

The four were questioned and examined. Schwarcz lied and said he had played for Bocskai in the first division. No sooner had the

---

[12] In Marsó.

[13] He actually said five in this account, but on various other occasions, including in Kelemen, *Gól a halál kapujában*, he said four, so it seems likely that is the true figure.

[14] In Marsó.

words left his mouth than, to his horror, he saw standing behind the SS officer an old acquaintance, Dezső Steinberger. Steinberger had been born in 1912 to a family of wealthy merchants in Balmazú- jváros, a small town 20 miles north-west of Debrecen. A 1929 survey lists it as having 13,223 inhabitants, of whom 318 were Jewish.[15] An Emil Steinberger, probably Dezső's father (although he seems also to have been known as Manó and is recorded on Dezső's birth certif- icate as Emanuel), a trader in oats and cereals,[16] is included on the Jewish council; he was later the owner of a mill.[17] Steinberger funded the local football team for whom he also played: according to the history on the club website, he 'did not know much about playing, but he was enthusiastic and devoted; he was an evangelist for football in Balmazújváros'. A team photo from as late as 1943 shows him, balding and bedraggled, in the middle of the back row.[18]

The Steinbergers, as well as two families they were connected to by marriage, Markovics and Friedlaender, and Sándor Schwarcz had been stripped of their land by a decree of April 1939.[19] Steinberger was deported to Auschwitz in 1944. He played in goal for one of the camp football teams and then began to inform on other prisoners.

At some point in the winter of 1944–45, the SS officer and physi- cian Josef Mengele, who would become notorious for the experiments

---

[15] *Magyar Zsidó Lexikon*, edited by Péter Újvári.

[16] Listed in a Hungarian business directory, *Magyarország kereskedelmi, ipari és mezőgazdasági címtára*, published in Budapest in 1924.

[17] He is described as such in a marriage notice for Emma, his daughter, in *Molnárok Lapja*, 19 February 1939. This is confirmed by an article in *Balmazújvaros újság*, July 2009.

[18] As detailed on the club website: http://balmazujvarosfc.hu/wp-content/ uploads/2016/05/bfc_klubtortenet.pdf

[19] In 'Selected Records of the National Land Mortgage Bank of Hungary (MOL Z), 1939-1945', RG-39.039M, held at the United States Holocaust Memorial Museum Archive.

he conducted on prisoners, found his car wouldn't start. Steinberger helped out and a grateful Mengele, impressed by his linguistic abilities, began to use him as a runner and general factotum. Steinberger's second wife said her mother had seen Steinberger at the camp and had described him as 'God' for the influence he wielded.[20]

The film director Béla Szobolits interviewed Steinberger in 1990. 'Prisoners who lost the ability to work would be gassed,' Szobolits said. 'Mengele would line up all the workers and go along checking their buttocks. If he saw there was no flesh there, he would decide the prisoner was finished and send them to a separate line to go to the gas chambers. As Mengele continued down the line, [Steinberger] was able to save some prisoners by pushing them back into the main line.'

Crucially for Schwarcz, Steinberger was well connected at Bocskai. 'He knew exactly who I was and he knew that Bocskai would never have considered signing me,' said Schwarcz. 'The recognition made me dizzy. I thought I was done, and the guards would cut me to pieces right there.'[21]

But Steinberger said nothing and allowed Schwarcz to carry on his pretence. It was, he said, 'a lie that saved my life'.[22] A football tournament was being set up to entertain the guards and to disguise the reality of what was going on at Auschwitz.[23] 'The SS officer,' Schwarcz said, 'felt me all over as if he was choosing a horse.'[24]

They were then taken behind the barracks and given a ball. 'First, two of my mates were tested,' Schwarcz said.[25] 'They were quite

---

[20] In Hungarian *FourFourTwo*, April 2018.

[21] From an interview with Mihály Sándor published on fociologus.wordpress.com.

[22] In Sándor.

[23] More detail on football at Auschwitz is given by Ron Jones, a Welsh soldier who was captured in North Africa and ended up a POW at Auschwitz, in the book he wrote with Joe Lovejoy, *The Auschwitz Goalkeeper* (Gomer, 2013).

[24] In Marsó.

[25] In Marsó.

clumsy in kicking the ball, their dribbling wasn't very great either. I saw from the facial expression of the two SS officers that they were dissatisfied, that my two mates failed the test…

'I was always extremely tense; I often used to have my heart in my throat before matches. I would only calm down when the referee blew his whistle … I had never been so nervous before. I knew that the stakes were high and I had to perform well. It was obvious for me: this is the place where human life is very cheap.'

To make matters worse, Schwarcz was wearing a prison uniform that hung from his thin frame and awkward wooden clogs. 'The camp's high-voltage fences with double barbed wire weren't very promising,' he went on. 'I couldn't figure out why the chimneys were emitting smoke but I could pretty much make out the figure of a German soldier holding a machine gun in his hand on duty in the nearby tower. I was the last one to go. The stress tensed my muscles. I was made to stand opposite the officer, who threw a high ball to me. I knew I'd never had problems with heading. Having hit the ball with my forehead with a light movement, it landed in the lap of the German; it went like a dream. The next task was to control the ball coming in the air without letting it bounce loose. I could do that, too. In the third round, a ball was thrown to me bouncing then another one rolled to me in a straight line and I was made to pass them back. I was sweating by the time I finished this.' But he passed.

Schwarcz was told he would play for the national team of the Roma being held at the camp and that he had a game the following day, a Sunday. As he returned to the barracks, Steinberger explained to him how the camp worked and why the chimneys were billowing smoke. Playing football, he told him, assured the players better conditions and food – he advised him to wear his kit at all times as footballers had a measure of protection – but came with a terrible risk. 'Here,'

Schwarcz said, 'an injured footballer is not taken to the sports clinic, but to the gas chambers.'[26]

That night, Schwarcz couldn't sleep, kept awake by the 'the wailing of German gipsies from the buildings next to ours.'[27] Between 1,000 and 1,500, he estimated, had been crammed together. At least, though, 'They had the privilege to have been able to suffer together with their loved ones.'[28] His own relatives, Steinberger had told him, had been killed within an hour of their arrival at the camp.

'Early morning on Sunday we went into another barrack to get changed,' Schwarcz said. 'The striped prison clothes were changed for long-sleeved ebony black jerseys, shorts, shin guards and football boots made of very high quality leather.'[29] For a moment he wondered whether he should wear the kit, given it had been made from clothing taken from other prisoners but then decided 'there was no room for sentimentality in Birkenau, the death camp'.[30]

Schwarcz was introduced to his teammates, nine Roma from Germany and Weigner, who had played professionally for Kispest.[31] 'We proceeded from the gipsy camp to the pitch with a military escort,' he said. 'On our way we could see a red-brick building which was Dr Mengele's empire... On the other side there was a double barbed wire fence. Beyond that stood the crematorium, and next to it the gas chambers. The chimneys were emitting sickening smoke even on Sundays...

---

[26] In Marsó.

[27] In Marsó.

[28] In Marsó.

[29] In Marsó.

[30] In Kelemen, *Gól a halál kapujában*.

[31] Or at least this is what Schwarcz said. I have been unable to identify the player and the Dénes, Sándor and Bába history lists no player called Weigner playing for Újpest.

'We tried to decide who to play in which position even though we had language barriers. We explained ourselves to one another by drawing in the dust and that's how I became the right-back. Twenty minutes later the opponents arrived in vivid green jerseys.'

At half-time it was 1–1. Schwarcz scored a free kick, but the opposition equalised almost immediately from a penalty. Schwarcz's side dominated but couldn't score and he saw the SS officer withdraw a revolver, as though threatening the consequences if they didn't find a winner. 'I wasn't a religious man,' Schwarcz said, 'but I do believe in God, to whom I said a prayer there from the bottom of my heart. And He heard me. Since then I've known that He always listens to prayers from the heart. I gave it my whole strength, all my skills as a player, I dribbled past two players and scored the winning goal.'[32] They were rewarded with 'a big piece of bread, some meat and a pot of potato soup'.

They won their next three games as well, despite a referee being beaten up by three SS officers who ran the opposition team after he awarded a penalty. But in the fourth game, Schwarcz's troublesome knee gave out. He was terrified what would happen if he couldn't play, but such fears soon became irrelevant.

The next morning, the team were locked into the barracks. 'When that happened,' Schwarcz said, 'inhabitants of complete blocks were taken away to be murdered. We were shaking all over. We could hear enraged barking and harsh commands. The dogs and their owners were working together, but even the noise they made couldn't drown out the wailing of people facing death. Children, their mothers, their fathers, the German gipsies. It was going on all day... And when it was over, the silence was so painful. All the nearby barracks stood

---

[32] In Marsó.

empty. Everybody was taken away. All my teammates died… My career as a footballer was over. The Slovakian barrack leader took the football jersey off me, gave me the prison clothes and threw me out.'[33]

On 2 August 1944, Schwarcz began working in the munitions factory at the camp but he did play one more game, several months later, for an international team against the German guards. By then he had lost a lot of weight and couldn't do much more than hang around up front, deliberately missing chances for fear of what might happen if he didn't. The guards won 8–0.

As the Red Army closed in, Himmler gave the order in November 1944 to end the massacres. On 18 January, nine days before Auschwitz fell to the Soviets, the camp was evacuated. Schwarcz was marched 160 miles through the snow to the camp at Gross-Rosen, struggling on as those too weak to keep up were shot. From there, the prisoners were packed into trains for the five-day journey to Mühldorf in Bavaria. Hundreds died on the way. Schwarcz worked in the cement factory there until the camp was liberated by US troops on 2 May. By then he weighed less than five stones.

* * *

The war was clearly drawing to a conclusion, but it was a long way from being over. The Allies, victorious in North Africa, had landed in Sicily on 10 July 1943. Mussolini was stripped of power and imprisoned 15 days later. The fighting went on until an armistice was announced in early September after the Allies had advanced into the toe of the mainland. By then, though, the Germans had reinforced their positions. They sprung Mussolini from jail and he set up a new fascist state in northern Italy. The fighting was fierce, the mountainous

---

[33] In Marsó.

terrain providing excellent defensive positions, but through 1944 the Allies slowly advanced on Rome.

The Red Army, meanwhile, crossed the Hungarian border in September 1944. On 15 October, Horthy signed an armistice with the USSR, but it was largely ignored by Hungarian troops. The Germans then kidnapped his son, and forced him both to abrogate the armistice and to depose Lakatos, appointing in his place the head of the Arrow Cross, Ferenc Szálasi. Horthy resigned and was sent to Germany, where he survived the war, eventually dying in Portugal in 1957. Szálasi, meanwhile, became leader of a German-controlled Government of National Unity. He handed over 50,000 Hungarians to the Germans but after that, to the astonishment of Eichmann, stopped the deportations and established the ghetto in the centre of Budapest. The Arrow Cross responded with its own campaign against Jews, murdering thousands and throwing their bodies into the Danube.

Arrow Cross thugs would parade up and down Budakeszi út, shouting right-wing slogans, firing guns in the air and threatening those in the Katalin Convent. They were led by a renegade Catholic priest called András Kun, a terrifying figure Gitta Mallász described as wearing 'black robes with a wide red belt stuffed full of daggers and revolvers'. He was believed to maintain a basement for torturing and killing Jews. One Sunday in November, a gang burst into the convent and forced the women at gunpoint into one room. They robbed them of their valuables and demanded their keys to go through the rest of their belongings.

As they waited, the telephone kept ringing; Sundays were the days when the women would receive calls. The Arrow Cross told them to answer and to tell whoever was on the other end that they were having a party and everybody was invited, trying to entice more Jews into their clutches. That Sunday, Erbstein couldn't get to a telephone but he had arranged for his former orderly to call and explain that he was unavailable. Susanna took the call and, adopting a high-pitched voice, did as she'd been instructed and explained there was a party. The former orderly realised something was wrong, and told Erbstein to call back. When he did, Susanna again answered at a higher octave than her usual tone. In the middle of the conversation, she dropped into her normal voice and said one word, '*Aiuto!*', the Italian for 'Help!'

The Arrow Cross waited for several hours to see if they had tempted any further victims over, then finally lined the women into columns and marched them outside into the cold. None had any doubt that they were being taken down to the river to be killed.

After hearing his daughter's message, Erbstein persuaded his former orderly to let him leave the camp. A work detail was quickly invented as cover and Erbstein sought out Valéria Dienes, his daughter's well-connected dance mentor. She got a message to Angelo Rotta, the papal nuncio. When he'd visited the convent, he had been shown round by Susanna, because of her fluency in Italian. He remembered her and called the Minister of the Interior, reminding him that the convent was owned by the Vatican and threatening a scandal. Eventually, another senior government minister, whose wife was a devout Catholic, persuaded him to sign an order demanding the Arrow Cross let the women go.

A car pulled up alongside the line of women and an argument broke out between the passenger – a young Vatican official called Verolino – and the Arrow Cross, who eventually backed down. The women returned to the convent, terrified that the building had been primed with bombs.

Jolán, Susanna and Marta Erbstein decided the convent wasn't safe and fled one night through the hole in the fence, leaving their possessions behind them. They told no one, not even Éva Kovács.

They made for Székely Bertalan utca, where Jolán's sister lived with her Catholic husband. 'It was extremely dangerous because we had no documents,' Susanna explained. 'If somebody had stopped us it would have been terrible. But, after walking and walking – it was very far from the villa – we arrived, and we were accepted at my mother's older sister's house.'[34]

Mallász also knew the Arrow Cross would return and set about making plans. She posted a couple of women to hide in bushes by the gate and keep watch and made holes in the fence to offer escape routes, covering them with leaves and branches. Complicating the issue was the fact that the next building along had been requisitioned by the SS as accommodation, who hadn't realised that the women in the convent were Jewish.

One day in early November, a Wehrmacht soldier had knocked on the door of the convent. There had been panic, but it turned out he was a friend of Hanna Dallos, having met her in Munich when both were art students. He was working as an illustrator for the military newspaper; Mallász saw an opportunity. Exploiting his fondness for Dallos, she persuaded him to commission some artwork from her. Even better, he provided her with a staff pass, stamped with a swastika.

That gave Mallász credibility in the eyes of the occupiers and she used it to gain the confidence of an SS corporal who was billeted next door. Because her mother was Austrian, Mallász spoke fluent German and was able to present herself as another foreigner in Hungary, somebody who had given up her art career for the war effort. She invited the corporal and a few others over for wine and cake, telling them to make a gap in the fence to use as a shortcut. She

---

[34] Cited in Bliss, *Erbstein*.

then explained about the threat of the Arrow Cross; the SS promised to protect them.

Sure enough, on 2 December the Arrow Cross returned with deportation orders. Mallász called on her friendly SS corporal. There was a stand-off, during which many of the women fled through the hole in the fence, across the garden of the house in which the SS were billeted and away. Mallász, acting as translator, deliberately confused the issue but she couldn't delay matters indefinitely. Eventually the Hungarian commander promised to leave if the SS commander told him to. They rang him and he told his corporal not to interfere. Only 13 women remained: 'those who are too old to flee, or too weak, and those who have made the decision not to flee,' as Mallász put it. Among them were Dallos and Strausz, who had decided they could not abandon their friend. All 13 were subsequently sent to Ravensbrück where 12 of them, including Dallos and Strausz, died. Father Klinda was badly beaten, a contributory factor in his death the following year.

* * *

Late in 1944, the 21-year-old Kispest forward József Mészáros, who would win the league title with Ferencváros in 1948–49, was sent by the Kispest president Imre Szokodi to a house in Buda. There in the cellar, he told him, he would find the former Hakoah and Ferencváros forward, more recently a player and coach at Marseille, József Eisenhoffer. 'We had just slaughtered a pig, and we were sure he would welcome a taste,' Mészáros said.[35] So he walked from

---

[35] Cited in Tibor Hámori, *Puskás, Legenda és valóság* (Sportpropaganda, 1982). It's not clear whether Eisenhoffer, who had converted to Judaism, followed a kosher diet and, if he did, whether sending him pork was insensitive or just a matter of necessity given the shortages in the city.

Kispest to Buda and delivered the meat. A second attempt to deliver food was not successful.

Eisenhoffer's return from Marseille had been reported in September 1941. 'I was a coach in France for nine years,' he said in an interview with *Nemzeti Sport* that was a fairly transparent attempt to advertise his services. 'I've already talked to Imre Senkey, the head of the Hungarian coaching committee, and he promised that if I could find a club, I would get a temporary licence. In the winter I'll do the necessary training course.'[36]

A few days later, though, no club had come forward and Eisenhoffer was making another plea for work, this time through the pages of *Képes Sport*. 'My current circumstances make it impossible for me to work at Kispest,' he said, 'but I would welcome the chance to take over any club, even one in the countryside, provided, of course, that there is no coach already there. I don't want to take anyone's place. If I can't find a team that needs a teacher now, I'll wait till next summer.'[37]

By the beginning of October, the MLSZ had still not granted Eisenhoffer a licence, but he remained in talks with Kispest about taking a coaching job. They came to nothing, though, and in February the following year, the MLSZ was forced to take action after Eisenhoffer had been found to be secretly working at Kolozsvári AC in what is now Cluj in Romania. 'Eisenhoffer had requested a licence,' the MLSZ secretary general András Gálffy explained, 'but he was not granted one because the Master Examination Coaching Committee did not accept his application for the course. After that we could do nothing other than forbidding him to work at KAC.'[38]

---

[36] *Nemzeti Sport*, 12 September 1941.
[37] *Képes Sport*, 23 September 1941.
[38] *Nemzeti Sport*, 11 February 1942.

Given Eisenhoffer's record as a player and a coach, that seems a baffling decision, but without knowing their reasons, it's very hard to make judgements. What he did for the next two and a half years is unclear. His wife was deported but Eisenhoffer was not, seemingly on the technicality that he was religiously but not ethnically Jewish, although it may simply have been a bureaucratic mix-up.

The next that is known of Eisenhoffer, he was hiding in a relative's cellar. For him, though, there was no escape. He was injured in an air raid and the wound became infected. Weakened by the lack of food, he could not be saved, and died in February 1945, around the time Budapest fell to the Soviets.[39]

* * *

Conditions in the camp on Timót utca, where Guttmann and Erbstein worked under the supervision of a sergeant who had served in the French Foreign Legion, were dreadful. 'If he was in a good mood,' Guttmann said, 'he only made us carry tarred stones to his bunker while we shouted, "We are shit, we are shit!" Was I a footballer from the national team, was I a successful coach? Was I a man? Who cared? You had to forget all about it!'[40]

After the Arrow Cross took over, many of those labour groups were handed over to the Germans. Around 70,000 were sent to Austria in November and December 1944. Guttmann and Erbstein somehow got wind of the plan – perhaps through his former orderly – and with four others, including the actor Sanyi Gál, plotted their escape. They watched the guards and learned their shift patterns. Their room was on the first floor and so for days before the escape

---

[39] Although the first confirmation of his death didn't come until 20 May in *Népsport*.

[40] In Hamori, *Régi gólok, edzősorsok*.

attempt they systematically softened the ground under the window before one night, as the guards changed, they jumped for it and ran into the darkness. Where Guttmann went is unclear: all he said was that 'kind people took the risk and hid me':[41] a best guess is perhaps that he went back to the attic above the hairdresser's.

Erbstein joined Jolán, Susanna and Marta at his sister-in-law's apartment in Pest. They were still in great danger. Erbstein's brother-in-law, Fülöp Béres, a signwriter, turned out to be a skilled forger and doctored the ID cards of dead relatives to provide documents for Jolán and Susanna.[42] Susanna was even able to keep the same forename, becoming Susanna Berés for the remainder of the war. In addition, she completed a Red Cross course and worked as a nurse for them, offering assistance in air-raid shelters. That provided another ID card that provided cover for her to be on the streets after dark. Marta, though, had no valid papers.

During air raids, as the rest of the occupants of the building made for the basement, Erbstein would stay in the apartment, Susanna using her Red Cross ID to go upstairs to check on him and take him food.

At one point, another resident told Susanna that the Arrow Cross were planning a raid as they'd heard Jews were hiding in the building – which at least proved their disguises were working. Terrified her father would be found, Susanna led him one day in early January through

---

[41] In Hamori, *Régi gólok, edzősorsok*.

[42] The husband of Erika, Erbstein's sister-in-law's niece, was a driver for the Swedish envoy Raoul Wallenberg who saved hundreds of Jews in Budapest. Shortly before Erika died in 2018, Susanna visited her in Madrid where she confirmed that, contrary to some accounts, she had no contact with Erbstein, his wife and daughters during the war and that Wallenberg, extraordinary hero though he was, played no part in Erbstein's survival. Indeed, there seems to have been a split in the family at the time: Erika did not attend Susanna's wedding in Budapest in 1946.

the rubble and chaos of the bombed streets to a so-called 'protected house' (under the control of a foreign embassy or legation) close to the Danube on the Pest side, probably in Újlipótváros, although she cannot remember the exact address.

A few days later, the Arrow Cross did raid the building, checking the papers of all the residents. Jolán and Susanna were sent to one side of the corridor, Marta pushed into a smaller group on the other. Susanna was about to try to argue her sister's case when a senior officer, for unknown reasons, intervened, took a close look at Marta's face, and sent her to join her family. The rest of the group she had been in were taken outside and shot.

* * *

After leading Ferencváros to three league titles, two Cups and the Mitropa Cup, István Tóth had gone to Italy where he had managed Triestina and Inter. In Milan, as well as completing a course in cinema management, he continued his socialising and could always be sure that if he hadn't managed to buy a ticket for the opera, one of the musicians would find a way of getting him in. Tóth's son, also called István, had been born in 1915 and was a good enough foot-baller that after his father had been sacked, Inter wanted him to stay on as a player. Tóth, though, sent him back to Budapest to complete his legal studies.

Tóth himself returned to Hungary with Újpest, then went back to Triestina before taking up a job with Elektromos, the Hungarian electricity company. It was while he was there that he arranged the first floodlit game played on Hungarian soil. He remained a highly respected figure, always happy to offer advice. Károly Sós, who would go on to manage East Germany, for instance, asked Tóth to assess one of his training sessions as he started out as a coach at Gamma, a small club based on a major optical factory. Tóth watched, then told him that although everything was fine from a technical point of view, there was no charisma, no inspirational connection between the coach and his squad, which confirms the impression that his great ability as a coach was his ability to inspire others.

During the war, Tóth served as a lieutenant in the Aviation Department at the Ministry of Defence and realised he was perfectly placed to steal documents that could be used in the preparation of false papers to help friends and family members avoid military service. From October 1944, his activities became rather more serious, thanks to his former Ferencváros teammate Géza Kertész.

Although Kertész's Atalanta had narrowly missed out on promotion to Serie A in 1938–39, their performances that season were enough to earn Kertész the Lazio job. They finished fourth in his first season there, but he was sacked six games into 1940–41. Kertész returned to Salernitana, where he replaced his compatriot Ferenc Hirzer, the former Juve striker. Then it was on to Catania again, then Littorio, before, in December 1942, Roma appointed him to replace Alfréd Schaffer. Kertész's preferred mode of play, though, was not a good fit for a team designed to play at pace on the counter-attack and Roma finished ninth.

He was dismissed and, when the Germans seized Rome in September 1943, Kertész decided, after 18 years in Italy, to return to Budapest where, that October, he was named manager of Újpest. After the German invasion of Hungary, Kertész became part of a group of around 20 people opposed to the occupation put together by Béla Jánosi, a well-known coach from Békéscsaba in the south-east of Hungary, who had led Újpest to the league title in 1934–35. Jánosi's brother Ernő and his nephew Miklós were also involved.

In the autumn of 1944, the Office of Strategic Services, the forerunner of the CIA, sent two agents of Hungarian origin back home. One went by the cover name Francis Moly. The other was Pál Kovács, a 42-year-old who went by the code name Stefano Cora or Steve Kora. He had left Hungary during Béla Kun's Communist Revolution of 1919, moving to Rome where he married and had two children.

There, he had got to know Kertész. Whether they had discussed forming some sort of resistance while they were still in Italy is impossible to know, but on reaching Budapest he contacted Kertész, who ended up hiding him for a time in the family home on Zichy Jenő utca. Kertész recruited Tóth and other friends into a resistance group known as 'Dallam' (the word means 'melody' in Hungarian).[43] It's believed there were 12 members, including three officers in the gendarmerie. They helped protect Jews and Communists, among them Hilda Gobbi, who would become a major film star in the 1950s, forged documents, distributed leaflets and observed German troop movements, sending encoded messages by courier to a radio operator in Slovakia. They also drew up plans to protect Budapest's bridges. They were aided by, among others, the great goalscorer Imre Schlosser; the former Ferencváros midfielder Zoltán Blum, whose jokes had so annoyed Béla Guttmann before the 1924 Olympics; the former Újpest defender Károly Fogl; the Gamma coach Károly Sós, who would lead Hungary to Olympic gold in 1968; and the striker Gyula Bodola, who had won two Romanian championships with Venus Bucharest and in 1943–44 helped Nagyvárad to the Hungarian title.

---

[43] These details are confirmed by *A magyar antifasiszta ellenállás és partizánmozgalom* [*Lexicon of Hungarian anti-fascist resistance and partisan movement*] (Kossuth, 1987), a book published in the declining years of the Communist regime with the intention of demonstrating that not all resistance to the Nazi occupation was Soviet-backed.

OSS archives[44] hold a document dated 1 October 1944 that says that the Dallam circuit would become operational from 7 October (with a radio operator called Steve Catlos). This presumably is when US involvement began although there is also an intriguing reference to 'Mallad' – apparently an alternative name for Dallam – as having been operational from 8 June. A week later an internal memo from HOLMIN to OLSON (probably Captain William A Holmin to Admiral Eric T Olson, both officers in the OSS) asked, 'Have you heard or contacted the Dallam circuit? This is an extremely important circuit. Be sure that it gets the very finest attention.'

There was already a US network in the area, a circuit called Dawes, an SO team led by Lieutenant James Holt Green that was established on 17 September. It had initially been involved mainly in air-crew rescue work but as 1944 went on, its role spread and it became the centrepiece of a number of networks, including not only Dallam, but also Day, Houseboat and Marlboro. On 25 October an urgent message was sent from Bari to Caserta: 'Chapin [a senior US officer in Italy] to Dawes for Tibor [Lieutenant Tibor Keszthelyi]… Your move with Catlos is approved. Tonight we will begin monitoring the Dallam circuit; if contact cannot be made, come in on the guard channel.' Later on, Olson was informed that 'monitoring of Dallam should begin this evening'.

Keszthelyi had been born in Rijeka (Fiume) in 1909. He emigrated to the US and lived in New Jersey, enlisting on 11 November 1942. He worked as part of what was known as the 'Bowery Team' which comprised him, Catlos, Kovács (Cora/Kora) and Moly. They joined up with the Dawes team and were sent into Czechoslovakia. On 27

---

[44] Every document referred to here is from the OSS section of the National Archive in Maryland, RG 226, Entry 154, Box 42, Fol. 642 'Dawes, Day, Dallam, etc.' (190/8/31/4).

October, Keszthelyi replied to Chapin that there had been 'no contact with Moly or Cora yet'. There is no further reference to Dallam in the files until 15 November, when there is an internal memo saying, 'It is reported that our circuits Dawes, Houseboat, Dallam and Day may have been picked up by the Germans.'

What prompted that concern is unclear, but nine days later, Chapin offered a fuller report: '2nd Lt Tibor Keszthelyi was in command of the Dallam team, which also consisted of Sgt Steve Catlos w/t [walkie-talkie] operator. On 7 October, Francis Moly and Steven Kora (cover names) were taken to Banska Bystrica, crossing the Hungarian border on 11 October via CRI underground, leaving courier link back to Tibor. Kora and Moly took identification and signal plan to a highly placed group in Budapest and were to inform Tibor by courier when they delivered. This group was burned when Horthy offered armistice terms and Moly's courier link was probably also burned by subsequent German military operations. There has been no word from either of them, for whom the courier link was the only contact.

'Tibor also had briefing on landing plans for the 15th AF flight to Budapest and was to signal in the first sortie if he reached Budapest. He had 4 signal plans, Dallam, an alternate Mallad, besides 2 for other radios known in Budapest, Marlboro and Stockton. There has been no contact with any of these as yet. Only Dallam has been monitored. Dawes #211 on 25 October contained the last information about Tibor.'

On 28 November, the Dallam circuit was suspended, although there were various attempts to resurrect it before it was finally abandoned on 26 January 1945.

Kovács, it turned out, had fallen for a local prostitute called Mari Bényi. He took to entertaining her at his apartment on Csengery utca and on a number of occasions, probably while drunk, he and Kertész boasted to her that their work with the Allies would make them important figures after the liberation. She told her pimp, an Arrow Cross officer called Gábor Dósa.

On 5 December, at around 4pm, Kovács visited Bényi. Dósa was already there, lying on the couch. Reluctantly, he left, but returned half an hour later with police officers. Some say Kovács was tortured, others that a notebook was found listing other members of the group. Either way, all of them were picked up the following day by the Arrow Cross and handed over to the Gestapo.

Kertész had never told his family what he was doing, using his work with Újpest as cover for his resistance activities. He seems to have taken training as usual on 6 December 1944 and then been arrested that evening. As a result, his pre-match comments on the upcoming match against Ferencváros appeared as usual in *Nemzeti Sport* on 8 December. They are heartbreaking in their banality. 'We only have one problem,' he said, 'and it is the injury to [the defender Sándor] Szűcs. I hope our "barnacle" will play, but I also have to prepare for the worst. If Szűcs is not playing, Balogh will play in the centre and Golács will be the right-back – he's been a good defender in the past on many occasions. The return of Kármán solves the issue of the inside-left position. We are ready.'

Újpest seemed to have no idea what had happened to Kertész and two weeks later their sporting director Sándor Majersky was still denying there was any problem. 'We have a coach under contract,' he said, 'and that is Géza Kertész. As soon as we can have him again, he can take the team again in accordance with his contract. Besides Kertész, our former player Jenő Vincze is also contracted to us as a coach. They, however, are "on duty" at the moment and so they cannot work for us. That's why we have decided as a temporary solution to give the job to Sándor Bíró, our oldest player, who has passed his regular coaching exam.'[45]

Tóth was at his home on Telepes utca on 6 December when the bell rang. 'My mother opened the door,' his son said. 'There were two men on the threshold. They had come to see my father and they told us he had to go with them urgently for some sports issue. I knew both of them: one was a director at the Electric Works and the other was an administrator for Carpathian Films.'[46] They, presumably, then handed him over to the Arrow Cross. Both, family legend has it, wanted to let him go but neither trusted his colleague sufficiently to make the first move.

Keszthelyi and the Dawes group continued to operate in Czechoslovakia. On 12 December, as he tried to borrow some horses in a village to transport stricken airmen, Keszthelyi was captured by German troops. He was tortured and the group rounded up. He, nine other members of the Dawes circuit, including Green, and two members of Day were killed in the camp at Mauthausen in late January 1945.

Tóth and Kertész were held initially in the prison on Fő utca, near the river in Buda. 'An armed guard accompanied me to cell 513,' said the director of the St Imre dormitory, who was arrested on 20 December. 'I sat on the edge of the bed that was empty. Under a pile of blankets on the other bed there was a man sleeping. A convicted evil-doer or a political prisoner? I had no idea. When dawn finally came my neighbour made a move. I waited nervously. He had been an inmate there longer than I. He had been alone, and he didn't seem to be happy about the fact that he got a cellmate. It was difficult to start a conversation. His mistrust dissolved only slowly. He didn't tell me

---

[45] *Nemzeti Sport*, 21 December 1944.
[46] *Népsport*, 23 December 1987.

why he was there but he did dare to ask the reason for my arrest. But later I came to love him very much.'

That was Tóth. Kertész was in the cell next door. 'Every day Potya-*bácsi* would call out to the cell next door in a half-whisper, "Géza, Géza," and then they would start a conversation. They talked about interrogations and escapes. I had to watch at the door to see if the guard was coming in our direction. I wondered who this Géza was. Sure, I was interested in it. My cellmate who was still somewhat mistrustful didn't disclose it to me at first. "It's a fictitious name," he said. "We just talk to have fun. I don't know him." … I marvelled at his optimism regarding their escape. Uncle Potya and his friend joined for a noble, patriotic cause: to perhaps prevent the bridges of Budapest from being blown up.'[47]

When the Soviets took over the Gestapo headquarters on Sváb Hill, the interrogations stopped. The prison was hit by a bomb on 3 January, after which Tóth and Kertész were moved, first to the parliament building and then to the basement of the Interior Ministry in Buda Castle. 'It is,' the director went on, 'almost impossible to describe the immense suffering and torture that they underwent, crammed together, going without food or water for days, their human dignity totally crushed.'

As the Soviets closed in, around a third of the prisoners were murdered. Tóth and Kertész were among them, shot by the SS at dawn on 6 February, five days before the city fell.

'I have felt guilty for a long time,' Tóth's son said, 'because I felt I was the cause of the tragedy. My father was invited to be a coach in South America. He was on the fence, my mother had already done the packing, and so they asked me to decide – and I said I would not

---

[47] Quoted in *Képes Sport*, 5 February 1985.

go. I would not leave my country, Budapest. So we stayed at home, and my father was taken away soon after.'

Tóth and Kertész were buried in a shallow grave in the courtyard of the castle. Ernő and Miklós Jánosi were also executed at around that time, although Béla was spared. As soon as the Soviets were in control, Tóth's wife Vilma went to the castle to try to find out if her husband was still alive. The heavy shelling the castle had sustained, though, meant the courtyard was covered in rubble. She had a nervous breakdown and spent three months in a sanatorium, but kept asking about her husband. In the spring of 1946, the graves were finally exhumed. 'In my father's pocket,' his son said, 'they found his notebook, his little comb, his hairbrush and he was wearing his watch which he was given after a match in Switzerland.' His little round glasses were also discovered with the body, broken into three pieces.

'My grandfather did not come home and the family did not know whether he was alive or dead,' said Lajos Péczely, Kertész's grandson. 'I think my mother was informed that they were probably buried in the courtyard of the Ministry and that the execution was very rushed, because the Germans were about to flee. My grandfather and Potya were buried alongside each other. My mother found it difficult to identify his corpse. It's a little hazy, but I think his gold watch was in his pocket, and I have now inherited it.' Tóth and Kertész were reburied on 3 April 1946.

A year after her husband's death, Vilma Tóth was presented with a certificate by the Hungarian government confirming her husband was an anti-fascist. On 7 September 1947, Tóth and Kertész were both awarded the Silver Degree of the Hungarian Liberty Order by the Hungarian president Zoltán Tildy. That should have made him a hero, but the paranoia of the Communists outweighed that. Tóth was perceived as having collaborated with the Americans and so the

Communist government stopped Vilma's pension and requisitioned the family home and their car.

Kertész's widow Rozália, meanwhile, was given a position running a restaurant as quasi-compensation to help her get by. 'When I was a very young child,' Péczely said, 'we visited her several times at the Hunting Lodge restaurant near the Arany János utca metro station. But Újpest, as his last club, has never remembered that my grandfather died as a martyr and never gave any official help to my grandmother.'

* * *

Soviet and Romanian troops had entered the eastern suburbs of Budapest as early as 7 November 1944, but it wasn't until 19 December that the offensive began in earnest. When a road to Vienna was seized on 26 December, the city was fully surrounded, trapping 800,000 civilians, 37,000 Hungarian troops and 33,000 German troops inside. The Arrow Cross leader Ferenc Szálasi had already fled.

Fighting was fierce as the Soviets pushed through Pest, extending even into the sewers. But after Csepel Island and its military factories were seized by the Soviets, Hitler gave the order, on 17 January, for German troops to abandon Pest and retreat to Buda, the hilly terrain of which offered better defensive positions, destroying bridges as they went.

György Kósa, the honorary president of the MTK Circle of Friends, was eight at the time and lived in the ghetto with his mother and grandparents, while his father was held in a prisoner-of-war camp by the Soviets after the labour battalion in which he had been serving was overrun. 'We could leave the ghetto only for one hour in the morning and one in the afternoon,' he remembered. 'We were starving. On the last two days no food was brought. We had one bowl of soup a day. Then suddenly, at 9:30 on 18 January, we could leave.

'There was a van with very young Soviet soldiers, almost children, and they gave out fresh black bread. It was the first real bread I'd eaten in months, but I had to step over corpses to get to it.'

German counter-offensives launched on 1 January and 7 January had been rebuffed, but a third, begun on 18 January, closed to within 15 miles of the Soviet encirclement. But fatigue and supply issues took their toll and, on 28 January, there was a general retreat; the city was left to its fate.

For two weeks the defenders held out despite ferocious artillery bombardment. A breakout was attempted on 11 February and the following day the city fell. According to Krisztián Ungváry,[48] around 38,000 civilians had died in the siege, 13,000 from military action and a further 25,000 from starvation and disease. There was little sense of liberation, with looting and rape widespread but, for Hungary, the war was over.

* * *

The Bavarian spa town of Prien am Chiemsee, 40 miles from Munich, the end of August 1945. A railway official entered a carriage and saw slumped in the corner a body. There was no obvious cause of death. Eventually, as more officials got involved, somebody recognised the corpse. It was Alfréd Schaffer, the Football King, and until recently the coach of Bayern Munich. He was 51.

Schaffer seems to have gone to Munich in late autumn 1944 to manage a wine bar. At some point in 1945, he took over Bayern, although it's far from clear whether he or the former player-coach Konrad Heidkamp was in charge when they won the Bavarian championship in 1944–45. The league, anyway, was suspended on

---

[48] In *The Siege of Budapest* (Yale University Press, 2006).

18 February 1945 because of the Allied advance and the growing frequency of air raids, with Bayern declared winners.[49] It was to escape the bombing that Schaffer had fled north-west to Prien.

The Americans had taken the area in April 1945 and the machinery of bureaucracy was not running entirely smoothly. No autopsy was performed on Schaffer.

It took time for news of his death to reach Hungary and when it did, the following January, *Népsport* initially reported that he had been killed in an air raid.[50] Three days later, it issued a correction: 'Béla Takács, who worked for Spéci [Schaffer's nickname] for a long time, has now told us that Schaffer was not a victim of a bomb attack but died after a long illness in Munich.'[51]

Various theories have emerged about Schaffer's death, but it seems most likely that he died either from untreated appendicitis or following a stroke: another life, another death, another body after so many.

---

[49] The Bavarian league at the time was divided into five sub-divisions. München/Oberbayern was the only one that came close to completing its matches; of the ten teams, one played no games and one played six, but the others all played each other. The other four sub-divisions were abandoned meaning that although Bayern had an unassailable lead in their section they had nobody to play against in the play-offs for the overall title.

[50] *Népsport*, 20 January 1946.

[51] *Népsport*, 23 January 1946.

III

CHAPTER ONE

ENDURING DARKNESS

Snow covered the ground and clung to the roof of Nyugati station in the west of Budapest. Outside, in the cold, Emil Östreicher waited. Budapest had fallen, the Germans were gone, the fascists were defeated and it was safe to see his mother Teréz again. Östreicher was a Jew and had been sent with a forced labour battalion to Ukraine. He had somehow managed to escape and had hidden out in a synagogue on Bethlen Gábor tér. On New Year's Day 1944, it was raided by the Arrow Cross, but he had escaped by jumping out of a window, fleeing down the street in nothing but his underpants.[1] The train carrying his mother pulled in. 'I will never forget it,' said Östreicher. 'Both of us had tears running from our eyes and I kissed her hand. Maybe it was for an hour, or it could have been just a few minutes.'

Östreicher had been born in Győr, near the (present-day) Slovakian border, in December 1914. His father was a goalkeeper for Mosonmagyaróvár, whose players would use the Östreichers' house as a changing room. But his father died before his mother had turned 40, leaving her to bring up Östreicher and his sister Lili, who was three

---

[1] These details are given in Iván Hegyi's book *Magyarok nagy pályán* (Sprint Kiadó, 2010) although it has not been possible to corroborate them.

years younger than him, alone. They were far from rich. 'I remember how our clothes were resewn endlessly,' Östreicher said.[2]

By his own admission, Östreicher was not 'a good student', but school gave him a chance to participate in sport. He rowed, he swam, he competed in athletics, he played football and, in January 1931, he came fourth in a figure skating competition at the Miklós Révai School in Győr. He failed his exams when he was 18, though, and feeling 'great shame' he decided to become a soldier. 'I applied for one of the toughest sections – for the scouts, for the pioneer infantry regiment,' he said. 'I was a pretty tall boy but as thin as my finger. Here I became strong. It was a tough, man-forming period, and we had to put 100–120 kg of wooden beams on our shoulders like a yoke.'

He left the army as a sergeant having served the standard five-year term, then worked as a weaver in a textile factory and delivered fruit before being called up for labour service. 'When the bullets are flying,' he said, 'dozens of deaths wait for your comrades, and you wouldn't give a penny for your own life. You would rather hide, even in a mouse hole, because of your fear. Throughout my life, I hated violence and vandalism, so I rejected Hitler from the first minute... There were critical days, weeks, dramatic lessons, until liberation came. But I got through this horrible frenzy, and thank God, my dear mother and my sister, Lili, also came through the horrors.'

But just because the war was over, it didn't mean the Östreichers' hardships were. They stayed in Budapest, where 'for a long time we lived on a bite of bread each day'. There were shortages of everything. 'It was the period,' Östreicher said, 'of swapping, wheeling and dealing, hole-in the-corner business.' He opened a restaurant called Kis Dongó

---

[2] *Nemzeti Sport* published an interview with Östreicher in six parts between 14 July and 8 August 1992. All quotes from him are taken from that unless otherwise stated.

[Little Bumblebee] on Régi posta utca by the river in the heart of the city and worked behind the bar. It made him very little money, but it did put him in contact with a lot of footballers, including three young players of immense promise: Ferenc Puskás, József Bozsik and László Kubala. 'The atmosphere was fantastic, especially after games,' Östreicher said. 'The lads came from every team and stories were told till dawn.' In that bar, connections were formed that would affect the whole course of European football over the two decades that followed.

It seems that Östreicher began to consider a career in football and in 1946 he became a director at Vasas after the Communist politician Gyula Hegyi, the head of the Ironworkers Union and the co-chairman of the MLSZ, had re-formed the football section of the club.[3] A year later, he left Vasas and became the Budapest representative of Győr, his hometown team, but then returned to Vasas to work as a dispenser.

The restaurant, though, was losing money and Östreicher closed up before he slid into bankruptcy. He worked briefly for a company trading in sporting goods and then was called up to the army again. As he began retraining, he was approached by Puskás and Bozsik, who told him that if he joined Honvéd, as Kispest had been renamed after being taken over by the army, he could avoid military service. At some point during the winter of 1949–50, he did, starting off as a treasurer, but then became technical director and finally, in 1956,[4] head of the football division of the club.

* * *

[3] He was included (as 'Emil Ösztreicher') in a list of directors published in *Népsport* (as *Nemzeti Sport* was renamed in April 1945) on 26 May 1946. There is also some suggestion he may have been involved at the club a year earlier under an assumed name.

[4] Östreicher, in the interviews in *Nemzeti Sport*, said 1955 but in his meticulous history of the club, *A Nagy Honvéd* (Alma Mater Zala Bt., 2013), László Rózsaligeti insists it was a year later.

As far as was possible through the war, Erbstein had remained in touch with the Torino president Ferruccio Novo, who had managed to keep the core of the pre-war side together and even added Silvio Piola, a star of the 1938 World Cup and still the all-time top scorer in Serie A. Although he was serving on the football committee at Vasas, with conditions in Hungary still so difficult, Erbstein was desperate to get back to Italy.

On 26 September 1946, he returned to Torino, although Jolán and his two daughters remained in Budapest. Gigi Ferrero, a player in 1938, had become manager and had led Torino to the first post-war *scudetto* and Erbstein was appointed alongside him as a 'technical high supervisor'.

By the late 1940s, Torino were playing a distinct W-M. In England, the system had already slid from its revolutionary appearance under Herbert Chapman to something far more staid, less focused on counter-attacking and determined still to prioritise old-fashioned wingers.[5] Erbstein, though, was part of a more general Hungarian movement that saw how off-the-ball running and an increase in pace could render the W-M something far more fluid. The local journalist Folco Portinari was given some of Erbstein's notebooks from the period. They are striking, focused in a way that appears very modern on the geometry of the pitch. Erbstein seems to have realised that there were defensive issues with his side and to have worked on a solution rooted in spatial awareness.[6]

The two inside-forwards were Ezio Loik and Valentino Mazzola, who had been signed as a pair from Venezia in 1942 – leading to the story that Erbstein had scouted them while making his illicit trips

---

[5] I look at this in far more detail in my books *Inverting the Pyramid* (Orion, 2008) and *The Anatomy of England* (Orion, 2010).

[6] More details are given in Bliss, *Erbstein*.

to Italy at the beginning of the war, although that seems extremely unlikely. Both were energetic but creative, ideal for the inside-forward role in a W-M. Behind them were two tough and direct wing-halves, Giuseppe Grezar and Eusebio Castigliano. 'The *quadrilatero*,'[7] Erbstein said, 'which represents the cornerstone of the *sistema* is made up of willing and snappy athletes, good hitters with an efficient head for the game.' Torino had won the league in 1945–46 and the following season they won it better, the margin of victory increasing form three points to ten. Erbstein was back.

*   *   *

Béla Guttmann returned to football in July 1945 when he was put in charge of the Budapest side Vasas, countering rampant inflation by insisting on being paid half in cash and half in food. It's likely that it was then that he met Emil Östreicher for the first time. But Guttmann was the same difficult character he had always been and after a matter of months he fell out with two club patrons who wanted inside knowledge of team selection.

Guttmann married Mariann in November 1945 – he was 46; she was 33 – but he had no intention of curtailing his itinerant lifestyle. In February 1946 he was appointed coach of Ciocanul Bucharest,[8] again making sure he was paid at least in part in vegetables. He left early in 1947 to return to Újpest, although the reasons why are unclear. It's possible he just wanted to go home, but the German journalist Hardy Grüne suggests he fell out with the Romanian authorities and was

---

[7] The Italian term for the square in the centre of the W-M.

[8] Founded as Maccabi in 1919, Ciocanul had been an overtly Jewish club until being forcibly disbanded by anti-Semitic legislation in 1941. It was re-formed following a merger under the new name in 1945, before another merger in 1948 with Unirea Tricolor to form the club that is now Dinamo Bucharest.

frustrated by the corruption within the Romanian game.[9] After all, as he admitted in an interview with *World Soccer* in 1961, Guttmann was not a man to let a slight lie. 'I always got offended easily,' he said, 'and my stubbornness didn't allow me to give in.'

That was the risk any potential employer took; with Guttmann, the flounce was never far away. But at the same time, he had a tremendous capacity to inspire players, at least in the short term. He was a disciplinarian, but he was also astute, alert to the psychology of his squad. At Újpest, he instituted a fines system to ensure punctuality and then deliberately arrived late one morning, paying the fine to make the point that they were all in it together.

Always alert for financial opportunities and aware of how precarious managerial positions were, particularly given his habit of walking out, Guttmann supplemented his income by opening a textile wholesale shop – perhaps lending credence to suggestions he had worked with Erbstein's textile business during the war. Some clubs might have worried about the consequences of him dividing his energies, but Újpest went on to win the Hungarian league title with a side good enough that when Hungary played Italy in May 1947, nine of their 11 were Újpest players.

Ten of the Italy side, meanwhile, all the outfielders, played for Erbstein's Torino. Hungary's coach was Tibor Gallowich – a 'fervent Communist' as Erbstein described him in a preview he wrote for Vallone's *Unità* – while Guttmann, who had been working as his assistant, was left in Budapest, much to his irritation. Italy won 3–2 with a last-minute winner from Loik, after which there was a celebratory banquet at which Erbstein played a prominent role, acting as a liaison with the Hungarians, making sure they felt at home.

---

[9] In *Die Trainerlegende* (Agon Sportverlag, 2001).

Manager of the champions, working with the national side and newly married, Guttmann seemed to have everything he could have possibly needed in Budapest, but he was never somebody who could simply settle. Hungary remained turbulent and the economic situation was critical, but his departure from Újpest was precipitated by his inability to hold his tongue. When a number of Újpest players were called up for international duty towards the end of the season, Guttmann relaxed training for those left at the club. An official protested, at which Guttmann told him to take over as coach, saying, 'I wouldn't want to get in the way of your career.'

He continued to work alongside Gallowich with the national side, taking temporary control for a 3–0 win away to Romania, and then, early in 1948, he was appointed as manager of Kispest. There he found a highly promising side boasting a 20-year-old Ferenc Puskás, whose father he had succeeded as coach, and a 22-year-old József Bozsik. They lost only two of the remaining 15 games that season, Puskás scoring a barely credible 28 goals.

But trouble was never far away. That November, in a game against Győr, Guttmann was so annoyed by the aggressive approach of the Kispest full-back Mihály Patyi that he told him not to go out for the second half, even though that would leave his side down to ten men. Puskás, used to getting his own way, told Patyi to stay on. The defender vacillated and eventually disobeyed his manager to play on. A furious Guttmann retired to the stands for the second half, most of which he spent reading a racing paper, then took a train home and never returned. He was subsequently banned for a month by the Association of Hungarian Coaches for walking out on his contract.

Without a club and with conditions in Hungary still extremely difficult, Guttmann sought to leave. He secured an exit visa in 1949

– the following year emigration was banned – and went to Vienna, but he really wanted to get to Italy, where Hungarian coaches were still in demand. He thought he had a job lined up at Roma but when that fell through Erbstein used his influence to secure him the manager's job at Padova for the following season.

* * *

The political situation in Hungary remained chaotic. The Soviets had established a provisional parliament in Debrecen late in December 1944, but had ensured that moderate parties were included alongside the Communists. An election was held in November 1945. The centre-right Independent Smallholders Party won 57 per cent of the vote, with the Communists on 17 per cent, but the Soviet commander in Hungary, the president of the Allied Control Commission, Marshal Voroshilov, refused to allow them to govern alone. Accordingly, the Smallholders formed a coalition with the Social Democrats, the left-wing National Peasant Party and the Communists. On 1 February 1946, Hungary was declared a republic and the leader of the Small-holders, Zoltan Tildy, a former priest who had opposed the alliance to Germany and had been forced into hiding after the occupation, named president. He appointed another Smallholder, Ferenc Nagy, as prime minister while the Communist leader Mátyás Rákosi was named as his deputy. Another Communist, László Rajk, became Minister of the Interior and oversaw the creation of the ÁVH, the secret police.

The Smallholders were constantly harassed, with a number of leading members arrested and charged with 'conspiracy against the republic'. In February 1947, Nagy's general secretary, Béla Kovács, was kidnapped, taken to the USSR, tried and sentenced to the Gulag. Three months later Nagy himself was forced to emigrate.

The Communists continued to struggle for popularity, though, and at further elections in August 1947, polled just 24 per cent despite widespread fraud. That led to a change of approach. In June 1948, the Social Democrats, which had been a servile ally since the war, was officially subsumed into the Communist Party. Soon after, Tildy was deposed as president and replaced by a cooperative Social Democrat, Árpád Szakasits.

The Peasant Party had been led since 1945 by Péter Veres, a highly respected politician and writer. During the First World War he had fought on the Italian Front and, on returning to Debrecen during the Soviet Republic, he served on the Balmazújváros Land Distribution Committee, the Workers Council and the Municipal Directorate, before becoming a prisoner of war in Romania. He remained politically active after his release and was repeatedly arrested by the Horthy government, while writing a number of literary works and articles celebrating peasant life. Veres was called up for forced labour details three times during the Second World War and spent much of 1944 hiding from the Gestapo and the Arrow Cross.

Veres helped hold the left-wing alliance together, despite the outrages committed against Kovács and Nagy, seeing Soviet backing as the best way of securing land reform, and after Nagy had been forced out, he was appointed Minister of Construction and Defence. In August 1947, he became Minister for Defence.

But Veres differed from the Communists on one key point: collectivisation. In 1947, the Peasant Party published a series of pamphlets in which Veres argued that 'the small Hungarian paradise demands individual farming and free production.' The following year he made the argument at greater length in his book *A paraszti jövendő* [*The Future of the Peasant*].[10]

---

[10] *A paraszti jövendő* (Jövő, 1948).

Veres became regarded as problematic and was targeted by the ÁVH. A secretary of Gábor Péter, the head of the ÁVH, a man called Bálint[11] was also from Balmazújváros. At some point, he realised that he knew somebody else from Balmazújváros, a man of base cunning and little scruple, whose father happened to have been a friend of Veres:[12] Dezső Steinberger.

As the Soviets closed in on Auschwitz, Steinberger had been on one of the death marches west. He seems to have spent time at Dachau, but ended up in Feldafing,[13] an emergency camp for displaced persons about 25 miles south-west of Munich established by the US army on 1 May 1945 to house mainly Hungarian Jews they had rescued from cattle trucks near the railway station at Tutzing. They were being taken from the concentration camp at Mühldorf-Mettenheim to be massacred in the Tyrolean Alps, but had been deliberately held up by the local Wehrmacht transport commander so that they could be saved.

Steinberger was interviewed by US forces because of his involvement with Mengele but no further action was taken and he returned to Balmazújváros. Contacted by the ÁVH, Steinberger and his brother Hermann agreed to work against Veres. 'Auschwitz,' Steinberger himself later admitted, 'only worsened my position because I was weakened in everything … I was weak in character, in will, in everything. Auschwitz burned everything.'[14] A few weeks later, Veres was forced to resign. In his book *Apám mellett, apám helyett* [*By My*

---

[11] It's not clear who this is or even whether Bálint here is a forename or a surname. It seems unlikely it was István Bálint, a leading figure in the ÁVH, because he was not from Balmazújváros.

[12] Various letters between the two are archived in Balmazújváros.

[13] This is confirmed both by *Hírek az Elhurcoltakról*, a Hungarian list of Jewish survivors of the war published in 1945, and by camp records.

[14] In *Futballdezső* (Hétfői Műhely Stúdió Alapítvány, 1991). Or, more accurately, in the trailer for the film; the documentary itself seems to have vanished.

Father, Instead of My Father],[15] Veres's son István outlines how his father's political career had been ended by information provided by the Steinbergers.

Eventually, in February 1949, all 'democratic' parties were merged into a single People's Front led by Rákosi and every other party outlawed. On 18 August 1949 a new constitution, modelled on that adopted in the USSR 13 years earlier, was ratified.

Rákosi had been taken prisoner during the First World War and, after escaping from a camp in the far east of Russia, had made his way to St Petersburg at the time of the revolution. That confirmed his Communist sympathies and he served in Béla Kun's government. When it collapsed, he escaped to the Soviet Union, but on returning to Hungary in 1924, he was imprisoned. He went back to Moscow in 1940, exchanged for Hungarian revolutionary banners that had been captured in 1849. There, he became a leading figure in the Comintern,[16] and was sent back to Hungary in January 1945 to head up the Communist movement. His two closest associates, Ernő Gerő and Mihály Farkas, had also spent significant periods in Moscow, leading to tension with those who had remained in Hungary during the war when Communism was outlawed. Those who had stayed tended to be more popular within the Party and were thus regarded as a potential threat. The most well known of them, László Rajk, the Minister for Foreign Affairs, was arrested in May 1949. At his trial in September, he gave a bizarre confession in which he admitted working for the unlikely triumvirate of Horthy, Tito and Trotsky. He later said he had been plotting to kill Rákosi and Gerő. He was convicted and executed, marking the beginning of the most oppressive period of Rákosi's rule.

---

[15] Published Kurucz Gábor, 1994.

[16] The organisation formed in 1919 to promote international Communism.

Over the following three years, there was a purge of supposedly undesirable elements within the Party as dissent was ruthlessly
suppressed. Around 2,000 people were executed and 100,000
imprisoned. There was a programme of industrial nationalisation
and an attempt to collectivise farms. The Soviet model was followed
slavishly, even when it made no sense to do so: Rákosi, for instance,
proudly declared Hungary 'a country of iron and steel', even though
it had no iron ore. Textiles, meanwhile, a traditional Hungarian
strength, were neglected. Wealthier peasants were declared class
enemies and persecuted, leading to a loss of expertise that exacerbated food shortages. Economically, the country remained a mess;
if there was a greater degree of stability, it came at the cost of an
authoritarian and repressive regime.

* * *

There were few of those problems in Turin. Erbstein had always been a
great raconteur and loved entertaining, gravitating to thinkers, artists
and academics, particularly those, it seemed, whose ideas had brought
them to the attention of the authorities. As well as the cultural critic
Raf Vallone, the poet Alfonso Gatto, who had been jailed in the 1930s
for anti-fascist activities, was a regular visitor to his apartment, but his
hospitality to the visiting Hungarians in 1947 prompted suspicion.
There appears to have been a whispering campaign against Erbstein,
accusing him of being a Communist spy, something that led, early in
1949, to him writing an article for a weekly sports supplement under
the headline, 'I am not a secret agent'.

On the pitch, though, Torino's success continued. There was a
third consecutive league title but, at the end of 1946–47, frustrated
by Novo's regular interference in team affairs (and given the close
relationship between the two men, it's not unreasonable to wonder

whether that might actually mean Erbstein's), Ferrero left, taking over at Fiorentina. 'By then,' he said, 'the introduction of any new player, even one of the youngsters, could not alter the team set-up or the balance of the game. There was just no risk of jamming a mechanism that was so close to perfection.'[17] The similarity to MTK 25 years earlier is clear.

The mechanism wasn't completely flawless, though. The former Torino midfielder Mario Sperone took over as coach, assisted by the director Roberto Copernico, who had maintained contact with Erbstein during the war through their textile businesses, and they immediately faced a major challenge. The defender Mario Rigamonti failed to show for pre-season having disappeared on a trip to Liguria on his beloved motorcycle. Nobody was overly concerned – he had gone missing before in times of stress – but with their new signing Sauro Tomà suspended following an offence at the end of the previous season, Torino needed him back. Sperone, in consultation with Copernico and Erbstein, reluctantly picked the 19-year-old Pietro Biglino for the opening game of the season at home to Napoli. But 20 minutes before kick-off, Rigamonti arrived. He'd set off from Brescia at 7am but had been riding so fast his engine had blown and he'd had to wait in Milan for a replacement.

It was typical of Erbstein's leadership that rather than disciplining him, he advised Rigamonti should go straight into the team. Torino won 4–1 and although Rigamonti was sent off in a 1–0 defeat at Bari the following week, he returned after suspension to play a key role in Torino's greatest season. 'Erbstein intervened with a hand on the shoulder for those who had done well,' said Umberto Motta, Torino's

---

[17] Cited in Bliss, *Erbstein*.

youth-team captain, 'and a look of irony, in a fatherly way, to those who had not been so good.'[18]

Erbstein was always willing to offer advice and more to his players. Mazzola, for instance, approached him after his marriage had become strained and he had fallen in love with another woman. Erbstein helped him file for divorce in Romania, where marriages were much easier to dissolve than in conservative Italy.

His expertise in international bureaucracy was a useful by-product of difficult personal experience. Just keeping his family together was hugely problematic. In October 1947, Juventus salvaged a 1–1 draw against Torino with a controversial penalty, leading to some pushing and shoving at the final whistle for which Erbstein and the Juve coach Renato Cesarini were both suspended for a month. Erbstein used the time away from the touchline to return to Hungary where Jolán and Marta were stranded, having had applications for passports turned down. By mid-November, the situation was still not resolved and it was announced that Copernico would remain in his temporary post as *tecnico* a little longer.

Erbstein secured a meeting with the sports minister Gyula Hegyi, the president of National Sports Education and Sports Committee (OTSB), whom he had met at that friendly between Italy and Hungary. According to Marta, Hegyi took a pair of blank passports from his desk and filled them in there and then. The next day, Marta left for school as usual, but then broke away from her friends, pretending to have left something at home. She took a tram to the station where she met her mother and, once again leaving most of their belongings behind, they headed south to Italy.

With Erbstein back in his post, Torino won seven and drew two of their next nine games. A 10–0 win over Alessandria took them

---

[18] Cited in Bliss, *Erbstein.*

five points clear at the top of the table at which, slightly surprisingly, Erbstein temporarily moved to the club his team had just hammered to try to save them from relegation. This was part of Torino's wider thinking, their attempt to create a structure that would sustain them at the top of the game. They had close relationships with Alessandria, Lucchese, Como and Vicenza, using them effectively both as feeder clubs and as places to park players who hadn't quite made the grade with them. Although Alessandria won their first two games under Erbstein 1–0, they didn't win again until the final day of the season by which time they'd already been relegated. In his absence, Torino had wrapped up their fourth straight league title, finishing 16 points clear at the top of the table.

* * *

The truck heading west through Hungary into the Sopron Mountains had Russian plates. Its occupants wore Russian military uniform and carried Russian papers but nobody inside was Russian. On board was László Kubala, a stocky 21-year-old centre-forward for Vasas widely regarded as one of the brightest young talents in the Hungarian game. His father, a bricklayer, was an ethnic Slovak, while his mother, a factory worker, had Polish heritage. He had been born in Budapest, though, and at 11 he had lied about his date of birth to play for the team of the local metalworks. By the age of 15, he was playing for Ferencváros; at 17 he made his debut for Hungary.

When he'd been a child, Kubala's father had given him a violin; he used it as a goalpost. He was preternaturally big, explosively quick and prodigiously technically gifted. His family couldn't quite believe how good he was. When Kubala came home with his first pay packet, his father assumed he'd stolen it and dragged him back to the club to apologise, only to be told that his son deserved every fillér.

Kubala joined Slovan Bratislava in 1946, married Anna, the sister of the coach, in 1947 and, a year later, compelled by military service to return to Hungary, signed for Vasas. His son Branko had just been born when he decided he had to get out. On a chilly Sunday in January 1949, leaving his wife and son behind, Kubala set off with others desperate to flee the hard-line Communist regime. If anybody stopped the truck, they claimed to be part of the munitions service of the Red Army. A few miles from the border, they abandoned the truck and walked through the snow. The Austrian authorities picked them up and took them to a detention centre. After three days, somebody recognised Kubala, and he was offered safe passage to any country he chose. The plan had always been Italy.

His wife and son escaped through Czechoslovakia, Anna swimming across the Danube while Branko floated in a tyre. Kubala waited for them in Udine. He was offered the chance to play for Torino in a friendly that April, but Branko had fallen ill and he had to decline.

Kubala signed for Pro Patria. At his first training session, as the rest of the squad set off on a run, he declined, saying he wasn't physically ready, and started doing a few tricks with a ball. The club chairman, impressed, offered him his watch if he could do 400 keepy-ups. He did, then jogged once round the pitch, continuing to keep the ball off the ground with a series of tricks.

However talented Kubala was, though, he could not evade the bureaucracy of contracts. He had walked out on Vasas and so FIFA banned him. Pro Patria released him, and Kubala joined Hungaria, a team of political refugees – mainly Hungarian although with a few Czechs, Slovaks, Russians and Croatians – based in Rome. It was coached by the former Slovan Bratislava manager Ferdinand Daučík, Kubala's brother-in-law.

Also in that squad was Gyula Zsengellér, the great Újpest goal-scorer who had played in the 1938 World Cup final. Although he didn't score as Újpest beat Ferencváros 5–1 on 19 October 1947, when he left the pitch that day, Zsengellér had scored 368 goals in 301 games for the club. He remains the third-highest scorer in Hungarian league history. The next day, though, he moved to Italy, the last Hungarian player to leave the country legally before the Communists closed the borders.

The threat of footballers defecting was taken extremely seriously by the Communist authorities and came to a head in the case of the Újpest and Hungary defender Sándor Szűcs, the player whose injury had caused such a headache for Géza Kertész on the day before his arrest. In 1948, Szűcs met the singer Erzsi Kovács. Both were already married but they fell in love. That went against Communist morality and the two were advised to separate. When they did not, they were subjected to a campaign of harassment until, in 1950, they decided to flee the country together. Szűcs was essentially entrapped by the ÁVH, arrested, convicted in a secret trial and executed in June 1951, while Kovács was sentenced to four years in prison. There seems little doubt Szűcs's punishment was exemplary, intended to dissuade other footballers from attempting to flee – and for more than five years, it worked.

Zsengellér joined Roma and spent two seasons there before moving to Ancona as player-manager. He led them to promotion to Serie B. The plan had been for Zsengellér to set up home and for his family to join him later, but that soon became impossible. His wife and son, Zsolt, were allowed to visit in 1948, but no visa was provided for his daughter, Anna-Maria, who stayed behind with her grand-mother's sister. Zsolt remembers his father urging his mother to stay in Rome, believing the Red Cross would ensure the family wasn't separated, but his mother didn't dare take the risk.

After his season at Ancona, Zsengellér moved to Colombia and the rebel league where vast sums were available to players and managers prepared to operate beyond the reach of FIFA. He was named player-coach of Deportivo Samarios in the city of Santa Marta, a team based on the remnants of Hungary who had been on a tour of South America. His salary would have been unthinkable in Hungary and he tried to divert some of that to his wife, sending her $100 in cash in a letter. But she was seen trying to change it on the black market, arrested at four one morning and sentenced to eight months in jail. She served six, during which time the children were looked after by sisters of their grandmother.

Zsengellér returned to Europe in 1953 and became manager of the Cypriot side Pezoporikos Larnaca, a role arranged for him by József 'Dori' Künsztler, a winger who had played for Újpest in the early 1920s before having great success as a coach with Panathinaikos in Greece and Apoel in Cyprus. Eventually, he accepted that it would be impossible to be reunited with his family and he divorced. He married a Cypriot woman and pursued an itinerant managerial career through Cyprus, Greece and Italy.

In the summer of 1950, Hungary toured Spain, playing a series of friendlies against Real Madrid, Espanyol and the national side. Kubala was brilliant. Against Espanyol, he took down a long ball from kick-off, flicked it over a defender's head and lashed the ball in on the volley. The Barcelona president Agustí Montal, sitting in the stand, supposedly turned immediately to the club secretary and told him to prepare a contract.

Madrid were also interested, and various legends have grown up about just how Barça landed him (probably, as Sid Lowe has argued,[19]

---

[19] In *Fear and Loathing in la Liga* (Yellow Jersey, 2013).

by nothing more complicated or controversial than looking at the contract Madrid had drawn up and offering more money) but they did, and also employed Daučík. The ban was still in place, though, and Kubala was allowed only to play in friendlies; even that he did under a false name so as not to draw attention to himself.

In April 1951, though, Kubala was given official political refugee status, something that was presented as a coup for Franco's Spain, and he made his official Barcelona debut against Sevilla at the end of that month in the first round of the Copa del Generalísimo. By the end of May, Barcelona had won the competition and Kubala's seven games for the club had brought six wins and a draw. On 1 June, he became a Spanish citizen.

Kubala was powerful and strong, so muscular that he seemed at times to be about to burst out of his shirt. 'You couldn't knock him over with a cannonball,' Alfredo di Stéfano said. But he was also skilful and imaginative, pioneering the staggered run-up for taking a penalty, and curling free kicks over and around the wall. He also liked to eat and drink. Once in Las Palmas, the coach Sandro Puppo threatened to fine anybody who stayed out late. Kubala handed over the money there and then. There were, inevitably, scrapes and on one occasion Kubala got into a fight with some US Marines, four of whom ended up being knocked into the sea.

But nobody cared. If anything, Kubala's robust social life only made him more popular. And whatever he did off the pitch, on it he was sensational. For Barcelona, 1951–52 is 'the year of the five cups' when they won the league, the Copa del Generalísimo, the Copa Eva Duarte[20] and the Martini & Rossi and Duward awards for scoring

---

[20] A precursor to the Super Cup, contested by the winners of the league and the Copa del Generalísimo between 1947 and 1953, although because Barça had done the double, they were simply awarded the trophy.

the most and conceding the fewest goals in the league. They also that summer won the Latin Cup, a tournament for the champions of France, Spain, Portugal and Italy.[21]

The following season, Kubala contracted tuberculosis and was sent to a small village in the mountains to recover. When he returned, Barça lay fifth in the table, but they came back to win the double again. His impact went far beyond silverware, though. Kubala was a star and made Barcelona popular. They had bought the land to build the Camp Nou before his arrival, so while the popular myth that it was built to accommodate fans who wanted to see him is inaccurate, it is true that it was he who filled it. That's why it is his statue that stands outside the stadium, and it's also probably because of him that Madrid were so desperate in 1953 to sign Di Stéfano when the Argentinian quit the rebel league in Colombia. They needed a superstar of their own.

Kubala added two more league titles and two more cups, but by the end of the decade, his lifestyle was beginning to sap at his pace. By then he had a manager in Helenio Herrera who resented his self-indulgence, his celebrity and, as he saw it, the way Kubala slowed the game down. He became player-coach in 1961 and left two years later for Espanyol, where he ended up playing alongside Di Stéfano, a pairing of two giants who had left their homes and ended up defining an era of Spanish football.

* * *

Torino went into their game at San Siro on 30 April 1949 four points clear of Inter. Without the injured Mazzola, Giuseppe Grezar and Virgilio Maroso, their approach was understandably conservative. 'Torino have the advantage of the better defence,' Erbstein said before

---

[21] A tournament for club sides from France, Italy, Spain and Portugal contested every year from 1949 to 1957 apart from 1954.

the game, before gently exerting pressure on the match officials in a way that seems very modern. 'I am not worried, especially if the referee keeps the game under control.'[22]

He did, and so did Torino. Despite being forced to use the inexperienced Rubens Fadini and Gyula Schubert on the left side of the *quadrilatero*, they drew 0–0 to maintain their advantage at the top of the table with just four games remaining. The draw all but secured a fifth successive *scudetto* and it meant Torino were relaxed enough to send a side to Lisbon to play in a testimonial for the Portugal midfielder Francisco Ferreira. That was the game that Kubala might have played had it not been for his son's illness.

Erbstein couldn't find a suitcase big enough, so borrowed Susanna's. She gave it to him on condition he brought it back and maintained his long-established custom of bringing her a doll from every country he visited.

Torino's arrival was front-page news in Portugal, a newspaper photograph showing a relaxed Erbstein walking across the airfield, hands in pockets, a bag slung over his shoulder, the wind whipping up his hair, their plane in the background. The game itself was anticlimactic. With the exiled king of Italy, Umberto II,[23] in attendance, and Mazzola and Grezar back after injury, Torino began well and took the lead, but an injury to Gabetta disrupted their rhythm and they ended up losing 4–3.

The following morning, the journalist Luigi Cavallero filed his report for *La Stampa*. 'The *granata* rose early to prepare for their return,' he wrote. 'In a few hours the plane that carried the management, players and journalists to Lisbon will take off on its return journey,

---

[22] Cited in Bliss, *Erbstein*.

[23] Who, as prince, in 1928, had pardoned Luigi Allemandi on his charge of match-fixing.

arriving at the Turin Air Field, weather permitting, at 5pm. May the clouds and the winds be favourable to us, and not shake us too much…'[24]

The flight left Lisbon on time. At quarter to five, Pierluigi Meroni, the captain, radioed the control tower in Turin. They were over Savona, he said. 'Within 20 minutes we will be in Turin.'

At 1702, the control tower put out a weather report: 'Clouds, intense bursts of rain, poor visibility, clouds at 500m.'

* * *

30 April 1949 was a damp day in Turin, the clouds sitting low over the mountains that frame the city. Marta Erbstein was almost 18 and to celebrate her upcoming birthday, her father had commissioned an artist to paint her portrait. That evening, she was at home with her mother, Jolán, waiting for the artist to arrive when the telephone rang. The news was dreadful.

At 1703, Torino's plane had crashed into the embankment behind the monastery of Superga. A group of monks, led by Don Ricca Tancredi, rushed out. Amid the wreckage they found a number of badly burned bodies. One monk opened a suitcase and found it full of *granata* shirts. Only then did they realise who had been on the plane. Everybody on board was killed. Erbstein, having survived so much, had not survived this.

Susanna was on a train and learned of her father's death when she overheard a conversation between two other passengers. Her suitcase, almost unmarked, was returned to her a few days later. As she observed grimly, her father always kept his promises. Eventually, she summoned the strength to open it. Inside, neatly wrapped in tissue paper, she found a Portuguese doll.

---

[24] *La Stampa*, 30 April 1949.

The bodies of the 31 victims were laid out in the monastery. In *La Stampa*, Giulio De Benedetti described 'a low chamber – bare – its whitewashed walls cracked here and there; on the ceiling a large condensation stain spreads into the strange shape of an octopus. Hanging from the centre, by a thread, there is a lampshade made of tin, but it is empty, broken, missing a light bulb; on the walls are small windows in wooden frames, but there is no glass; the floor is tiled, cold; in the corner a crack stretches towards the centre of the room. They were placed side by side, almost on top of each other, in this mortuary, with a name as cold as its walls: morgue – the name of death, who welcomed the youth of Turin.'[25]

For several days after the crash, just as after the trauma in Cleves, Marta was unable to speak. One woman in the city hanged herself in grief. More than 500,000 turned out for the funeral; soldiers had to be deployed to hold them back. Torino completed the season, fielding their youth side. Their opponents did the same and the *scudetto* was won by five points. Torino hadn't lost a home game in six years.

---

[25] As quoted in Bliss, *Erbstein*.

CHAPTER TWO
INEXCUSABLE IMPROVISATION

A little over 200 miles south-west of Budapest, as Hungary struggled with the aftermath of German occupation, the former Ferencváros centre-half Márton Bukovi made a tactical adjustment in Zagreb that, seven years later, would lift Hungary to unimagined heights and humiliate England at Wembley. Pulling his centre-forward a little deeper may not seem like much, but it was the vital step in the development of the *Aranycsapat*.

Bukovi, having won four league championships, three Cups and a Mitropa Cup as a player with Ferencváros, moved to Sète in France – 'a dirty, provincial sailors' town that I grew to love' as he described it[1] – where he added a league and cup double in 1934, before retiring the following year at the age of 34. He had never been quite the same since breaking a leg in 1930 – an injury he described as 'the greatest tragedy that can befall a footballer, like an opera singer losing his voice'.

---

[1] Unless otherwise stated, all Bukovi quotes here come from a series of interviews he gave to *Šport* newspaper. They stretched over a barely credible 90 issues (unfortunately the first six appear to be missing from the National and University Library in Zagreb), which itself suggests the importance he had assumed.

He was, presumably, looking for a job at that point anyway but, if the surely romanticised version of events he gave to the Croatian newspaper *Šport* is to be believed, happenstance gave him a significant nudge. He found a new flat in Sète that overlooked a square that reminded him of Tisza Kálmán tér in Budapest. Children would play football and he would quietly watch them. One day, a boy called René, the most talented player there, hit a passer-by with the ball, sending his hat flying. The man – 'fat, possibly alcoholic' – was furious and threatened to report the children to the police. René, weeping, apologised and begged him not to, at which Bukovi intervened. Diplomacy, though, was never his greatest attribute and he ended up slapping the man hard across the face.

René, it turned out, was an orphan who was looked after by his sister. Bukovi, perhaps recognising something of his own early life, took René to a nearby café and bought him some cake. They were soon joined by the other children who asked for autographs and then begged Bukovi to coach their team. He agreed to work with them for half an hour a day. It was then, he said, that he first felt 'the calling'. Bukovi revelled in the role and the team soon began to draw spectators as he encouraged them to play passing football on the ground, he said to minimise the chance of them breaking windows or lights he would have to pay for. Eventually, an official from Sète came to take a look. Before he left, he had offered Bukovi a job as a youth coach.

'What I'm about to say may be unpleasant, but I simply want to,' Bukovi said in 1943 – which seems to have been true of most conversations throughout his life; he habitually rejected what he should say and instead said what he felt he had to say. 'Players rarely think about football. I did think. I made up systems, asked coaches, wanted to know. I thought about the ways of training, often unsatisfied with the practices we had.

'I felt that we needed to work with more of a plan, that what we were doing was an inexcusable improvisation, that coaches didn't recognise anything new and would simply drill in the same thing they did when they were players. What I'm really trying to say is that I always had a magnet drawing me to the coach's calling. A man carries that germ and then gets infected, even though he didn't think about it, or didn't have that firm intention, and he finds peace in the calling that suits him best. And I wanted to be a coach. And yet, it only happened by accident. If it hadn't been for René and the square, and for that passer-by, or maybe for my wife's desire for a new flat, maybe my spark would have died out and I would have become a mechanic for a living.'

After a few months with Sète's youth team, Bukovi took a holiday with his wife and children to Budapest. Ferencváros offered him a contract to continue playing and he had a meeting with Henrik Fodor, the club secretary of MTK. 'I didn't have a very favourable opinion of Fodor and neither did other players,' Bukovi said. 'He was a bit of an odd fellow. Always sombre, he reminded me of my schoolteachers when they looked for a victim. He was a bully. He'd force his will upon people. But he was conspicuously kind that time.'

Bukovi, though, decided that for the sake of his wife it was time to settle down and end his playing career. MTK offered him a job, but Bukovi didn't want to coach anybody he had played alongside. A frustrated Fodor invited him to his office at the MLSZ and threw a bundle of envelopes at him. Each contained a request from abroad asking the Hungarian federation for help. Bukovi chose Yugoslavia, where he was appointed manager of Građanski Zagreb, a club that had already had two Hungarian coaches: Imre Pozsonyi had spent a season there in 1925–26 immediately after leaving Barcelona, and György Molnár a season in 1932–33.[2]

---

[2] They had also been coached by Arthur Gaskell, a former teammate of Hogan's, who had managed Hakoah, and by Dombi Kohn, later manager of Bayern and

Molnár had been replaced by the Irishman James Donnelly, who introduced the W-M and in that sense prepared the groundwork for Bukovi. Građanski's board, anyway, had been convinced that the W-M was the future and insisted Bukovi should implement it. He, though, was sceptical about just how much progress Donnelly had made and about the board in general. 'They believed that systems won games,' he said, 'and that all of the football's secret is in some school and not in the players' feet, their feeling for space, sense of collectivism, devotion, strength, condition, speed and so on. They wanted the lads to play in a more modern way. They wanted me to implant some novelty which would surprise opponents. Something in the style of Mandrake the Magician.[3] A wand, and now the team will play like this. A wand of different colour – and a different system…

'It was clear that I couldn't just [implement the W-M] overnight and thought it would have been premature for us anyway,' he said. 'But I told them I would start immediately. Luckily they didn't know much about football, because what we practised was something entirely different. It was the Italian system.' That is, the *metodo* rather than the *sistema*, the halfway house between the old-fashioned 2–3–5 and the British W-M in which the inside-forwards were withdrawn but the centre-half had not retreated to become primarily a defender.

But then, after the 1935–36 Yugoslav championship had been abandoned following a dispute over its format, a friendly was arranged against Liverpool for May 1936.[4] Bukovi feared not only that Građanski would lose but that everybody would realise what he

---

Barcelona.

[3] Mandrake was a syndicated comic strip created by Lee Falk, later more famous for the Phantom. In *The Encyclopedia of American Comics*, Ron Goulart describes Mandrake as the first superhero.

[4] Nine days after they had played Građanski, Liverpool lost 3–2 to Beogradski SK, a game they played shirtless because of a clash of colours.

was implementing was not the W-M at all. 'Ahead of the game, all the Zagreb papers wrote how Građanski would face Liverpool playing "the English way", in a W-M system,' Bukovi said. 'Someone translated the articles for Liverpool and they were fully convinced that what awaited them would be something they were very familiar with. When they realised that what we were "selling" them was something else, it was already too late.'

Građanski won 5–1. 'The whole town buzzed about how Bukovi had given the English a taste of their own medicine and I kept quiet. No one spoke of the Italian school.'

Or, at least, no one spoke of it until the post-match banquet, when Liverpool's right-half Matt Busby pointed out the truth.[5] 'The English betrayed me,' said Bukovi. 'At the post-match banquet they revealed … how we misled them.'

Liverpool had just finished 19th out of 22 teams in the English top flight, but this was still regarded as a near miraculous success. Liverpool were impressed enough to invite Građanski for a return fixture that November. Liverpool won the rematch 4–0, and Građanski went on to have a disappointing trip, also losing to Doncaster, Wolves and West Ham, and drawing 4–4 against Hearts. Nonetheless, Bukovi made great use of the tour to study the English interpretation of the W-M which he found confirmed his own impression that football in central Europe was too mannered and needed to be more direct.

---

[5] Bukovi doesn't say specifically that it was Busby. That detail comes from the journalist Zvonimir Magdić who knew Bukovi well and attended the banquet, which was held at a restaurant called Grozd on Savska cesta. That Bukovi says 'English' shouldn't be taken as meaning it was not Busby, who was a Scot: for one thing, he is clearly speaking of 'the party of the English team'; and for another the differences between the constituent parts of the United Kingdom seem of very little concern to outsiders. To old football men of central Europe, 'English' is almost invariably used as a synonym for 'British'.

'We introduced the defender-centre-half, a role that suited [Ivan] Jazbinšek best. The full-backs had to forget about marking inside-forwards and transfer their attention to wingers. The half-backs grew into builders and, together with inside-forwards, took over the focus of the play. The advantage of the W-M is that you can create chances already from your own half. Playing in the old way, you needed too many short moves to outsmart the opponent. The strength of the English way of playing was in being able to advance quickly up the pitch and skip the majority of the opponent's defensive belt. An old-school centre-half would only watch the flight of the ball, powerless to do anything. Now it was the complete opposite as our centre-half Jazbinšek possessed distinct qualities for such a role; he could hold opponents by himself. I won't exaggerate if I say I never found a greater master of the role. In my opinion, he is the greatest defender-centre-half Yugoslavia ever had and there were only a few who can stand comparison to him in world football.'

The lessons of England learned, Bukovi made Građanski a dominant force in Yugoslav football, winning the league title in 1936–37 and 1939–40 before the championship was brought to an end by the war. The 1937 championship was sealed with a 4–0 win in Belgrade against BSK. 'Not only did we win the championship with that victory and end the Serbian club's two-year domination, but it was important to me for other reasons,' he explained. 'When I first came to Zagreb I had no idea about the struggle of Croatian people. It was only then that I found out and saw that through sport, especially through football, a real political struggle is fought.

'Građanski was then considered a people's fighter. Croatians felt Građanski's defeats as their own and rejoiced in the team's wins. We won in front of 20,000 home fans, among them [Milan] Stojadinović, the Prime Minister at the time,[6] who only came to congratulate BSK for beating the Croats. Our players fought not only to win the championship, but also to prove what Croats can do and what they mean. The people understood that and it was little wonder that more than 20,000 came to welcome us back in Zagreb, carrying the winners on their shoulders from the train station to Trg Jelačića.[7] Those were unforgettable moments, the most beautiful and the dearest I had in my sporting life.'[8]

His introduction of the W-M had been controversial and, in 1943, he was asked if he still believed it was the most effective formation. 'I will be up until I perceive some other system as better,' Bukovi said. 'I had doubts about it for a long time but I eventually came to realise its advantages and accepted it. They criticised us for it but today everyone plays it. I noticed children playing in fields are lining up in this new system and everyone is marking their man. The system is, after all, accepted by all European teams. Many German teams use it, Hungarian clubs as well as their national team, all except Ferencváros and NAC. I believe that a new system will emerge after the war. Systems change and have to change, like everything else in life...'[9]

What he did not say, though, was that it would be he who would lead that change. 'Márton Bukovi recognised the voice of times earlier than anyone else in Hungary,' the veteran journalist László Feleki wrote on his death in 1985. 'As the Građanski coach in Zagreb, he had great success with the most modern playing system. Bukovi could

---

[6] He was Serb.

[7] The large central square in Zagreb, in which stands a statue of Josip Jelačić, a noted military general and the leader who abolished serfdom in the country in the mid-19th century.

[8] *Šport*, Issue 6, 1943.

[9] *Šport*, Issue 6, 1943.

always step over his own shadow and evolve.'[10] Reinterpreting his own role as a centre-half following the change in the offside law had perhaps led Bukovi to question other fundamentals of the game. 'As a leader,' Feleki went on, 'there was a treasure in his hands: the confidence of the players. And he gained this because the players knew all his words and advice were worth their weight in gold.' It helped that he was a superb linguist, speaking not only Hungarian but also good Italian, French, German, Serbian, Croatian, Polish and Russian.

That is not to say, though, that Bukovi was an easy man. He himself acknowledged that he could be tough with players. 'I demanded discipline,' Bukovi said. 'I was not lenient with anybody, I was critical and demanded a lot.'[11] As he saw it, rules were rules. Jazbinšek was a supremely dedicated professional and a a great favourite of Bukovi, but he fined him once anyway when he arrived home after the club's 11pm curfew because there'd been a power cut in the cinema and he waited to see the end of the film after electricity had been restored. 'I think my methods at first did not seem very sympathetic,' Bukovi went on, 'but wherever I worked every player liked me. I also made it clear to club leaders from the outset: the responsibility is mine alone, so do not try to interfere with my business.'

Yet to portray Bukovi merely as crotchety, cantankerous and sure of his own mind is to do him a gross disservice. He was also brave and principled, a man of profound intregrity. Građanski's groundsman when the war began was a Jewish refugee called Max Reisfeld who had fled Nazism in Vienna. When the Ustaše seized power in Croatia and began implementing anti-Semitic legislation, Bukovi was among the club officials who helped hide Reisfeld and his family beneath a stand, bringing them food and provisions. Građanski's stadium was in an

---

[10] *Képes Sport*, 5 May 1985.
[11] *Népszabadság*, 18 December 1983.

industrial area that was frequently raided by the Ustaše who saw it as a centre of Communist resistance, but the Reisfelds survived undetected for four years and were able to return to Vienna at the end of the war.

Marika Lantos, the wife of the MTK and Hungary defender Mihály Lantos, got to know Bukovi well when her husband worked as his assistant at Olympiacos between 1965 and 1967. Bukovi's wife wasn't with him when he arrived in Greece, she recalled, but 'he needed a woman to look after him'. He couldn't cook, so Marika would make him dinner on a small electric stove in the bathroom of the hotel room she shared with her husband. 'We were always worried the food smell would overwhelm the place,' she said. Bukovi 'liked breaded meat very well done, almost dry, with ratatouille'.

When Bukovi arrived in Greece, Lantos's son was five years old. Bukovi doted on him, bought him a bicycle and would take turns with Lantos to head the ball at the boy while he dived about on the bed pretending to be the Újpest and Hungary goalkeeper Antal Szent-mihályi. But Marika Lantos recognised there were others who didn't see that side of Bukovi. 'He was a hard man,' she said, 'precise, strict and consistent. He demanded order and discipline. It didn't matter who a player was; he would always tell him what he thought of him. That might be why many didn't love him. He could be reserved and grumpy but he had a heart of gold. He was like a bad mother-in-law: he commented on everything and always found fault. He meant well, but he couldn't understand that he needed to make distinctions between people. He just said what he wanted to say.'

Bukovi's very particular habits are perhaps best demonstrated by his love of film. He didn't have a television but would visit the cinema after training several times a week. 'He hated going with anybody though,' Marika said, 'so he would ask at the box office if his wife were already there. If she was, he would go to another cinema.'

There's no reason to believe Bukovi's marriage was anything other than happy, but he never seems to have been too concerned by the prospect of spending time apart from his wife, whom he had married in 1933. Ferencváros had offered him their manager's job in the summer of 1942, but he rejected them, even as his wife returned to Budapest to give birth to their son. Eighteen months later, she was still in Hungary and he was still in Zagreb but, she hopefully told *Nemzeti Sport*, he was about to return home.[12] He did not, though, and as the Germans invaded Hungary, she and the child moved instead to Zagreb.

In June 1945, the war in Yugoslavia over and Tito's Communists in control, Građanski, along with several other clubs, were disbanded and their archives destroyed as punishment for having played in the fascist-backed wartime league. A new club, Dinamo, was founded to represent Zagreb, and took on Građanski's colours, stadium, the bulk of their fan base and many players. Bukovi, who had been coaching a military unit in exchange for food, agreed to be manager after a number of senior players appealed directly to him.

Dinamo did well in their first season, 1946, and ended up facing Lokomotiva in a game to decide the Zagreb championship. 'It was not an ordinary game for the football in our country – nor, I dare say, for the world,' said Bukovi. 'On that day, for the first time a striker with a special role appeared on the pitch. It was then that Yugoslavia first heard about the withdrawn striker and I'm pretty sure it was also a first of its kind in the world. And a successful one, too!

'Dragutin Hripko played the role. He played it closer to well than to poorly, but far from ideally. As a footballer he never achieved great quality, but I always spoke about him when asked about a withdrawn

---

[12] *Nemzeti Sport*, 20 February 1944.

striker. He was my lab rat... I can clearly remember how the Loko-motiva players didn't know how to handle him. On that day, the role of a new striker could be played by an average player. That may have been true a little later as well; you could have a mediocre footballer in that role, but afterwards, when teams had read that book, it could only be entrusted to extremely talented individuals.'

There had been prototypes of what today would be known as the false nine before, notably G.O. Smith of the Corinthians in the 1890s, Luis Ravaschino at Independiente in the 1920s and Matias Sindelar with the Austrian Wunderteam of the 1930s, but none had previously pulled the centre-forward so far back that he became a midfielder. This was a huge step in the evolution from W-M to 4–2–4. A Zagreb championship match changed everything.

Bukovi was already loved in Zagreb. He had managed an unofficial independent Croatia during the war and been assistant manager of Yugoslavia. He had won league titles and now he was not merely teaching his players the best of what was happening abroad but leading new developments. Eventually, though, in April 1947, Bukovi decided he had to leave – despite the Dinamo Zagreb directors hiding his passport to try to persuade him to stay[13] – and he returned to Budapest to become manager of the recently refounded MTK.

But Bukovi was far from the only Hungarian great to have survived the war by spending it outside of Hungary.

---

[13] His wife tells the story in *Nemzeti Sport*, 11 February 1983.

CHAPTER THREE

THE CITIZEN OF THE WORLD

IFK Norrköping were relegated out of Allsvenskan, the Swedish top flight, in 1937. It was no great shock; they'd never been a dominant force. This was their second relegation since the national league had been founded in 1924 and they'd never finished higher than sixth. They weren't one of Sweden's bigger sides; they weren't even the biggest side in Norrköping. Their city rivals IF Sleipner had been ever-presents in the top flight and would go on to win the league in 1938, when they provided five of the Sweden squad that went to the World Cup in France.

Relegation may not have been particularly surprising but at an angry AGM the Norrköping members voted to remove the board. The result was chaos. The Swedish football federation (SvFF) demanded an audit because they hadn't been paid the 1,100 kroner they were owed as their share of gate receipts. That investigation revealed debts had risen from 4,000Kr to 13,650Kr while the club was continuing to give players 20Kr per game when the second-flight allowance was 10Kr. As the club faced ruin, the board was ousted and a new one elected.

Norrköping's best player, Torsten Johansson, was named as coach and chairman. He'd made his debut at 17 under the great goalscorer Imre Schlosser, effectively becoming his apprentice. 'He

THE NAMES HEARD LONG AGO

made me as a footballer,' Johansson said. 'I don't know what I had been before his arrival.'

The club treasurer was Carl-Elis Halldén. He was portly and garrulous, had lost an arm to polio and was nicknamed 'Nalle' – 'Teddy Bear'. After a year, Halldén became manager with the outspoken Sigge Andersson, another former player, taking over as treasurer. Between them, the three transformed the club.

IFK Norrköping had been a middle-class club, recruiting players from the local grammar school and often losing them when they left Norrköping to go to university. But Nalle Halldén changed all that. He was regional overseer for Tipsjänst, the state-run football pools, and used local agents, mainly tobacconists, as scouts, collecting reports from local papers and gossip and funnelling them back to him. In 1939–40 IFK Norrköping were promoted and the following season, as they finished seventh, Sleipner were relegated. The balance of power in the town had shifted.

IFK Norrköping decided that to press home their advantage they needed a full-time coach. István Wampetits, the Hungarian manager of Degerfors IF, a former Bocskai player who had managed Debrecen before moving to Sweden in 1937, recommended his fellow-Hungarian Lajos Czeizler.

In 1909, Czeizler, aged 16, had left his home town of Heves to become a banker in Budapest. His background is something of a mystery; extensive research has failed to yield any information about his parents or any siblings, or what religion he was. What is known is that his life changed one morning as he played football in the grass space between two houses on István út. Béla Révész, a coach at MTK, was standing nearby, waiting for a tram that had been delayed, idly watching the game. Three of the players, he thought, including Czeizler, showed promise, and so he took them to the stadium for a trial.

Czeizler signed for the club and played as a goalkeeper in their reserve sides. He was small and slight for a keeper and had notably tiny feet. 'We got kit handed down from the first team,' he said, 'but I was unable to find boots that fit. They were usually three sizes too big and of no more use than galoshes.'

Fortunately, the English forward Joe Lane, who also had small feet, saw Czeizler's predicament and gave him his boots. They were 'used and heavily worn' but 'to me,' Czeizler said, 'they were a godsend and I used them for three years until they totally fell apart.'

Czeizler fought during the First World War, being promoted to lieutenant. He stayed with MTK until 1919 and then, fleeing the turmoil in Budapest, spent a season with SC Germania Schwechat in Austria, playing a handful of games at right-back. He moved to Poland, becoming assistant to Imre Pozsonyi at Cracovia before in 1923 taking over at the Łódź side ŁKS.

Czeizler stayed at ŁKS for five seasons, then went to Italy where he coached Udinese, Faenza, Lazio (as assistant to Ferenc Molnár), Cremonese, Catania and Casale. He returned, in 1935, to ŁKS where he spent two seasons before moving north to Sweden. He did well with Karlskoga IF and Hallstahammars SK, largely in the second flight, and got to know Wampetits who was working at Degerfors, six miles from Karlskoga. He suggested Czeizler should look for a club with greater resources.

Hallstahammar were relegated from Allsvenskan in 1939. 'I became rather disillusioned at Hallstahammar,' Czeizler said, 'but I was approached by Reymersholm in the spring of 1941. They were freshly promoted and negotiated with me and the Austrian Richard Kudelka, who eventually got the job. That was disappointing. Then came the offer from IFK Norrköping, which I happily accepted. We faced Reymersholm in our first league game in 1941–42 and won that battle 5–1. Afterwards I was told that they regretted not choosing me. The reason? They thought I was too old.' He was 48 but, bald and a little pudgy, he probably looked older.

Czeizler was very grateful for the opportunity, well aware of his fortune in finding a neutral country during the war. 'The best gift football gave me,' he said in 1966, 'was that it freed me from the Second World War. It was enough for me to fight in the first one.'[1]

In total Czeizler spent eight years at IFK Norrköping, his longest stay anywhere in a career that would last 44 years. He found a system there that already suited his way of thinking. When Johansson had retired, the club had done away with the attacking centre-half; there was, effectively, a W-M already in place. Czeizler, though, demanded more, pushing the amateur regulations of Swedish football to their limits. He made it a policy to sign almost exclusively players who had been forwards at their previous clubs on the grounds that they tended to be technically more gifted. He would then convert them into whatever position he actually desired.

In Norrköping, Czeizler inherited a goalkeeper in Torsten Lindberg and a stopper centre-half in Einar Stéen who were both physically imposing and were both employed as policemen. Also on Norrköping's police force was the Olympic wrestler Ivar Johansson; it was a common profession for sportspeople who remained technically amateur. Both stayed throughout Czeizler's time at the club, as did the captain and right-half Birger Rosengren, who would arrive at games around quarter of an hour before kick-off on a bicycle, his boots in a cardboard box on the rack above the rear wheel.

'We listened more attentively to Lajos than to the local, Swedish teachers,' said the forward Georg 'Åby' Ericson, who would later coach

---

[1] *Football*, May 1966.

IFK Norrköping himself before leading the Sweden national side at the 1974 and 1978 World Cups. 'It's true that in the 1940s, the skills of Swedish coaches were still in their infancy, but we were impressed by Lajos not for his preparedness, but rather for his humanity... Think about it, in the midst of the Second World War, a citizen of the world appeared among us. A man stepped into a small town in isolated Sweden with a multilingual culture and character, and brought the spiritual treasures of Central and Southern Europe. He presented the masterpieces of Hungarian and Austrian football, talked about Italy and Poland – in other words, he opened our eyes.

'Like simple children we listened to him with our mouths open. Perhaps I was the best at listening, since I was often only the 12th person in the team. But we also influenced Lajos. Especially with our extraordinary work and discipline. Iron discipline reigned and we followed his instructions without fear. And that mentality he liked. And he liked humour more than the whip.'[2]

It worked. In 1942–43, for the first time in their history, IFK Norrköping, helped by Halldén's remorseless pestering of army commanders to release players on match days, won the league.

The following season, as Malmö emerged as a serious force, IFK Norrköping came fourth. Serious action, evidently, was needed. They already had the forward Knut Nordahl but he was a creator rather than an out-and-out finisher so they signed his brother Gunnar, a physically imposing player with a ferocious shot who had scored 58 goals in 77 games across four seasons for Degerfors. IFK persuaded him to leave his job at a steel mill in Degerfors to become a fireman in Norrköping. 'Never chase the ball,' Czeizler told him. 'Stay on the halfway line and conserve your energy. You need it when we attack.'

---

[2] In *Nemzeti Sport*, 6 November 1991.

Nordahl went on to become perhaps the greatest striker in Sweden's history, the only man to be top scorer five times in the Italian top flight. He was in no doubt about the importance of Czeizler to his career. 'I wouldn't call him a magician,' Nordahl wrote in his 1954 autobiography. 'But he was a great man who, for some reason, had chosen to invest his powers and intelligence in football. My admiration for him as a human being and a friend is immense and I am quite certain he would have succeeded and become one of the very best, no matter what he decided to do…

'Lajos does not possess Wampetits's eye for the technical and skilful details but he is on the other hand an astute tactician with some other capabilities that, added together, made him an ideal football coach. Most of all I admire his level-headedness, his ability to stay calm without losing his temper, no matter if we win or lose. Criticism is delivered, yes, but later in the week and in a thoughtful way. He never used big words. He still makes us listen. The man carries an air of respect and we try our very best, just for his sake…

'To me he has become a father figure.'[3]

* * *

IFK Norrköping won the title again in 1944–45 and 1945–46, when they also beat a touring Newcastle side 5–0, as well as drawing 2–2 with Charlton. Beating professionals was a huge psychological step forward for Swedish footballers, even if they did have to acknowledge that English sides, having just come through the war, were a long way from being at their best.

But there were further improvements to be made. Czeizler had spotted the gifted inside-forward Nils Liedholm playing for Sleipner.

---

[3] *Guld och gröna planer* (Bonniers Folkbibliotek, 1954).

The two sides shared Idrottspark, occupying dressing rooms at opposite ends of a corridor. In some training sessions the clubs used one end of the pitch each, so it was easy for Czeizler to monitor Liedholm's progress. Eventually he approached him, telling him he was wasting his time with Sleipner and promising that if he joined IFK he would soon replace the ageing Karl-Erik Grahn of Elfsborg in the national team. Liedholm was flattered but wasn't convinced he would get into the starting XI at IFK Norrköping, so he began plotting.

The man he needed to supplant in the IFK Norrköping line-up was Åby Ericson. Ericson had hurt his knee in 1940 in a game for his regiment but hadn't initially realised how serious the problem was. He didn't see a doctor for three months and when he did he learned he had snapped his posterior cruciate ligament while his cartilage was badly damaged and had to be removed. In the early 1940s, Ericson was a frustrated figure, in constant pain, regularly travelling with the team as a reserve and seemingly only really happy when playing the piano in local vaudeville productions that he himself arranged. In 1944–45, he made 13 appearances but was 12th in the list of appearances made, meaning he missed out on a medal as only 11 were awarded.

'Nils Liedholm wanted me to joined Sleipner,' Ericson explained in his 1977 autobiography. 'We had played a few games together during our military service and it had worked out well. I thought it a good idea... Above all, I thought it would be nice to be a first-team regular.' Players moving between clubs had to go 90 days without playing so Ericson sat out the mandatory period and wrote a letter to Halldén. 'Why did I ever consider leaving the club I loved so much?' he asked.

'It's frightening to be a fringe player. Those awful Sundays when I wasn't even allowed to travel with the team. I wandered aimlessly in Norrköping, knowing exactly what they were up to.[4]

---

[4] Georg Ericson and Åke Stolt, *Inlägg från Åby* (DEWE-Forläget, 1977).

After a few games, though, Liedholm joined IFK Norrköping and Ericson realised he had been the victim of a scam to get him out of the way. Furious, he sat out another 90 days before returning to IFK Norrköping.

* * *

In 1947, after winning a third straight league title and a fourth in five years, IFK Norrköping toured England. The BBC offered short-wave commentary in Swedish and invited the team, in their kit, to the TV studios. Liedholm made his debut against Charlton as the previous inside-right, Knut Nordahl, was shifted to right-back to accommodate him. IFK Norrköping won 3–2. On that tour they also beat Sheffield United 5–2 and, in front of 47,000 at St James' Park, Newcastle 3–2.

The following season, after yet another title, they beat Chelsea 4–1 and Hibs 3–1 in friendlies, drew 4–4 with Austria Vienna and lost 5–1 to the great Dinamo Moscow. Ericson finally became a regular as an ageing side won the title again, although his bad luck struck again as he was injured before the end of the season meaning he collected his medal in a suit. Even worse, he missed the Olympics, at which Sweden took football gold.

The Olympics alerted the rest of the world to Sweden's talent and, within six months, Nils Liedholm and Gunnar Nordahl had both been signed by AC Milan. Waiting for them was their former coach, Lajos Czeizler, who had been appointed at the beginning of the season.

CHAPTER FOUR

THE EXILE

When the war ended, György Orth was in Argentina, managing Rosario Central. His life by then had become that of an unhappy wanderer, moving constantly from club to club, yearning always for home but for one reason or another never quite able to return. He had never really recovered from the knee injury sustained in September 1925 playing for MTK against Wiener Amateure.

He had returned to training early in 1926, slowly and carefully, focusing first on exercises to strengthen the leg. That summer MTK went on tour to Portugal. It could have been Orth's chance to prove he was back, but he went down with tonsillitis and missed most of the tour, although he did score with the injured leg against Vitória. But the world he knew was slipping away. He hated Hungarian football's adoption of professionalism in 1926, feeling it encouraged physical play, placing too high a premium on victory. He struggled to impose himself. Occasionally there would be a trick, a glimmer of what he had been. He was inspired in a 13–1 win for Hungary over France in June 1927, but the margin of victory itself undermined the achievement: this had not been a tough game against tough opponents.

'The best balls from Orth come from his sports shop,' ran the joke in the music halls. He began to study coaching manuals, aware the end was close. Kálmán Konrád had returned from Austria to become the darling of the media. And at MTK there was a new forward, seven years his junior, Jenő Kalmár, who was beginning to challenge for his place. Training became harder and harder. He applied to become a referee but was told that as a professional player he was barred. His marriage to Vilcsi Mihály broke down. Orth became increasingly gloomy and, in 1928, he wrote to Alfréd Brüll, the president of MTK. 'My knee is bad, president, it's impossible to play football with it any more,' he said. 'You know, what it means to me to say this... I've been fighting for three years to get back my old skills... It's not working!'[1]

He offered to work for the club, but neither they nor the MLSZ could find him a role, and so, after getting married again, to another actress, Anna Füzess, a divorcee nine years his senior, he joined Budai 33 as a player-coach. There was one final, glorious performance, directing a 7–0 win over Bástya, but the injury flared before the next match and Orth knew it was over.

In February 1930, a combined MTK-Ferencváros team took on the Czechoslovakian side Teplice at the stadium on Hungária út. Orth, the collar of his overcoat turned up, watched the first half from the back of the stand. At the beginning of the second, he walked wearily down the stairs, pausing every now and again to absorb the scene, and made for the exit. At the gate, he took one final lingering look back. This was his farewell to Hungary. He had decided to accept an offer to become the national coach of Chile.

Hundreds came to the station that night to see him off on the first stage of his journey, an express to Vienna. 'I didn't have any problems at home,' he told waiting journalists. 'I didn't have problems with the business either, but in the shop I always felt that I did not have a talent

---

[1] In Fekete, *Orth és társai*.

for this... I wasn't born to be a salesman... I kept saying that I could *teach* football more enthusiastically than stand behind the counter... I didn't want to be a coach at home, I wanted to become a *football teacher*... They don't need me at home...'

His wife did not go with him; his second divorce was announced the following year. The move was a great wrench, separating him as it did not only from his wife but from his beloved mother, who remained the dominant female presence in his life.

When, early in 1932, his salary was reduced by 20 per cent as the Chilean federation sought to cut costs, Orth immediately threatened to go back home, at which his salary was restored to its original level. There must be a suspicion, though, that he would have welcomed the excuse to return to Budapest. 'Orth is also very popular off the football pitch,' a letter from a Hungarian based in Santiago to *Sporthírlap* noted.[2] 'They wouldn't hold a ball or any kind of social gathering without him. He lives like a small king. He owns a car and is over 100kg but because he is in such good shape, you can't tell. He writes a letter to his mother in Budapest almost every day.' Orth's mother would often take those letters to newspaper offices to pass on her son's gossip.

Orth did return to Hungary in September 1932 and after a few weeks became coach of the Debrecen club Bocskai. But with the economic crisis continuing, he soon decided to accept a job in Italy with Messina. 'My poor son,' his mother said. 'He promised not to leave any more. It's true that I am still a mother and I only feel good when my son is next to me. I am old [she was, probably, 71] and my son is all my support and hope.'[3] A neighbour, Stefánia Beja, to whose daughter Orth was godfather, remembered her complaining,

---

[2] Published 19 March 1932.
[3] *Sporthírlap*, 1 December 1932.

'Oh, Stefike, first the prima donnas took my son away, then foreigners persuaded him to go abroad.'[4]

He was in Messina for only a season. Visiting Milan, he met an Austrian dancer, Anny Elsinger, and she soon became his third wife. They moved on, via Aquila, to Pisa. His mother, travelling with Bocskai as they embarked on a tour of Italy, came to stay. 'He is a very good boy, even trying to read my thoughts,' she said. 'Whenever he gets home, he hugs me, picks me up and dances around the room with me. We are always cheerful when he's at home, playing around all day.'[5] But, homesick, she went home after only a few weeks. She told Beja that she couldn't get used to 'the climate and the greasy food'.[6]

Presumably to his mother's relief, Orth soon went back to Budapest. But his mother had complained of an 'aching stomach' from the moment she returned from Italy. 'She became thinner and thinner,' Beja remembered[7] and died in May 1935, and the following year Orth moved to Germany. As a foreigner, Orth needed an extraordinary coaching permit but after he had been personally recommended by Hans von Tschammer und Osten, the head of the German Reich Commission for Physical Exercise, it was granted and he took charge of Nürnberg on 1 November. They reached the national final in his first season only to lose to Schalke, then got to the play-offs the following year, where they were edged out by the eventual champions Hannover.

Orth left the following November, two years after he had arrived. He and Anny headed across the Atlantic once more as Orth again became manager of Chile. That lasted four months, after which Orth

---

[4] Hámori, *Régi gólok, edzősorsok.*
[5] *Sporthírlap*, 22 December 1932.
[6] Hámori, *Régi gólok, edzősorsok.*
[7] Hámori, *Régi gólok, edzősorsok.*

returned to Europe. In August 1938, he came to Budapest, which was in the grip of a ferocious heatwave that claimed several lives. The great Hungarian racing driver László Hartmann had just been killed in an accident in Tripoli and the general sense of unease as Hitler and Mussolini postured and provoked was heightened by a minor earthquake. Orth stayed at the Hotel Britannia, where MTK used to hold their balls, and where he had met his first wife. But with Budapest on edge, he was soon off again, this time taking a job as manager of Metz.

From Metz he went to Catania and Savona before in 1942, the Chile national team came calling again. Orth spent two years in Santiago, then moved to Argentina with San Lorenzo and Rosario Central, and Mexico with Deportivo Guadalajara and the national side, during which time he seems to have taken Mexican citizenship. In 1947, Ferencváros toured Mexico, and Orth spent almost a month with old friends, most notably the former MTK forward Zoltán Opata who asked if he would consider returning home. 'I don't have anybody in Pest,' he said. 'I have no children and my current wife is Austrian…'

But after that, Orth did start writing to former MTK teammates: Opata, Ferenc Kropacsek, the Konrád brothers and his oldest friend György Molnár. In *Orth és társai*, the journalist Pál Fekete suggests those letters, written in scrupulous, formal Hungarian, were essential in trying to ward off homesickness. 'It is almost as if he hadn't written the lines, his memories of old times and his own adventurous life, to the addressees but to himself,' said Fekete. 'They show how deeply he treasured the almost fading memories which emerged from the depths of his soul one by one. It was often astonishing how precisely this wanderer of the world remembered tiny details – names and events – which almost completely faded in the memory of those living at home.'

But the letters were not happy, and neither was Orth. The sense of weariness that had gripped him following his first move to Vienna never really seems to have gone away. After Mexico, Orth moved on, twice more managing Chile, running a football school connected to Boca Juniors, and then taking on the national side of Colombia. 'He took problems home with him,' said his wife. 'He would put his elbows on the table, lean on them and think hard. He would toss and turn in bed and come up with newer and newer ideas.'

Orth spoke regularly about his desire to return to Hungary and would spend hours trying to tune his radio to hear Hungarian programmes. 'Since we last saw each other at the entrance of Hotel Britannia in 1938 I have travelled half the world,' Orth wrote to Molnár in April 1956. 'Since I didn't like anything any more in Chile, I accepted an interesting job here: besides being a coach I also run a refereeing course; I teach football at colleges and to university students and I prepare the team of the county for the league championship... I feel those 45 years spent in football: if I think of the ball, I feel tired. My wife is tired of housekeeping, and both of us are tired because of the Latin American environment. Cali has a tropical climate and it's not good for us. Our goal is to survive this one year here. And returning to Mexico, to finish with this occupation for good.'

Two months later, he was just as downbeat. 'You say about my photograph that my posture hasn't changed,' he wrote. 'There are a lot of things in which I haven't changed. Mainly in my emotions I haven't! I intend to go to Mexico from here. There I'll see what I want to do. Perhaps – but I don't think so, because I am very bored of this – I will continue to work as a coach for one or two years. But after that they won't be able to take me out to the pitch, not even with a lasso.'

He went to Lima to take charge of the Peru national side but before long he was counting the days till the end of his contract there as well. 'I have been here for 13 and a half months and I am bored to be in one place...' he wrote. 'I have a good life, but I like to wander around – is this supposed to mean that I am not old? No, it isn't. But because I don't have much time left, I wouldn't want to spend my time in one place, but a bit of it here, a bit of it there.'

And yet he was successful, leading Peru in 1957 to their first-ever victory over Argentina and then, in May 1959, to a 4–1 win over England. He had planned to return to Europe but at that the Peruvian football federation (FPF) demanded Orth should sign a new contract. 'Since I wanted to leave and I did not want to stay, I raised my price hoping that they wouldn't accept my offer,' he wrote to Molnár. 'I was wrong! They accepted it! And renewed my contract... I had to cancel my booking for the voyage to Europe... With a heavy heart!'

By December he was regretting it again. 'I think about my resignation more and more often,' Orth wrote to Molnár. 'I think my retirement – making myself retired – should occur in 1964–65. Perhaps as two old smokers we could celebrate it together.' He liked the money and the security the job brought, though; by his own admission the spontaneous generosity he had shown as a child became a penny-pinching caution later in life.

In August 1960, Orth did at last return to Europe as Peru qualified for the football tournament at the Rome Olympics. By chance, they were drawn in a group with Hungary, whom they faced in Naples on 29 August. The two teams travelled down from Rome on the same train, and Orth spent most of his time with the Hungarians, reminiscing, telling jokes and stories. He had been given leave by the FPF to stay in Europe for three months after the Olympics and arranged with Hungarian officials, including Gyula Hegyi and Sándor Barcs, finally to visit Pest again.

But at the beginning of October, the MLSZ received a letter from Vienna, where Orth was staying with his brother-in-law. 'Neither my wife nor I are in an acceptable condition health-wise and physically speaking...' he wrote. 'The unusually cold and rainy autumn weather has taken its toll on both of us... I'm afraid, more serious consequences may follow and I'm suffering from such a lumbago that I can't walk straight... I need to take care of myself lest I be confined to bed for a long time.'

Anny, though, remembered no such illness when asked by Hámori. She recalled how her husband 'happily ran to the embassy' to get the visa after meeting the Hungarians on the train. They were on their way to Budapest when they stopped in Vienna, at which he had second thoughts '"But why?" I asked him. "You were looking forward to this day so much!" He didn't give me a reason, his only answer was, "Depression."'[8] The Budapest of 1960, of course, was very different to the Budapest he had last visited in 1938, but you wonder what other reasons were at work. Was it that he could not bear to visit a city with so many reminders of his mother, or was it his own past he couldn't face, the ghosts of his own greatness?

Orth went back to Peru but by the time he got there, the public mood had turned against him. They had gone out in the group stage of the Olympics and Orth had been blamed, particularly for his fraternising with the Hungarians, who had ended up beating Peru 6–2. 'The newspapers don't see things the right way,' he wrote to Molnár. 'They don't see that nothing more could be expected of this team. In cases like this, it's always the coach who is at fault.'

Disillusioned and physically run-down, his taste for Europe rekindled by his break, Orth accepted when the Lisbon-based club

---

[8] In Hámori, *Régi gólok, edzősorsok.*

Sporting offered him the manager's job in 1961. He and his wife crossed the Atlantic again but by the time they arrived, a new president had replaced the one who had offered him a job and had already appointed as coach the Brazilian Otto Glória. The new president did, though, acknowledge that Orth's contract was valid, so arranged for him to become manager of Porto on a lower salary, while Sporting made up the difference.

His former MTK teammate Béla Guttmann, who 40 years earlier had nearly persuaded him to join Hakoah, was manager of Benfica at the time, and the two became close. 'I spend a lot of time with Béla Guttmann,' Orth wrote to Molnár. 'He often calls me on the phone, but on these occasions it's always him that speaks...'

He began to talk again of visiting Budapest, but his health continued to deteriorate. 'I almost forgot: I had a pain in my chest,' he wrote to Molnár. 'I think it's my heart. I was examined and told that it's nothing. They said I had a bad cold and I'm getting injections. I don't know where I could have caught this, I do take care of myself... Guttmann had warned me of the danger after he got rheumatism in his shoulder.'

On 8 January 1962, Orth went to Lisbon for a television interview. He had lunch with Guttmann beforehand and told him he had a pain in his chest, the result, he thought, of bronchitis. Guttmann urged him to quit smoking. The following day, Orth returned to Porto, seemingly recovered. On 11 January, he took training, came home and took the dogs for a walk. He returned saying he felt unwell, but nonetheless went out for a haircut. When he got back, he was exhausted and sweating. Anny put him to bed but soon after, he suffered a heart attack. 'If I recover,' he told his wife, 'I will never smoke another cigarette.'

Those were his last words; within a few minutes, Orth was dead, aged just 60. He had not been home for 22 years.

CHAPTER FIVE
THE GOLDEN HARVEST

Richárd Weisz was a big man. He had won an Olympic wrestling gold in 1908, had been national champion seven times in a row and had also won four national weightlifting titles. In a photograph from 1905, he looks like a stereotypical strongman from the previous century, with an upturned moustache above a vast slab of chest. He survived the war in the Budapest ghetto and, after the Soviet invasion, he gathered together a number of other former MTK members and set about re-establishing the club.

There were a number of difficulties, even beyond the fact that a large number of MTK's members had been killed. Weisz himself died in December 1945, aged 66, but he at least lived long enough to see the re-formed football section of the club complete their first league season back after dissolution, finishing sixth.

Another issue was finding somewhere to play after their ground had been confiscated. As the surviving members set about building a new home, the football section played at Ferencváros's stadium, old rivalries left aside. Barely had it been completed when the stadium was seized once again by the state as the Communists ruled in 1949 that all football clubs should be nationalised.

For many clubs that was a decision that eased profound financial difficulties, but it also meant huge upheaval. Some were elevated, some repressed, and the identities that had been forged before the war were blurred. Ferencváros, with their perceived inclination to the right, were deemed particularly suspect and there was a deliberate attempt on the part of the authorities to downgrade them. Although they had won the league in 1949, on 16 February 1950 Ferencváros were taken over by the state food workers union, ÉDOSZ, taking on their name and losing their green-and-white colours. A year later the club was renamed again, as Kinizsi, after a great warrior of the late 15th century.

MTK, meanwhile, initially became Textiles, named for the union that supported it, and then, as the ÁVH took an interest, Budapest Bástya [Bastion]. They went through a spell of being Textiles again, before settling on Vörös Lobogó [Red Banner] until 1956, when they reverted to MTK.

Without question, the biggest beneficiaries of the upheaval were Kispest. The club had been formed in 1908 when Kispest had still been a small town separate from Budapest and their only success had been the Hungarian Cup in 1925–26. They'd produced two players for the Hungary squad at the 1934 World Cup, but were never a big club. The emergence of Ferenc Puskás and József Bozsik, both of whom made their debuts in 1943, had raised the level and from the end of the war they hadn't finished outside the top four when, in 1949, they were taken over by the Hungarian Ministry of Defence to become the army team. They were renamed Honvéd, literally 'defender of the homeland' but also the word for a private in the army.

Gusztáv Sebes, who had been appointed national coach in 1949, succeeding Tibor Gallowich after a brief period when the team was run by a three-man committee of which he had been part, had seen how the great Italy side of the 1930s had been largely built around one club and, given the opportunity by nationalisation, wanted to impose a similar structure in Hungary. Honvéd, in not being part of the traditional elite while having in Puskás and Bozsik two young players who would form the basis of his side, were the perfect choice.

Sebes was similarly well suited to his role. The son of a cobbler, he had worked as a union organiser in Budapest and then at the Renault factory in Paris before returning to Hungary in 1927 and spending 13 years as a player at MTK, taking over briefly as coach after Gyula Feldmann's stroke in 1940.

His managerial expertise, though, was always more in leadership than in tactical detail. He was a politician and an organiser rather than somebody naturally at home on the training field or the bench – which, arguably, is exactly what Hungary needed at that time; it's hard to imagine somebody as blunt as Márton Bukovi or as volatile as Béla Guttmann, for all their genius, being able to navigate the various Communist Party committees. 'Sebes,' said the MTK and Hungary forward Mihály Vasas, 'would never have been a coach if he had not been at Honvéd with those players. He got really lucky.'

In 1946 Sebes was named head of the Hungarian coaches authority and two years later he became chairman of the Hungarian Olympic Committee. He was, Marika Lantos insisted, 'a committed socialist': there was no artifice or cynicism about his leftist rhetoric, which meant that he had very clear ideas about how people should behave and how things should be done.

On one occasion, for instance, he supposedly took the MTK winger Károly Sándor aside and told him that if his wife were a properly socialist woman she would wear less lipstick. Sándor, a skilful individualist with a reputation for speaking his mind, retorted that his wife's make-up was none of Sebes's business which, it's said, was one of the reasons Sebes was reluctant to select him.

That said, Sándor also had a reputation for self-indulgence on the pitch, a love of tricks that didn't fit the team ethic Sebes was always so keen to drive. 'Sándor didn't drink,' said his former MTK teammate László Bödör. 'He wasn't sociable. He sometimes left training and went to the racetrack. He loved gambling on horses and cards. Technically, he could do anything, but he was very individualistic. That's why he didn't play for the national team.'

Besides, there are also examples of Sebes being tolerant of the views of others. At the 1954 World Cup, for instance, players were allowed to take their wives to the final in Bern. Lantos was unmarried so took his mother. 'A lot of the women,' his future wife Marika said, 'were religious and took the opportunity to go to church in Switzerland. [Lantos] was about to go in when he saw Sebes. They stepped back, but Sebes was adamant they should enter. He told them he didn't believe in God but that he also didn't judge and that they should go in.'

And Sebes remained, always, fundamentally a football man, as Tibor Nyilasi, the great Ferencváros and Hungary forward of the 1970s, recalled. 'When I was a kid,' he said, 'Sebes lived in the same area of Budapest as me. He would come down to the square where I played football with my friends, and take us up to his flat, give us sandwiches, and show us Super-8 films of [old Hungary] games. It was him who recommended me to Ferencváros. He was like a grandfather. He only lived for football. In the hard times of the 1950s his voice was heard in important circles.'

Sebes's organisational skills and political acumen were vital. Shortly after taking the national team job, Sebes realised he needed a central defender who was both physically powerful and capable of playing the ball out from the back. Hungary had just such a player, the Vasas defender Gyula Lóránt. Unfortunately, he had been caught in March 1949 with three other players trying to follow his former teammate László Kubala in defecting to the West and was imprisoned in the Kistarcsa Central Internment Camp. Before a game away to Austria that October, though, Sebes appealed to the Interior Minister János Kádár for clemency, giving his personal guarantee that Lóránt would not abscond while in Vienna. Kádár was persuaded, and Lóránt played brilliantly as Hungary beat their neighbours for the first time in 12 years.

As the army club, Honvéd could conscript whomever they wanted and accordingly brought in Sándor Kocsis, Zoltán Czibor and László Budai from Ferencváros, Gyula Lóránt from Vasas and the goalkeeper Gyula Grosics from Teherfuvar. Sebes was effectively able to use Honvéd as a training ground for the national side.

Honvéd won five of the seven championships after nationalisation, with the other two going to Bukovi's MTK, but of far greater significance was what Sebes was able to achieve at national level. The Hungary side of the early 1950s, the *Aranycsapat*, was one of those rare examples of a generation flowering together. It wasn't just that there was a handful of exceptional players, it was that they fitted together, complementing one another's abilities – a process facilitated by the fact so many of them had been collected at one club so they could train together on a daily basis.

And at the heart of the side was Puskás, one of the all-time greats of the game. He was chubby and one-footed, but as his supporters have always said, if you have a left foot that good, why would you use your right? He frequently over-indulged off the pitch, but that was part of his charm. He wasn't some impossible Adonis, living on another plane of athletic possibility, he was an everyman who brought joy and lived joyously despite the privations of the Hungary in which he grew up. There are countless stories of his behaviour after matches, from the England captain Billy Wright watching in awe as he demolished a cheeseboard to his night out in Glasgow with the brilliant but dissolute Scotland inside-forward Jim Baxter that ended with Puskás exercising his passion for 'visky' and 'jiggy-jig' in a scullery at a house party in Drumchapel.

That *joie de vivre* was summed up by his nickname '*Öcsi*' – 'kid'. It was seemingly bestowed by the forward Gyula Zsengellér, who was a great friend of Puskás's father. Although they played for different clubs, Zsengellér at Újpest and Puskás senior at Kispest, they would meet up on Mondays, which was always a rest day after match day on the Sunday, to have a hot bath and drink wine. Zsengellér would often run out of money for the tram and end up having to walk the eight miles back from Kispest. Zsengellér played alongside his friend's son when he received his first call-up for the national side as an 18-year-old against Austria in August 1945 and laid on a tap-in for his first international goal. As he played the pass, he supposedly said, 'Go on, *Öcsi*, knock it in.' Because it seemed so fitting for Puskás's cheek and vivacity, the name stuck.

Cocky and confident as he was, there was also a naivety about the young Puskás. Before another friendly against Austria in Vienna in 1946, for instance, the players were given bananas. Puskás had never seen one before so when he saw Zsengellér pretending to eat one without peeling it first, he was taken in and took a large bite, before spitting it out, cursing his father's friend.

He would learn and before long was the centre of dressing-room banter, not only teasing his teammates but also even the most senior politicians. At one national team retreat on Margitsziget, for instance, he saw the Minister of Defence, Mihály Farkas, dressed in a white general's uniform and said, 'I thought you were the ice cream boy arrived at last.' Everybody else there held their breath – Farkas was, after all, one of the main architects of Rákosi's repression. But the general just laughed: Puskás could say what he liked.

It would be wrong, though, to assume that just because he was cheery and relaxed, Puskás did not think about the game, or was merely a turner of tricks blessed with an extraordinary left foot. He was exceptionally technically gifted, of course, but what made him quite so important to the *Aranycsapat* was his tactical brain. 'If a good player has the ball, he should have the vision to spot three options,' the right-back Jenő Buzánszky said. 'Puskás always saw at least five.'

Perhaps recognising his own lack of tactical nous, in 1949, Sebes appointed the former MTK full-back Gyula Mándi as his assistant. Mándi had retired as a player in 1937, with ten league titles and 32 international caps to his name. That he had survived the war was thanks in no small part to his brother-in-law, György Szomolányi.

Szomolányi was the managing director of a paper mill that was converted to produce the wooden stocks for rifles and had a certain latitude in whom he was able to employ. In 1942, he saved Mándi from a Jewish labour detail by giving him papers to work in the factory. Two years later, though, Mándi couldn't avoid labour service. Finding himself bound for Ukraine, he scribbled a postcard to Szomolányi and threw it from the train taking him east. Somebody found it and posted it but when it arrived, it was torn, and all that could be made out was the word 'KELPUSZTA'. Szomolányi realised this must be Ekelpuszta, where there was a transit camp. He put on his officer's uniform from the First World War, strode into the camp and insisted he needed five men for an essential task. Impressed by his air of authority, the guards told him to take his pick. Szomolányi selected

Mándi and four others, including the elderly husband of a sister of Mándi's wife. He, though, refused to go, nominating instead a young father of four. He was never heard from again.

Having survived the war, Mándi became coach of the lower league side Ganz TE, and also set up a shop in Budapest selling shirts. He had been noted as a player for his positional sense and that translated as a manager into tactical acuity. Bukovi was too much his own man to work alongside Sebes but Mándi, aware of the need to support his family and with far less of a coaching pedigree, was happy to operate as Sebes's assistant.

The partnership worked. Hungary suffered a 5–3 defeat in a friendly against Austria on 14 May 1950, after which they won nine games and drew one in the build-up to the 1952 Olympics. Hungary had competed once in the Olympic football since the embarrassment against Egypt in 1924, losing their only game 3–0 against Poland in 1936, but Communism had given them a huge advantage: all their players were technically amateur and so they were able to select their strongest possible squad. Between 1952 and 1980, every Olympic gold medallist in men's football was Communist – and after France triumphed in Los Angeles in 1984, the USSR won it again in 1988.

Mándi received his official suit for the Games, but at the last moment he was refused permission to travel after it was decided his shirt shop made him an agent of private enterprise. Nonetheless, Sebes telephoned him every day for tactical advice. Hungary beat Romania, Italy and Turkey before facing the defending champions Sweden in the semi-final. They hammered them, 6–0. 'It was one of those days,' said Puskás, who scored the opening goal. 'Once we'd hit our rhythm we were virtually irresistible.'[1]

---

[1] In *Puskás on Puskás*, ed. Rogan Taylor (Robson, 1998).

In the final, they faced Yugoslavia, who had beaten the USSR after a replay in the first round. Tito's government had manoeuvred itself into a position of independence from Moscow, inflating the political tension to the extent that when the USSR had lost to Yugoslavia in the first round, the defeat had so enraged Stalin that he disbanded the CDKA side that had provided the bulk of the squad. Sebes, similarly, on the morning of the final received a telephone call from Rákosi warning him that defeat could not be tolerated.

But Hungary were unstoppable. In front of 58,000 in Helsinki, late goals from Puskás and Czibor gave Hungary a 2–0 win. 'At that time,' Buzánszky said, 'Miss Universe was a Finnish woman.[2] In itself receiving the gold medal was a wonderful feeling, but it was a great bonus to have Miss Universe handing over an olive branch and giving us a kiss. I was so overcome with the moment I had to look in the paper the next day to see if she really was as beautiful as I remembered.'

It was the semi-final, though, that stood out. Sir Stanley Rous, the president of the Football Association, had been so impressed that he had offered Sebes a friendly against England. That was still regarded as a great honour, but when Sebes reported the approach to the MLSZ, he was told that Rákosi was concerned by the possibility of defeat. Nonetheless, when European football federation leaders met late in 1952, a friendly was arranged for November 1953.

By the time of the meeting, Hungary were even better than they had been at the Olympics, having made a vital change to their line-up. That September, Hungary played Switzerland in Bern in the Dr Gerő Cup, a tournament for central European national teams that ran between 1927 and 1960. Having gone 2–0 down early on, Sebes brought on Nándor Hidegkuti to replace his MTK teammate Péter

---

[2] The 17-year-old Armi Kuusela had won the inaugural Miss Universe contest in Long Beach, California five weeks earlier.

Palotás. By half-time, Hungary were level; they went on to win 4–2. Hidegkuti got the fourth, but it was his general involvement, the way he dropped deep to link with the midfield and facilitate the interplay of the other forwards, that made him undroppable.

Having Hidegkuti operate as a withdrawn centre-forward, of course, was Bukovi's innovation. At MTK, he had had the muscular Romanian Norbert Höfling as his centre-forward, but when he was sold to Lazio in 1949, Bukovi reverted to the deep-lying centre-forward system he had used in Zagreb. 'The centre-forward was having increasing difficulties with a marker around his neck,' Hidegkuti explained. 'So the idea emerged to play the No. 9 deeper where there was some space.

'At wing-half in the MTK side was a fine attacking player with very accurate distribution: Péter Palotás. Péter had never had a hard shot, but he was never expected to score goals, and though he wore the No. 9 shirt, he continued to play his natural game. Positioning himself in midfield, Péter collected passes from his defence, and simply kept his wingers and inside-forwards well supplied with passes... With Palotás withdrawing from centre-forward his play clashed with that of the wing-halves, so inevitably one was withdrawn to play a tight defensive game, while the other linked with Palotás as midfield foragers.'[3]

Hidegkuti, it turned out, was even better suited to the role. Puskás may have been the greatest player in that Hungary side, but it was Hidegkuti and his capacity to enact Bukovi's re-imagining of the role of the centre-forward that made Hungary so difficult to play against. 'Hidegkuti had a special type of intelligence and excellent technical ability,' said his MTK teammate László Bödör. 'He could always

---

[3] In Stratton Smith and Eric Batty, *International Coaching Book* (Souvenir, 1966).

control the ball and see the spot on the pitch to go to. He was good in the air and on the ground and was a great finisher. He could score goals from positions others would never have dreamed of. Finishing is an innate ability; it can't be learned. Hidegkuti adapted to the deep situation. He couldn't score so many goals playing that way but he created space for the inside-forwards.'

Hungary played eight further games between the Switzerland win and the trip to Wembley, winning six and drawing two, but it was England that dominated Sebes's thoughts. They may have lost embarrassingly to the USA at the 1950 World Cup, and they may have been left behind by tactical evolution, hobbled by a conservatism rooted in their veneration of the winger, but England was still the mother of football, still the country that gave the game to the world. And at home, they remained unbeaten against continental opposition; even away they had hammered the reigning world champions Italy, a team featuring seven players from Erbstein's Torino, 4–0 in 1948.[4] And they had world-renowned players, such as Stanley Matthews, who had reached his apotheosis six months before the Hungary game by inspiring Blackpool to victory in the FA Cup final, and Stan Mortensen, who had scored a hat-trick in that game.

Sebes was meticulous in his preparation, using Honvéd as a training ground and exploiting the political situation to demand that opponents in the league adopted 'English' characteristics when playing his side. 'His role,' Buzánszky said, 'was absolutely decisive. It was like arranging cogs in a wheel – everything had to fit.'

He wanted to ensure that nothing could surprise his players. 'Sebes got hold of some English footballs,' Buzánszky went on, 'so we could get used to the kind of ball that absorbed moisture and

---

[4] For more on that game, arguably England's greatest ever performance, see my book *The Anatomy of England*.

got heavier as the game went on. He also knew the Wembley pitch was 74 metres across, and widened the pitch at one of our training grounds so we could get used to Wembley's dimensions.' He even used smoke machines to replicate the fog for which London was at the time notorious.

On 15 November 1953, ten days before the game at Wembley, Hungary used the English balls for a friendly in Budapest against Sweden. They were poor, and could only draw 2–2. Troubled by that performance and the impact a hugely critical reaction in the Hungarian media could have on confidence, Sebes changed his travel plans and decided that rather than flying to London, the squad would travel by train, stopping off in Paris on the way for a warm-up game against the works team of the Renault factory where he had worked before the war. 'It was a big boost for morale,' Buzánszky recalled. 'We won 18–0 and that proved to us that we weren't that bad.'

England, meanwhile, had selection problems. Only three players – Billy Wright, Matthews and Mortensen – remained from the side that had demolished Italy five years earlier. Tom Finney was injured, Tommy Lawton was 34, Wilf Mannion was 35 and Neil Franklin had broken his contract to go and play in the rebel league in Colombia. George Robb, who had played at the 1952 Olympics, came in for Finney on the left, while Ernie Taylor was included at inside-right to link between his two Blackpool teammates, Matthews and Mortensen, at right-wing and centre-forward respectively. With hindsight, it looks a slow, unbalanced side.

Their preparation had been no more impressive than Hungary's: a late equaliser salvaged a draw against a Rest of the World XI in October, and then a drab 3–1 win over Northern Ireland in the Home Championship. Most significantly, the Rest of the World had troubled England by deploying Gunnar Nordahl as a deep-lying centre-forward, a gambit that left the England centre-half Derek Ufton 'a fish out of water', as the Austrian journalist Willy Meisl put it, [5] much as José Lacasia had confounded Harry Johnston two years earlier when Argentina had beaten England 3–1 in a representative game in Buenos Aires.

But Hungary felt no great confidence. Sebes had tried to relax his players the evening before the game by taking them to a revue theatre to see *Pardon My French*. 'If you want to see girls in feathers, sequins and spectacular settings,' as the *Mirror* put it, 'they are all here. And if you want girls without the feathers and sequins, they are here, too.'[6]

Tension, though, remained high. 'There was great anxiety on the bus before the game,' said the Újpest defender Pál Várhidi, who was on the bench that day. 'Before other matches players would chat with each other, but this time there was silence.' They were more advanced than England, though, in almost every way. Where England's warm-up consisted of some desultory stretches and a few potshots at the goalkeeper, Hungary had an energetic routine. It may look rudimentary by today's standards, but at the time it was revolutionary, and perhaps explains why Hungary so often raced into early leads in games.

Their kit, too, was much more modern than England's. 'When we walked out at Wembley that afternoon, side by side with the visiting team,' said the England captain Billy Wright, 'I looked down and noticed that the Hungarians had on these strange, lightweight boots, cut away like slippers under the ankle bone. I turned to big

---

[5] In his book *Soccer Revolution*. Willy Meisl was the brother of the Hugo Meisl, who had run the Austrian game before the Second World War. He had migrated to the UK in 1934 and was a devout Anglophile, if perennially frustrated by the insularity and conservatism of England's football establishment.

[6] The *Daily Mirror*, 25 November 1953.

Stan Mortensen and said, "We should be all right here, Stan, they haven't got the proper kit."' Perhaps the Hungarian boots wouldn't have worked had their game been based on thumping their way through the quagmire of an English league pitch in February, but it was not; it was based on technique, passing and speed of thought, all the ideals promoted at MTK in the years immediately after the First World War.

It took Hungary just 45 seconds to score, Bozsik laying in Hidegkuti to give Hungary the lead. Jackie Sewell levelled, but Hidegkuti soon added his second before Puskás got the game's most famous goal, taking Zoltán Czibor's cross on the edge of the six-yard box before dragging the ball away from Wright's attempted challenge, slamming the ball home as the England captain hurtled past 'like a fire-engine heading to the wrong fire', as Geoffrey Green put it in *The Times*.[7] A deflected Bozsik free kick made it 4–1 and Mortensen pulled one back to make it 4–2 at half-time.

But 4–2 was no reflection of the play; Hungary had been utterly dominant, with Hidegkuti pulling away from Harry Johnston, the England centre-back, to control the game from a deep-lying centre-forward position. Just as England had been unable to deal with Lacasia and Nordahl, they had been unable to deal with Hidegkuti. 'To me,' Harry Johnston, the England centre-back, wrote in his autobiography, 'the tragedy was the utter helplessness ... being unable to do anything to alter the grim outlook.'[8] If he had followed Hidegkuti, it would have left a huge hole in the middle of the back line; by leaving him, it meant Hidegkuti was free to create the play. The W-M, at least as practised by England, was too inflexible to cope when opponents didn't match up with a similar formation.

---

[7] *The Times*, 26 November 1953.
[8] *The Rocky Road to Wembley* (Sportsmans Book Club, 1954).

Bozsik knocked in a fifth soon after half-time before Hidegkuti completed his hat-trick with a smart volley from Puskás's lobbed cross. Alf Ramsey converted a penalty to make it 6–3, but the truth is that Hungary could have scored more if they hadn't eased off, spending long periods of the second half playing keep-ball as England chased vainly after them. 'To be honest,' Buzánszky said, 'Kocsis was nowhere near his best. If he had shown his real form, the result would have been even more cruel.'

The symbolism was lost on nobody: modern, vibrant, Communist Hungary had gone to the Empire Stadium, whose design consciously evoked Lutyens's work in New Delhi, the jewel of the Empire, and had devastated any lingering thought of English superiority. Sebes insisted his side played 'socialist' football, and it was the case that their success stemmed from their teamwork and their capacity to interchange position, a clear contrast to the rigidity and individualism of England. In the stands sat Jimmy Hogan, a guest of honour of the Hungarians. For him, a visionary rejected in his own land, this was a vindication in which he took little pleasure. 'We played football as Jimmy Hogan taught us,' said Sebes. 'When our football history is told, his name should be written in gold letters.'[9]

But the symbolism was perhaps not entirely apt. Grosics, for one, was uncomfortable with the attempt to marry football to ideology. 'Football cannot be named after political systems,' he said. 'It is true that the political leadership in Hungary fully exploited our success for their own good, but it would be going too far to say that Communism or the socialist system had anything to do with the Hungarian success.' Nationalisation had made Sebes's job easier and

[9] Taylor, *Puskás on Puskás*.

was of undeniable short-term benefit to the national side; the long-term consequences for Hungarian football as a whole were rather less beneficial.

And besides, the belief that Communism represented an exciting step into modernity was becoming increasingly difficult to maintain. The Five-Year Plan that Rákosi, aping Stalin, had announced in 1950, which sought to increase industrial output by 380 per cent, had no chance of success. Even if the goals hadn't been impossibly ambitious, Hungary was exporting large quantities of raw materials to the USSR and was paying war reparations of around a fifth of the annual national income, while the purges had savaged Hungary's professional classes. The early 1950s saw a marked fall in the Hungarian standard of living: by 1949 disposable income had reached 90 per cent of the level it had been at in 1938 but by 1952 it had fallen back to roughly two-thirds.[10] Even if people had had money, there was little in the shops to buy, with major shortages of bread, sugar, flour and meat.[11]

Under Rákosi, thousands had been arrested and either executed or sent to camps. Education had been thoroughly politicised and the role of religion diminished. Hungary in the early 1950s endured a brutally repressive regime.

Stalin's death on 5 March 1953, though, changed the atmosphere. Rákosi, like Stalin, had generated around him a cult of personality and, as one crumbled, so the other didn't seem quite so secure. Communist leaders in Moscow, particularly Georgy Malenkov, who was Stalin's immediate successor, recognised Rákosi's unpopularity

---

[10] Figures from 'The Transformation of the Hungarian Economy', a paper prepared by the Institute for the History of the Hungary Revolution (2003).

[11] Sándor Bognár, Iván Pető and Sándor Szakács, *A hazai gazdaság négy évtizedének története 1945–1985* (Közgazdasági és Jogi Könyvkiadó, 1985).

and ordered him to stand down for Imre Nagy. Like Rákosi, Nagy had been taken prisoner in the First World War and had become a Communist in Russia. He had returned to Hungary in 1921, but on another visit to Russia in 1930, he had rejoined the Communist Party. He later became a Soviet citizen while working in the Soviet Statistical Service. Nagy returned to Hungary after the Second World War and served as Minister of the Interior under Tildy. After the Communist takeover he was appointed Minister for Agriculture and Speaker of the National Assembly.

Nagy accordingly took over as prime minister, but Rákosi stayed on as general secretary of the Hungarian Working People's Party, leading to a rancorous power struggle as Nagy imposed a series of reforms. He slightly relaxed state control over the economy, reduced taxes and quotas for peasants and increased the production and distribution of consumer goods. At the same time he released thousands of political prisoners and reduced the power of the ÁVH.

Six months after thrashing England, Hungary did it again, this time at home in the Népstadion in Budapest. Football was fulfilling its role in making Hungarians feel good about themselves. England, mystifyingly, made no move to counter Hidegkuti and were beaten even more convincingly, 7–1 this time. Over a million Hungarians applied for tickets for the game and although the official attendance was a touch over 105,000, it was likely even more packed in. There were even stories of spectators in the ground using carrier pigeons to send their tickets back to friends and relatives outside.

'In a way 1954 was more important because it proved what had happened at Wembley was not just chance,' Grosics said. 'Never before or since has there been such interest in Hungary in one match. In those days of dictatorship, it was football that united people in Hungary with the 5 million Hungarians living outside the borders.

There was a feeling of togetherness in the Hungarian nation, something to grab hold of and tie ourselves to.'

It wouldn't last.

CHAPTER SIX

THE HIGHEST LEVEL

Superga was a disaster from which Torino have never recovered. Having had to rebuild their entire squad, it was a remarkable achievement even to finish sixth, as they did in 1949–50. Juventus, their city rivals, ran away with the title, finished five points clear of Lajos Czeizler's Milan, and 21 clear of Torino. For a while, though, Béla Guttmann's Padova kept pace with them. A third of the way through the season, Padova were second in the table, but after a 2–0 defeat to Juventus in December, they collapsed, at one point in the spring losing eight in a row. When they lost again to Juventus to slide to 15th, Guttmann was dismissed, with the club accusing him of having taken a kickback to sign the Yugoslav goalkeeper Zvonko Monsider. Guttmann sued – unsuccessfully – and his licence was suspended by the FIGC while the case was investigated. Mariann, his wife, was so upset by the stress that she briefly returned to Vienna.

Guttmann took charge of Unione Triestina in the summer of 1950. It was not a much sought-after position. Financial pressures led to the bulk of the first-team squad being sold off before the start of the season and one director supposedly said that anybody who could keep the squad that remained in Serie A deserved a statue. Guttmann's side began well with a 2–2 draw at Juventus and early wins over Torino and Roma. A familiar pattern began to emerge, though, as good autumn form fell away as the season went on. There was a run of ten games without a win and only a victory over Novara on the final day kept Triestina up. Cleared of wrongdoing over the Monsider signing by the FIGC, Guttmann signed an improved contract that summer but he was sacked in November after a 1–0 defeat to Torino left Triestina second bottom of the table. Once again, he would be helped out by an old friend.

* * *

For Imre Hirschl, winning the Argentinian double at River Plate in 1936 had been a high he could never repeat. After leaving the club in 1938, he returned briefly to Gimnasia, then cycled through jobs before, in 1943, there came an incident that forced him to leave Argentina.

A disciplinary meeting of the Argentinian Football Association held on 13 January 1944 found that Florencio Sola,[1] the president of Banfield, had used Hirschl as an intermediary in an attempt to bribe the Ferro Carril Oeste goalkeeper Sebastián Gualco[2] with 2,000 pesos before a game between Banfield and Ferro in September 1943 (it finished 1–1 and Gualco didn't play). Hirschl was one of nine men convicted of 'amoralidad deportiva' – sporting immorality – and give a permanent suspension from any direct or indirect activity with AFA or clubs affiliated to AFA. The ban was overturned by the General Inspection of Justice on 10 May that year, but sufficient stigma remained that it would be six years before he could return to Argentinian football.

Hirschl had been working with a group that helped new arrivals from Europe, and through that work met Heddy Steinberg, who had been born in Budapest in 1917. Her father, Oskar, committed suicide

---

[1] Banfield's stadium is named after him.

[2] His middle name, inappropriately enough, was Inocencio.

in 1924, while her mother, Paula, emigrated with her. Hirschl married Heddy in 1939. As well as his daughter Gabriela, they had a son, Tomas, born in 1958. He died in a car accident in Buenos Aires in 1996.

It's not clear whether Hirschl had ever formally divorced Erzsébet after her return to Budapest, or whether the fact they lived 7,500 miles apart was seen as separation enough. After the death of their son, Péter, in 1940,[3] Erzsébet stayed on Semmelweis utca with György Scheer, a jeweller who had married one of the two daughters of Erzsébet's sister Irén, who had died from heart problems in 1926, and Irén's husband Sándor Spitzer, who had been a witness at Erzsébet and Imre's wedding. Erzsébet survived the war and died in 1971.

Banned in Argentina, Hirschl went first to Brazil, where he managed Cruzeiro, and spent the rest of the decade as an itinerant coach, never staying anywhere long, never really able to impose his ideas. But then, in 1949, he was named manager of the Uruguayan club Peñarol, who had first tried to appoint him nine years earlier.

Peñarol were one of the two great clubs of Uruguay – only they and their great rivals Nacional had won the league since the introduction of professionalism in 1932, but by 1949 they were at a low ebb. Nacional had won the league in 1946 and 1947, meaning they had won six of the previous eight championships, and Peñarol's appointment of the English coach Randolph Galloway[4] in 1948 had proved unpopular. He had tried to impose the W-M, but Peñarol, with their

---

[3] And possibly before; the records are unclear.

[4] Galloway was one of the diaspora of British managers in the early to middle part of the 20th century. Born in Sunderland in 1896, he had served in the army, playing rugby and winning various sprint contests before switching to football, playing as a centre-forward for Derby County, Nottingham Forest, Luton, Coventry and Tottenham before, in 1929, setting off for Spain where he became coach of Sporting Gijón. He had a stint at Racing Santander, returned home and lived in Nottinghamshire with his wife, before taking off in 1946 to become manager of Costa Rica. More details are provided in Rory Smith's book *Mister!*

slow defenders and preference for zonal marking, struggled to adapt. Although they won 15 out of 19 games in 1948 before a players' strike brought a premature end to the season, both fans and certain senior players were unconvinced.

Hirschl arrived to great excitement, with 1,500 fans turning up to watch his first training session, held on 8 May 1949. He gathered together 40 players from the senior, reserve and youth squads and slowly made his selection. To widespread surprise, at the final training session before the first friendly of the season, he told directors that he was planning to give a debut to the rapid 22-year-old winger Alcides Ghiggia, preferring him to a couple of forwards with national team experience.[5]

Ghiggia would become a revelation on the right of the fabled *'escuadrilla de la muerta'* [the death squad] forward line: Ghiggia, Hohberg, Míguez, Schiaffino, Vidal. That side, known as *la Máquina* [the Machine] – seven years after the River Plate team built on the foundations Hirschl had left garnered the same nickname, celebrating the sense of the team being a finely tuned mechanism in which every cog had its role – passed undefeated through 1949, winning all three domestic competitions, their superiority symbolised by the *clásico de la fuga* [derby of flight] in October when Nacional, losing 2–0 at half-time and down to nine men, refused to return to the pitch to play the second half.

The extent to which Peñarol's *Máquina* was Hirschl's creation is disputed, but nobody doubts the impact he had over tactics and training. Ghiggia said that before his arrival a practice session tended to consist of the players jogging round the pitch a couple of times to

---

(Simon & Schuster, 2016).

[5] More detail on the extraordinary atmosphere around that final training session and the announcement that Ghiggia would start is given in Andreas Campomar, *¡Golazo!* Riverrun, 2014).

warm up and then having a game. Hirschl, though, introduced drills 'a la europea', just as he had in Argentina. 'The regimen was very hard,' said the defender Juan Carlos González, 'and we practised three times a day.'[6] That was unheard of in Uruguay at the time. Hirschl had his players practise heading with a ball hung on a rope from a device that looked like a gallows and dribble in and out of poles while performing specific exercises in the gym. There was individual training for goal-keepers and a board set up at the side of the pitch against which players would kick the ball with their weaker foot. Some complained, but Ghiggia said, 'I didn't get bored because I knew it was good for me, and I accepted everything he told me.'[7]

Hirschl had achieved success at River Plate with his own version of the W-M and he continued that approach in Montevideo. For Ghiggia, Hirschl was 'a man of very precise and original ideas', who possessed an 'enormous discipline and a tactical and distinctly attacking football'. Hirschl's football was direct, based around playing balls behind the opposing full-backs for his explosive wingers to run on to. There was a focus on the team as a cohesive unit, with exces-sive individualism discouraged, all the classic values of the original MTK style filtered through the 1925 change to the offside law and the subsequent switch to W-M. According to the sociologist Rafael Bayce, it was in 1951, Hirschl's third and, in that spell, final season at the club when the W-M reached its peak in Uruguay as Peñarol again went unbeaten in winning the championship.[8]

---

[6] In Nelson Dominguez, 'Juan Carlos González', in *Estrellas deportivas*, no. 90, (La Mañana & El Diario, 1979).

[7] Unless otherwise stated, all Ghiggia quotes here are taken from Atilio Garrido and Joselo González, *El gol del siglo* [*The Goal of the Century*] (El País & Tenfield, 2000).

[8] Rafael Bayce, '*La evolución de los sistemas del juego*', *100 años de fútbol*, no. 22, (Editores Reunidos, 1970).

There were sceptics, notably the goalkeeper Roque Máspoli and the captain Obdulio Varela, who initially doubted just how much of a difference Hirschl had really made – 'he had a million players to choose from,' Varela would say – but Ghiggia was not the only one to see his role as vital. 'Eighty per cent of the team was Hirschl,' said the inside-left Juan Schiaffino.[9]

Hirschl was strict, to the point of keeping a black notebook with him at all times, jotting down infractions to remind himself whom to fine. Varela complained that Hirschl demanded so much control over his players that he 'would make you stand naked in the gym to see what you'd done the night before'.[10] But gradually Varela began to warm to his manager, particularly after they reached an agreement that the centre-half could self-diagnose his persistent leg injuries and decide whether he was able to play or not.

His greatest influence was over the squad's younger players; throughout his career, Hirschl showed a preference for working with youth he could mould to his conception of the game. Ghiggia described him as 'the best coach I ever had', saying he commanded respect not just because he was the manager but because 'he integrated, mingled with the team and told jokes.'

He was also prepared to accept being on the receiving end of pranks. 'I was a very bohemian kid,' Ghiggia recalled. 'I was always joking with Emérico, who had a lot of books, and I would often sneak into his room and tear out the last pages of the novels, so the poor guy never knew what the end of the story was.'[11]

That helped foster team spirit, as did the amount of time the players spent together at the club headquarters at Los Aromos. They

---

[9] In 'El Peñarol de 49' in *El libro de oro de Peñarol*, no. 3, (1987).

[10] In Luciano Álvarez, *Historia de Peñarol* (Aguilar, 2014).

[11] In *Nemzeti Sport*, 31 October 2014.

would meet for their *concentración* on a Thursday, staying there for three nights before the match on a Sunday, and were then given the option of staying the night after games as well. Directors and coaching staff would go home, giving the players freedom. According to Ghiggia they would go out and eat ice cream or, at times, buy meat for a second dinner at 1am.

So dominant were Peñarol in 1949 that Hirschl began to be touted as a possible national coach; after all, it was clear that when the squad for the 1950 World Cup was announced early in 1950, it would be packed with Peñarol players. The club launched a campaign to have Hirschl appointed, what the historian Atilio Garrido, in his book on Uruguay's victory[12] called '*Operación Hirschl*'.

Garrido frames the issue as a largely political dispute, Peñarol keen to emphasise their superiority by having their man appointed, while Nacional were desperate to avoid what would have been perceived as further humiliation. The battle became personal. Officially, Nacional were opposed to Hirschl taking charge because of his demand to have complete control, but others suggested he only wanted the job out of vanity.

The politicking dragged on. The incumbent national coach Enrique Fernández resigned in March 1950 (to become manager of Nacional) and Hirschl was appointed to replace him. Crucially, he restored Varela to the national squad. But with Nacional resisting, Hirschl was soon ousted. There were protests and counter-protests. Peñarol withdrew their players from a national team tour of Chile and then a group of Peñarol players led by Varela – by then, clearly, fully adjusted to his manager's methods – threatened to quit the national team unless Hirschl were reappointed.

---

[12] Atilio Garrido's *Maracaná: La historia secreta*, (Atilio Garrido, 2014).

Nacional continued to resist and eventually brought up Hirschl's ban from Argentinian football for match-fixing. As Peñarol defended Hirschl, other Uruguayan clubs, notably Liverpool, Rampla Juniors, Danubio and Wanderers, sided with Nacional and a couple of clubs accused him of having tapped up their players the previous season, encouraging them to join Peñarol in 1950. In late April, just before the South American World Cup qualifiers began in Brazil, Hirschl was secretly named coach by the Uruguayan Football Association (AUF). Nacional protested and called an extraordinary meeting at which they won a vote for Hirschl to be un-appointed again.

As it turned out, Argentina, Peru and Ecuador all withdrew from the qualifiers, meaning Uruguay, Paraguay, Bolivia and Chile qualified automatically for the finals. Uruguay used the time when the qualifiers would have been played for a series of friendlies. Without a coach, Varela effectively took charge, implementing the marking system and basic tactics he had learned from Hirschl. Results were mixed, but there was one 4–3 victory over Brazil that showed the World Cup favourites were not invincible.

Eventually, after much further wrangling, the AUF accepted that it would never be possible to appoint Hirschl and so, on 23 May, just over five weeks before the tournament began, they named Juan López, who had no connections with either Peñarol or Nacional at that stage, to lead the national team into the World Cup.

The tournament that year featured a final group of four teams. Uruguay faced Brazil in the last game, needing a win to claim the World Cup from the hosts. In front of more than 200,000 Brazilian fans at the Maracanã, it seemed a foregone conclusion, and Brazil took the lead. But Schiaffino levelled after 66 minutes and then, with 11 minutes remaining, Ghiggia cut in from the right to scuff a shot past Moacir Barbosa in the Brazil goal. Uruguay pulled off the greatest of upsets. It became known as the Maracanazo, and it continues to haunt Brazil. (It's not unreasonable to suggest that it was in part the trauma of that game that led to Brazil's hysteria and subsequent collapse, 7–1 in the semi-final against Germany, when they next hosted the tournament, in 2014.)

To what extent was it Hirschl's triumph? That is very difficult to say. Six of the players who started the final match, including both goalscorers and Varela, whose leadership was vital, played for his Peñarol. Varela, rather than López, was the tactical brain of the squad, adopting a more defensive approach against Brazil, and he clearly had learned from Hirschl. And yet nothing in the contemporary Uruguayan media coverage gave Hirschl much credit. But then his involvement didn't fit the prevailing narrative. As the newspaper *El Bien Público* had it, the 1950 World Cup was the victory of 'Uruguayan players and Uruguayan tactics'.[13] They were the tough little nation standing up to their bigger neighbours, sustained only by their innate stores of *garra*, that mystical quality of toughness and streetwise-ness (the word literally means 'claw') that supposedly characterises Uruguayans. In that interpretation of the victory, there was no room to acknowledge the influence of a Hungarian.

Ghiggia, though, had no doubt about Hirschl's importance. 'He came to us from Buenos Aires,' he said. 'He was a real expert. He understood the language of footballers, he was very prepared, he knew everything about football. He was an intelligent man and we loved him very much… He never talked about Hungary or Budapest; he was always talking about how great Buenos Aires was.'[14]

Hirschl returned to his beloved Buenos Aires with San Lorenzo in 1951, but with his health failing, something he blamed on the

---

[13] *El Bien Público*, 19 July 1950.
[14] *Nemzeti Sport*, 31 October 2014.

stress associated with the job, he decided to quit. This, he realised, was the perfect opportunity to return the favour Guttmann had done for him in São Paulo 21 years earlier. He sent a telegram to his old friend telling him that he would soon have to give up the job, effectively offering him the position. Guttmann travelled across the Atlantic to accept but arrived too late. By the time he got there, Hirschl had already been forced to resign and had been replaced by Francisco Corsetti.

Hirschl kept working in football, acting as scout for a number of sides, including AC Milan, and returned to coaching only twice: first with Peñarol in 1956 and then, as a favour to the club president Antonio Vespucio Liberti, to River Plate in 1961, only to be hounded out over his conviction for match-fixing by a campaign led by the then-editor of *El Gráfico*, Dante Panzeri, whose voice, Hirschl said, was enough to make him feel sick. He died in 1973 and is buried in the Jewish cemetery at La Tablada in Buenos Aires.

In Buenos Aires and without a job, Guttmann spoke to Boca Juniors but was unable to secure a deal and ended up coaching Quilmes in the second flight. He had little success there and was seemingly already contemplating a return to Europe when another telegram arrived, this time from the Újpest former wingman, József Künsztler. He had just left the Cypriot side Apoel and wanted Guttmann to replace him. Guttmann lasted three months there before a much bigger offer lured him away: AC Milan.

* * *

Under Czeizler, Milan had been noted for the directness of their style. He would drill his players early in the week and then give them a couple of days to rest before matches to try to ensure they were both fit and fresh for games. With the Swedish attacking trident of

Gunnar Gren, Gunnar Nordahl and Nils Liedholm – the Gre-no-li, as they became known – Milan scored 18 goals more than any other side in Serie A in 1949–50, and thrashed Juventus 7–1 in Turin, but still ended up as runners-up behind Juve.

The following season, though, Czeizler's Milan did win the league, the club's first championship since 1907. Despite winning none of their final five matches of the season, they picked up a scarcely credible 60 points from 38 games (at a time when it was still two points for a win) and yet still only sealed the *scudetto* on the penultimate weekend when Inter lost at Torino. For the second season running Nordahl finished as top scorer as they racked up more than 100 goals. Milan also that season became the first Italian winners of the Latin Cup.

After finishing second behind Juve the following season, though, Czeizler was replaced by Mario Sperone, who had worked with Erbstein in various capacities at Torino. He had brought Milan its first Serie A title, and yet Gianni Brera, the great – if at times prejudiced – Italian football journalist of the age, argued that he would have won three 'had he only honoured the defence'.[15] For Brera, who was weirdly obsessed by the perceived physical inadequacies of Italian football, the Gre-no-li had brought a muscularity with which Italian defenders could not cope, but they had also been tactically naive. His principal exhibit in support of his argument was the derby in November 1949 when Milan had led 4–1 after 19 minutes but had kept attacking and had ended up losing 6–5.

For Czeizler, there followed a difficult season as technical director of Padua. Two coaches had already been sacked before he was ousted with the club battling relegation; they eventually survived by winning their final two games of the season. It didn't

---

[15] In '*Quel genio che vines tropo poco*', his obituary of Gunnar Gren, published in *La Repubblica*, 16 November 1991.

harm Czeizler's reputation too much, though, and he was given a similar role with the Italy national team to lead them into the 1954 World Cup. Qualification was achieved with two wins over Egypt but the tournament itself went rather less smoothly. Italy lost 2–1 to Switzerland and then beat Belgium 4–1, necessitating a play-off against the Swiss. Unable to handle *la verrou* [the bolt], the early sweeper system pioneered by their Austrian-born coach Karl Rappan, Italy lost 4–1, which perhaps indicates that Brera's doubts about Czeizler's tactical capacities were not without substance. He was dismissed after the tournament.

Sperone lasted a season at Milan but a third-place finish behind Inter and Juve saw him replaced by Gren as player-coach. Gren didn't last long, though, and neither did his successor, the former Milan player Arrigo Morselli, and it was after another third-place finish that the technical director, Antonio Busini, turned in the summer of 1953 to Guttmann.

Milan struggled to match a powerful Juventus side, but still had a strong squad, with the Danish forward Jørgen Sørensen joining Nils Liedholm and Gunnar Nordahl as Gren left for Fiorentina. 'Since I had outstanding players,' Guttmann said, 'I gave them the order, "Attack!"'[16]

He also instituted two training sessions a day, accusing his big-name players of having gone soft. 'The duration and severity of training had been defined by the top stars,' he said. 'Nobody should cross the boundaries of comfort.' As so often before, his confrontational approach had an immediate positive impact. Milan finished third and Guttmann was offered a new contract. They finished third again in 1953–54 but that summer there was money available for

---

[16] Cited in Bolchover, *The Greatest Comeback*.

transfers and Milan signed the great Uruguayan Juan Alberto Schiaffino, the skilful Argentinian winger Eduardo Ricagni and the commanding defender Cesare Maldini. It may have been a team packed with talent, but it remained emphatically Guttmann's side. When Ricagni refused to swap positions with Sørensen in one game, Guttmann transfer-listed him, at which the player apologised.

Milan won their first seven games of 1954–55, and they were four points clear of Bologna in second at the beginning of February. A 4–3 defeat at Triestina shouldn't have been enough to derail them, but the following week Milan faced Sampdoria, who by then were managed by Czeizler.

A couple of days before the game, Czeizler invited Guttmann for a night out in Milan with their wives. It did not go well. 'In a Milan bar,' *La Stampa* reported, 'there was an altercation between the two Hungarians. The two wives intervened, one of whom threw a bottle at the other.'[17] There seems a general consensus that it was Czeizler's wife, a Hungarian he had married in Sweden in 1948, who had attacked Mariann. Witnesses described the two couples 'punching and screaming'. Sampdoria, exploiting Czeizler's knowledge of the Milan squad, won the game 3–1.

Milan were still top of the table, but two days later, Guttmann was told to report to a board meeting after training. Discussions went on for five hours before finally, at 2am, he was asked into the boardroom and told his contract had been terminated. A club spokesman explained the decision had been taken because of 'misunderstandings between Guttmann and the team, a situation that had been dragging on for weeks and which had recently deteriorated, resulting in a reciprocal feeling of distrust'.

---

[17] *La Stampa*, 12 February 1955.

It was the same story as at Padova and Triestina, with early success followed by rancour, as though Guttmann's training methods or his personality were too intense to be endured for long. Guttmann, meanwhile, blamed Czeizler, accusing him of having plotted with the assistant coach Ettore Puricelli to get his old job back, not that he mentioned him in his succinct farewell to the media. 'I have been fired,' Guttmann said, 'even though I am neither a criminal nor a homosexual. Goodbye.' From then on, he supposedly insisted on a clause in his contracts that he could not be sacked if his side were top of the league.

Milan went on to win the title and his players, however fractious their relationship with Guttmann may have become, had little doubt who deserved the credit. Milan played Honvéd in a post-season friendly and invited Guttmann as guest of honour, presenting him at the post-game banquet with a plaque hailing him as the coach of the champions.

* * *

By the mid-1950s, Guttmann had become good friends with another Hungarian Jew living in Milan, Dezső Steinberger. After bringing down Peter Veres, Steinberger had moved to Budapest. He requested but was denied a passport and so, acting on the advice of the mysterious ÁVH secretary Bálint, he trained as a magician as it was easier for qualified entertainers to travel abroad. Steinberger was granted a passport in 1949 and left for Italy with six female dancers. For the following decade he arranged for troupes of Hungarian dancers to travel to Italy; ÁVH records make clear this was a flimsy cover for trafficking prostitutes. By the time Guttmann met him, he had adopted the name by which he remains notorious, a name that, oddly, was suggested to him by Veres: Dezső Solti.

When Guttmann first met him, Solti was making a living from a number of ill-defined occupations. He was a theatre impresario, he helped arrange tours for travelling football teams and he worked with various Italian clubs including, eventually, Inter. He described himself as a 'manager' for which perhaps the most generous interpretation is 'fixer'. According to his memoir, Solti was first employed by the Inter president Angelo Moratti in 1956. They soon fell out, seemingly over his failure to persuade the former Honvéd coach Jenő Kalmár to join the club, after which, Solti claimed, he began 'helping Real Madrid with their European Cup games'. But Solti inveigled himself again by, he claimed, introducing the Argentinian Helenio Herrera, at the time the manager of Barcelona, to Moratti in 1960. Herrera subsequently presided over Inter's greatest period of success.

Solti played a central role in that – perhaps rather too central. Inter won the European Cup in 1964 and 1965 and on both occasions concerns had been raised over incidents in the semi-finals. In 1964, Inter's Luis Suárez had escaped sanction for a bad foul that put the Borussia Dortmund right-half Dieter Kurrat out of the game (this in the days before substitutes). The Yugoslav referee Branko Tešanić, subsequent investigations suggested, had been put up at Inter's expense, while pocketing his UEFA expenses, and had been given a gold watch to ensure Inter progressed.

The following year, Inter overcame a 3–1 first-leg deficit to beat Liverpool 4–3 on aggregate, with one goal scored after the ball was kicked out of the hands of the goalkeeper Tommy Lawrence as he prepared to clear, and one struck in directly from an indirect free kick. The referee then was the Spaniard José María Ortiz de Mendíbil; as the British journalist Brian Glanville pointed out almost a decade later in the *Sunday Times*, Italian teams seemed to do remarkably well when he was in charge.

The evidence in those cases, persuasive as it is, is circumstantial. In 1966, though, there is direct testimony, because the fix failed and

Inter lost in the semi-final to Madrid. In his remarkable 1983 book *Csak a labdán van bőr* [*Only the Ball has a Skin*][18] the Hungarian journalist Péter Borenich details how Budapest became the centre of the nexus of corruption in European football in the 1960s and 1970s. Seventeen years after the event, he persuaded the referee of that 1966 semi-final second leg, György Vadász, to go on the record about what had happened.

Solti, Vadász explained, had approached him in Milan and stayed with him all day to ensure nobody from Real Madrid could approach him. When they were left alone, he offered him enough money for 'five, six Mercedes' to ensure Inter progressed. Solti also took Vadász and the two linesmen to meet Moratti at his villa. Inter's owner gave each of them a gold watch and suggested Solti should buy them electrical goods. But Vadász refused and Madrid went through with a 1–1 draw. At the end of the game Solti berated him, accusing Vadász of denying Inter three clear penalties and threatened to have him struck off the FIFA list. Vadász never refereed another international match.

By the time of Borenich's revelations, Solti had already been banned from European football over an offence that had taken place ten years earlier, by which time he was working with Juventus.[19] On 27 January 1973, the Portuguese referee Francesco Marques Lobo was at home in Lisbon listening to music on his record player when he received a telephone call telling him that 'an Italian gentleman',[20] a 'follower of football' who was in town for an international the

---

[18] Péter Borenich, *Csak a labdán van bőr* (Magánkiadás, 1983).

[19] The club for a long time denied this, but Glanville and a US freelance called Keith Botsford uncovered a letter signed by him on behalf of the club, which was published in the *Sunday Times*.

[20] Unless otherwise stated, all quotes in this section are drawn from Brian Glanville's account of his *Sunday Times* investigation into Solti in *Champions of Europe* (Guinness, 1991).

following day,[21] was keen to meet him at the Ritz Hotel and had messages from mutual acquaintances. Lobo was instantly suspicious and asked why the messages couldn't be passed on over the telephone. The caller said they were of a 'personal nature' and had to be conveyed face-to-face. Lobo said he was about to eat his dinner and would call back later. He immediately rang Sousa Loureiro, head of the Portuguese refereeing association, who told him to keep the appointment, but to confine any conversation to polite small talk.

Lobo went to the Ritz and there, in room 142, met Solti and a much younger blonde woman. Solti passed on a message from an Italian friend, then congratulated Lobo on being appointed as a referee for the World Cup the following year. This was the first Lobo had heard of his selection, but Solti claimed to have been told by Artemio Franchi, the Italian president of UEFA. Franchi had also told him Lobo would be chosen to referee the second leg of Juventus's European Cup semi-final against Brian Clough's Derby County. Lobo was led to understand that Solti knew people who could be very beneficial to his career.

Solti then suggested that it would be helpful to Lobo if he went to Turin to watch the first leg, so that he could fully understand how 'hard' English football was. He'd already booked flights for him, he said, to travel from Lisbon to Madrid and from there to Milan. He produced a car key from his pocket and dangled it in front of the referee. 'The implication was,' Lobo said, 'that when I left Italy I would not have to fly back, but would have a car of my own to drive back in.' He then openly offered $5,000 in cash if Lobo helped Juve win the second leg.

---

[21] It's not clear what game this was. Portugal did draw 1–1 in a World Cup qualifier against Northern Ireland the following day, but that match was played in Coventry.

Derby had lost the first leg 3–1. There was little obviously untoward on the pitch, although another referee than the West German Gerhard Schulenburg might have been stricter in dealing with Juve's aggressive right-half Giuseppe Furino, and it was an unfortunate coincidence that both Derby players who would miss the second leg if cautioned, Archie Gemmill and Roy McFarland, were booked, the latter for very little apparent reason. But at half-time, Peter Taylor, Derby's assistant manager, saw the West Germany international Helmut Haller, who was on the Juve bench that night, approach Schulenburg. Taylor had already been warned by the Welsh former Juve great John Charles that Haller had visited Schulenburg before the game. Perhaps it was just two compatriots having a chat, but if so, why was Taylor intercepted 'by a group of tough-looking Italians' as he approached? 'I believe it was corrupt and dirty,' Taylor said.[22]

On 4 April, Solti rang Lobo. As Lobo worked for Portugal's national telecommunication company, it was a simple matter for him to record the call. He spoke Portuguese; Solti a mixture of Italian and Spanish. They agreed to meet in Lisbon, and then again in Paris on the way to Derby. Solti confirmed the agreed fee was $5,000.

Lobo refereed the game fairly, awarding Derby a penalty that Alan Hinton missed and then sending off Roger Davies for punching Francesco Morini. He submitted evidence of the attempt to bribe him to his referees' association, who sent it to the Portuguese football federation who sent it to UEFA. No action was taken against any of the clubs, but Solti was – eventually – banned from involvement in European football, while Lobo was omitted from the list to referee the 1974 World Cup, ostracised just as György Vadász had been.

---

[22] In Peter Taylor, *With Clough by Taylor* (Sidgwick & Jackson, 1980). For more on how that defeat haunted Taylor and, more particularly, the Derby manager Brian Clough, see my book *Nobody Ever Says Thank You* (Orion, 2011).

Almost two decades later, in March 1990, the film director Béla Szobolits spent a day with Solti in Milan for his documentary *Futball-dezső*.[23] He is much more sympathetic to Solti, who was 79 at the time of the interview, than most. 'He was good-humoured with a mischievous look in his eyes,' Szobolits said. 'He talked a lot about women. He was very religious, sensitive, easily moved.

'He lived alone in a very average two-bedroom apartment in Milan. A middle-aged Italian woman cooked and cleaned for him. Every day he got up at 7am, put on his kippah and prayed for an hour. He would read passages from the Torah. There was a Jewish jeweller of about his age from Romania who came round between 10 and 12 every day. Solti would have lunch alone and sleep. Then, he read the newspapers and went into the town centre for an ice cream. He read philosophy after that. He would have his evening meal, then stand in the window looking over the city, taking in the fresh air, before going to bed after midnight.'

Szobolits and Solti went to a game together at San Siro that evening. The director remembers the crowd rising to applaud Solti when he was spotted in the VIP area; his importance to the club's past successes was widely recognised.

---

[23] The film itself, slightly mystifyingly, has gone missing. It's the only one of Szobolits's films of which he does not have a copy. It was always assumed that István Kardos, the head of the production company Hétfői Műhely Stúdió Alapítvány, had the master print, but when he died, it could not be found. Kardos had not, as he was required to do by law, submitted a copy to the national film archive. A number of people remember seeing the film on television in around 2011, but the television company does not have a copy, and nor do any of the various film institutes, libraries and archives contacted. Even more frustratingly, there were at some point tapes of around 24 hours of interviews conducted by Szobolits, which may still exist somewhere. Thankfully, Szobolits's memory seemed good, stimulated by an exercise book he had found in which he had jotted notes as he conducted the interiew with Solti.

But in what did that lie? He worked hard, of that there is no doubt, chasing down leads on possible signings, oiling the wheels of the transfer market. But the match-fixing? Solti admitted he had at times given gold watches to referees. "'Football is a game of fine margins,'" Szobolits recalled him saying. "'All we did was try to ensure those were not against Inter. If a free kick is going to be given one way or the other, we wanted to make sure we were seen as the victim not the opposition.'"

* * *

In April 1955, Guttmann went out with Solti in a car he had had imported from the US. Guttmann didn't have a licence but was driving nonetheless when he lost control. The car hit two students on the corner of Via Pellizzo da Volpedo and Via Mosè Bianchi. One, the 17-year-old Giuliano Brene, was killed instantly; the other, the 18-year-old Graziella Brianzoli suffered serious injuries and had to spend a month in hospital.

Guttmann and Solti fled the scene. Arrest warrants were issued and a week later, Solti was picked up by police in the Austrian Alps around 180 miles from Milan. He wrote a letter to the chief prosecutor assuming sole responsibility for the crash. Guttmann was officially absolved.

Witnesses, though, contradicted Solti's statement and, in November 1955, by which time he was at Vicenza, Guttmann was charged with manslaughter, as was Solti. The case finally came to court in March 1957. Guttmann, by then, was in South America. In the dock, Solti retracted his confession, saying he had feared that Guttmann would kill himself and that he had reached an agreement with him that he would take the blame if Guttmann compensated the families. It wasn't until March 1960 that the court convened again. Guttmann was in Portugal while Solti was working with Inter, although both were described as 'untraceable' in the court document. Solti was acquitted while Guttmann was convicted *in absentia* and sentenced to six months in jail for manslaughter and causing injury through negligence, the sentence to be commuted if 4 million lira were paid to the families.

* * *

Three months after the car crash, Guttmann was appointed manager of newly promoted Vicenza for the start of the 1955–56 season. His time there followed the familiar pattern: a promising start followed by collapse. A third of the way through the season they were second behind the eventual champions Fiorentina, but by the beginning of April a run of four straight defeats had left them third bottom. Whether Guttmann was sacked or whether he resigned remains unclear. Guttmann himself claimed there had been a dispute over who was allowed in the dressing room at half-time, leading to him being pushed out, which certainly would have been in character, but Bolchover speculates that he might have been trying to leave the country to avoid his trial for manslaughter.[24] Certainly by May 1956, Guttmann and Mariann were back in Vienna. They applied for Austrian citizenship, describing themselves as 'stateless' having fled Hungary, and were granted it on 28 September.

Just as he ceased to be Hungarian, though, circumstances conspired to place Guttmann in charge of a Hungarian side for the final time.

---

[24] In *The Greatest Comeback.*

CHAPTER SEVEN

THE UPRISING

Five yards outside the box, Ferenc Puskás slowed slightly, waiting for Mihály Tóth's angled pass to reach him. He was in behind Werner Liebrich, who couldn't get back. Karl Mai was steaming across from his right, but wasn't going to get there in time. The captain of Hungary had just the goalkeeper Toni Turek to beat. Puskás let the ball run across his body on to his left foot, steadying himself. Exposed, Turek stood poised on the edge of his six-yard box. From level with the penalty spot, Puskás shot, losing his footing on the damp surface as he did so. It didn't matter. His shot was firm and low and skidded under the dive of Turek. It was 3–3. With four minutes of the 1954 World Cup final remaining, Hungary had, it seemed, pulled level. In extra time, their extra class, surely, would tell.

As he followed the ball into the net, Mai waved both hands above his head. Liebrich, turning back to the halfway line, exhaustion and disappointment scoured on his face, pointed at Puskás. Turek lay face down in the mud. But the appeals of the two defenders were heard. The Welsh linesman Mervyn Griffiths, a controversial, authoritarian figure, belatedly raised his flag, and the English referee Bill Ling ruled out the goal: offside.

The video footage is frustratingly inconclusive but Puskás was furious. 'I couldn't believe it,' he said. 'It was almost a minute afterwards when he raised his flag. I could have murdered him. To lose the World Cup on such a decision just isn't right.'[1]

But lose the World Cup they had. After four years unbeaten, the *Aranycsapat* had lost the one that really mattered.

* * *

Hungary had gone to the 1954 World Cup in Switzerland as favourites. They thrashed Luxembourg 10–0 in a warm-up game, then beat South Korea 9–0 in their first match in the group stage. West Germany, in their first tournament since the Second World War, were dismissed with almost similar ease, beaten 8–3, meaning Hungary had scored 34 goals in four games. They looked unstoppable.

But with the score at 5–1 in that group game, Puskás was caught from behind by Liebrich, a centre-half at Kaiserslautern. It was a foul that would reverberate far beyond the confines of a football pitch in Basel. At that moment, Hungarian football began its decline. Puskás was forced to leave the field with what X-rays would later reveal was a hairline fracture of the ankle. He missed the next two games and was clearly not at his best when he returned for the final – against West Germany.

Inevitably, that led to allegations Liebrich had targeted Puskás. He had, after all, switched positions with the right-half Jupp Posipal ten minutes before the foul. There is a significant difference, though, between a physical player being deployed against the opposition's best creator and a calculated plot to injure him. Sebes thought the foul had been a deliberate ploy, but then an organiser like him perhaps

---

[1] In Taylor, *Puskás on Puskás*.

assumed everybody was constantly drawing up plans as he himself did. In *Captain of Hungary*, Puskás wrote of 'a vicious kick on the back of my ankle ... when I was no longer playing the ball'[2] but as time eased his frustration he eventually concluded his injury was the result of clumsiness rather than malice. Hidegkuti, in his autobiography, called it 'a correct challenge, and quite accepted in football... He was just trying to tackle Puskás, who strained his ankle.'[3]

Although subsequent events lent Liebrich's foul a momentousness, at the time it paled beside the ferocity of the quarter-final against Brazil. That game should have been feted as a meeting of the two most tactically advanced sides in the world, between two teams beginning to move on from the Danubian W-M of the 1930s towards a 4–2–4, but history remembers it as the Battle of Bern.

In driving rain, Hungary raced into a two-goal lead inside seven minutes with strikes from Hidegkuti and Kocsis, and Djalma Santos pulled one back with an 18th-minute penalty. When the English referee Arthur Ellis awarded Hungary a penalty on the hour, Brazil protested furiously. Substitutes and coaches invaded the pitch and were only removed after the intervention of police. Lantos converted to make it 3–1, after which the game became increasingly violent. 'They behaved like animals,' said Ellis. 'It was a disgrace. It was a horrible match.'[4]

Amid the mayhem Julinho pulled it back to 3–2 but by then the game had come to seem almost an irrelevance. Bozsik retaliated after a foul by Nílton Santos and as punches were exchanged both were sent off. Djalma Santos, spitting and gesticulating, chased Czibor behind Ellis's back and Humberto Tozzi was sent off for kicking

---

[2] *Captain of Hungary* (Cassell, 1955).
[3] *Óbudától Firenzéig* (Sport, 1962).
[4] In an interview in the *Independent*, 9 June 1998.

Lóránt. Kocsis added a fourth with two minutes remaining, but the final whistle wasn't the end of it.

The Brazil midfielder Pinheiro was hit on the head by a bottle thrown from the Hungarian bench, and fighting continued down the tunnel and into the Hungary dressing room, leaving Sebes requiring four stitches to a cut above his eye. 'This was a battle; a brutal, savage match,' he said. 'Brazilian photographers and fans flooded onto the pitch and police were called to clear it. Players clashed in the tunnel and a small war broke out in the corridor to the dressing rooms – everyone was having a go; fans, players and officials.'[5]

The semi-final against Uruguay was an epic, one of the greatest games ever played. Goals from Czibor and Hidegkuti had Hungary 2–0 up a minute into the second half, but Juan Hohberg scored twice in the final quarter of an hour to take the game into extra time. Puskás spoke of the 'tremendous heart' his side had shown.

But then came the final and the greatest disappointment Hungarian sport has known. For Germany, what happened on 4 July 1954 was the Miracle of Bern, the moment at which the nation emerged on to the international stage again after the horror of war. 'Suddenly Germany was somebody again,'[6] said Franz Beckenbauer. 'For anybody who grew up in the misery of the post-war years, Bern was an extraordinary inspiration. The entire country regained its self-esteem.'[7] Hungary, though, has never come close to those heights again.

In retrospect the warning signs are clear. There was the accumulated weariness of the exhausting games against Brazil and Uruguay.

---

[5] Gusztáv Sebes, *Örömök és csalódások* (Gondolat, 1981).

[6] *'Wir sind wieder wer'* ['We are somebody again'] is essentially a slogan about the German experience in the 1950s. In the original, familiarity means it perhaps sounds less dramatic than it does in English.

[7] In the film, *Das Wunder von Bern* (Sönke Wortmann, 2003).

There was the issue of Puskás's fitness, although on the morning of the match he was cleared to play. The night before the final, brass bands practising for the Swiss national championships disturbed Hungary's sleep. Police mysteriously prevented the team bus from reaching the stadium, leaving players to battle their way through the crowds to get to the dressing room. And it rained persistently for the 36 hours before the match, turning an already soft pitch into a quagmire, something that both hampered their passing game and placed even greater strain on weary limbs.

But everything began well enough, goals from Puskás and Czibor giving them a 2–0 lead within eight minutes – it's impossible to be sure that it was the result of Sebes's belief in the value of warm-ups, but it meant Hungary had taken a 2–0 lead in every game at that World Cup. But two minutes after Czibor's goal, West Germany pulled one back, Max Morlock sliding in after József Zakariás had half-blocked a cross, and then Grosics flapped at a Fritz Walter corner, allowing Helmut Rahn to volley an equaliser. With just 18 minutes played, it was 2–2.

West Germany's line-up featured only five of the players who had played in the 8–3 defeat in the group stage. Perhaps it was a case of Sepp Herberger slowly working his way towards his most effective XI, but the story has grown up, supported by Herberger's assistant Helmut Schön, that Herberger, confident of getting through the group, deliberately fielded a weaker side for the meeting in the group stage so he could learn about Hungary without giving much away about his own side. Certainly Herberger adapted to Hidegkuti's role in a way that had been beyond the wit of England, using Horst Eckel to man-mark him.

As a result, Hidegkuti's influence was limited, but he still hit the post. And this is a fact that is often lost in the talk about

Herberger's cunning or Hungary's tiredness, or even the later reports that the West German side had taken amphetamines:[8] Hungary, fundamentally, were unlucky. Kocsis hit the bar and the West Germany keeper Toni Turek made a number of fine saves, but a third goal would not come. And then, with six minutes remaining, Bozsik was muscled off the ball by Hans Schäfer and when his cross was headed out by Mihály Lantos, Rahn gathered the loose ball, cut on to his left foot and shot low past Grosics.

But luck is never an adequate reason to those who have suffered a major disappointment. There must always be a search for explanation, ideally scapegoats who can carry the blame. Even in its headline *Népsport* said the team selection was 'wrong'.[9] In the days and weeks that followed, Kocsis and Hidegkuti both wondered what might have happened had Puskás not played but then, as Puskás pointed out, he had scored one goal and had another controversially ruled out – and it wasn't as though he was the most mobile or hard-working of players even at peak fitness.

His inclusion, though, had had a knock-on effect as Sebes brought in the industrious Mihály Tóth on the left wing to cover for Puskás's lack of fitness, which meant Czibor switching from left to right to replace László Budai, who had played well in the semi but had been generally out of sorts. Although Czibor's pace troubled the West German right-back Werner Kohlmeyer, the wingers were considered to have been so ineffective in the first half that at half-time, Gyula Hegyi ordered Sebes to swap them over. There were plenty happy to blame the coach. Why had he indulged Puskás? Had he overcomplicated his tactics to

---

[8] 'Doping in Deutschland von 1950 bis heute aus historisch-soziologischer Sicht im Kontext ethischer Legitimation,' report by Humboldt University, Berlin, and the University of Münster, 2013.

[9] *Népsport*, 5 July 1954.

accommodate him? Had he even, self-servingly, made the switch to emphasise his own genius as a leader? What if the MTK winger Károly Sándor had been included in the squad? And why, given he had not been selected, had he travelled to Switzerland with the official party? Was it really just because Puskás liked playing cards with him?

None of which seems entirely fair: after all, Sebes had just overseen a run of 32 wins and four draws in 36 games over almost four years in which Hungary had won the Olympics and twice hammered England. 'It was our own fault,' Puskás said. 'We thought we had the match won, then we gave away two stupid goals and let them back into it.'[10]

This was a defeat with ramifications far beyond football. 'The reaction in Hungary was terrible,' said Grosics. 'Hundreds of thousands of people poured into the streets in the hours after the match.' What became apparent was that if crowds were big enough, the authorities could not control them; it was a reminder of the power of the people. 'On the pretext of football,' Grosics went on, 'they openly demonstrated against the regime. The atmosphere was so bitter it could be felt months later. In those demonstrations, I believe, lay the seeds of the 1956 Uprising.'

Not that there was anything organised or co-ordinated about the demonstrations. The crowds attacked the apartments of some players and even journalists, enraged by rumours – that perhaps had their basis in what had happened in the World Cup final 16 years earlier – that the game had been thrown for a fleet of Mercedes. It was – preposterously, given Sebes's daughter was ten at the time – suggested that Mihály Tóth had been selected for the final only because he was the manager's son-in-law.

---

[10] In *Puskás on Puskás*.

The accusations of complacency perhaps had a little more substance. At least two players and possibly as many as six broke a curfew to meet the wives and girlfriends who had been allowed to travel to Bern for the final. Czibor later claimed that his room-mate had blundered back in at 6am having spent the night with a hotel maid and complained that he had had to work twice as hard as usual during the game to cover for him, although that is hard to substantiate. Circumstantial evidence pours doubt on his complaint: neither of his two room-mates, Péter Palotás and Ferenc Machos, played in the final. Czibor also said that the guilty party had never played for Hungary again; of those who played in the final, that applies only to Zakariás.

Nine months earlier, after the victory over England, Hungary had returned to Keleti station to a rapturous reception from tens of thousands of fans. This time, it was considered too dangerous for them to head directly to Budapest and they were diverted instead to the northern town of Tata.

Although they were able to go back to Budapest soon enough, and went unbeaten for a further 18 games – meaning that of 51 matches played between May 1950 and February 1956, they lost only one, the World Cup final – something fundamental had been broken in Bern. The spirit of the side never fully recovered and neither did their relationship with the public.

That the national team engaged in widespread smuggling was little secret but it had been regarded as reasonable reward for their achievements; almost overnight, it became seen as evidence of their self-indulgence. Puskás, who had been a universal hero, was barracked at Honvéd away games, Sebes's son was beaten up at school and Grosics, who had always been something of an outsider, was arrested having been accused of 'conduct incompatible with the laws and morals of the Hungarian People's Republic'.

Grosics had never quite fitted with the squad. While the other players relaxed by watching westerns, he would work through chess problems. He was prone to anxiety and a hypochondriac, something that led to him being substituted late in both wins over England. In training sessions he would wear a red beret because he believed it brought him relief from a brain disease from which he thought he was suffering. That he was a very gifted goalkeeper, one of the first prepared to leave his line to dominate his box and beyond, cannot be doubted but Grosics was also erratic and eccentric.

He had been arrested in 1949 when he had planned to leave the country illegally. He felt since that moment he had lived always under greater scrutiny than other members of the *Aranycsapat*. 'I was born into a religious family,' he said, 'and that wasn't a good sign at all at that time. I never made any secret of what I thought about the government. My family – especially my mother – had intended that I should be a Catholic priest. I was raised in that spirit, and that was one of the reasons I was not trusted.'

Late in 1954, Grosics was arrested again and placed under house arrest. Once a week a large black car would arrive at his door to take him off for interrogation by the ÁVH. A couple of years earlier, before Nagy's liberalisations, the sanctions might have been more severe. But at that time nothing was certain. The death of Stalin had seemingly set the Communist bloc on a path away from authoritarianism. But as Georgy Malenkov began to find himself outmanoeuvred by Nikita Khrushchev in Moscow, so Rákosi's star began to rise again. On 9 March 1955, the Central Committee of the Hungarian Working People's Party condemned Nagy for 'rightist deviation'. Newspapers joined the attack, blaming Nagy for Hungary's ongoing economic difficulties and on 18 April he was dismissed by a unanimous vote of the National Assembly and subsequently banished from the Party.

Sebes, meanwhile, found his political status waning as the hier-archy of the Communist Party evolved. Opposition to him found its leader in István Kutas, a former handballer and athlete, who in 1949 became vice-president of the National Sports Education and Sports Committee (OTSB) with responsibility for Sports Education. He would later become editor of *Képes Sport* and then, between 1973 and 1978, president of the MLSZ. He was a highly adept politician, wilier than Sebes, and set about undermining him. That could be petty in form, so whenever anybody referred to the 'Golden Squad' in his presence, he would correct them and insist it was a 'Silver Squad', or it could be serious. It was on Kutas's initiative that, in 1955, Gyula Mándi was replaced by Pál Titkos, the MTK forward who had scored in the 1938 World Cup final. That he had nothing personal against Mándi was made clear in 1957, when he granted him a permit to coach in Brazil; this was about internal politics around the national team. The structure Sebes had created around him was slowly dismantled. In the September, he himself was prevented from taking his place on the bench at a match in Switzerland and his secretary was dismissed.

Results deteriorated. Hungary lost 3–1 to Turkey in a friendly in February 1956 and the *Aranycsapat* rapidly lost its sheen. There was a draw against Yugoslavia, then defeat to Czechoslovakia and when Hungary lost to Belgium in a friendly in June, Sebes was sacked. He was replaced by a five-man committee headed by Bukovi, which recalled Grosics to the team.

Rákosi didn't last much longer. He had himself been undermined by events in Moscow as Khrushchev denounced Stalin in the 'Secret Speech' of February 1956 and condemned the propagation of cults of personality. The same month, Béla Kun, who had fled to Moscow after Horthy's Nationalists had seized power only to be swept up in Stalin's purges and executed as a supposed Trotskyist in August 1938, was exonerated (although in 1956, the Soviet authorities would say merely that he had died in prison in 1939; the full truth was only admitted in 1989).

Visiting Soviet leaders removed Rákosi on 18 July 1956 and he left for Moscow, never to return to Hungary. Gerő was installed as his successor, but he was too closely implicated with the faults of the Rákosi regime, provoking resistance. The convictions of Rajk and the others condemned by the show trial of 1949 were overturned and on 6 October Rajk was reburied, an event attended by tens of thousands in a mass protest against the regime. A week later, Nagy was readmitted to the Party.

On the afternoon of 23 October, more than 20,000 demonstrators, at that point mostly students, gathered by the statue of the national hero József Bem in a square just south of the Margaret Bridge. Péter Veres, the former Peasant leader who had become head of the Writers Union, read a manifesto to the crowd, demanding independence from foreign powers and the implementation of democratic socialism. It went nowhere near far enough for protesters who, after cutting the Communist coat of arms from the centre of their Hungarian flags, marched across the Danube to the parliament building. By the time they got there, at around 6pm, their number had swelled to 200,000.

Two hours later, Gerő issued a speech condemning the protesters and rejecting their demands, to which the demonstrators responded by toppling a 30-foot high statue of Stalin that had been erected in 1951. At the same time, a group surrounded the Magyar Rádió building. When a delegation of students was detained after attempting to enter to broadcast their demands, the crowds called for their release. The ÁVH fired on protesters, killing several. The Hungarian Army was sent to support the ÁVH, but numerous soldiers ripped the red badges from their caps and sided with the demonstrators, who became increasingly confident, setting police cars on fire, attacking Communist symbols and seizing guns from armouries.

The Hungary squad, which had recovered a little of its self-esteem with five successive victories under Bukovi, including a symbolic away victory over the USSR, was in Tata preparing for a game against Sweden. Bewildered by events in the capital, they spent most of their time listening to the radio, trying to work out what was going on. When the game was called off, most of them returned to Budapest, although they had no idea whether it was safe to do so.

On the night the protests broke out, Gerő requested the intervention of Soviet troops and by 2am on 24 October tanks had already entered Budapest. The protesters set up barricades and in the days that followed there were sporadic outbursts of violence as revolutionaries targeted the ÁVH. 'I didn't expect anything,' said the MTK winger László Bödör. 'I didn't understand what was going on. I was living in the tenth district [Kőbánya, in south-east Pest] so I rode my bike into town to watch what was happening. They were shooting. I was there when the statue of Stalin was pulled down. They were hanging people up by their feet on Köztársaság tér [today, II János Pál pápa tér]. The worst fighting was by the Corvin Cinema. Young people had guns and threw bottles filled with petrol. On Üllői út there were burnt-out tanks and where there were bodies, they covered them with some sort of white paint to stop infection.'

On 25 October, there were armed clashes outside the parliament, which led to the collapse of the government. Gerő and the former prime minister András Hegedüs, who had been pushed aside for Nagy, fled to the USSR. János Kádár, a lifelong Communist who had led the Hungarian party during the war, was named general secretary in Gerő's place.

Although Nagy appealed for calm, armed units began a campaign against Soviet troops. Grosics was heavily involved. He was there by the statue of St Imre on Gellért Hill when troops again opened fire on demonstrators, and subsequently allowed his house to be used as an arsenal by rebels. 'I had a lot of problems getting rid of the arms afterwards,' he said. 'Fortunately, I had a good friend in the army, a captain, who came in a small truck and took the weapons and grenades away. That was my small contribution.'

The most radical of the rebels were led by the former military officer Béla Király, who was married to the niece of the former prime minister Gyula Gömbös. He had been sentenced to death under Rákosi's government, later commuted to life imprisonment, before being released as part of Nagy's programme of pardons earlier in 1956. They attacked the Central Committee of the Communist Party, killing dozens suspected of being sympathetic to Soviet rule (although Király himself was in hospital at the time).

A ceasefire was declared by Nagy on 28 October and as Soviet troops retreated to garrisons in the countryside, fighting died down. On 1 November, Nagy announced Hungary's withdrawal from the Warsaw Pact, released a number of political prisoners and legalised political parties that had been banned.

The Soviets, though, then decided further intervention was necessary, and sent 12 more units of the Red Army to join the five that were already in Hungary. By 9:30pm on 3 November, Budapest was encircled; tanks entered the city again in the early hours of 4 November. At 5:20am, Nagy broadcast a plea to the West for help, but none came and at 6am Kádár proclaimed the Hungarian Revolutionary Worker-Peasant Government.

Fighting continued for a week. It was at its fiercest in Újpest and Csepel and largely involved working-class youths from the poorer areas of Budapest. 'Uncultivated, rude, often anti-Semitic, many of them joined for adventure and the spirit of the fight,' wrote the historian William Lomax.[11] Many probably spent their weekends on the terraces at Ferencváros, which by then found itself a profoundly anti-establishment club. The students and writers who had initiated the Uprising greeted them, Lomax said, with a mixture of 'shame and admiration'.

However hard they fought, though, against the Red Army the outcome was inevitable. Perhaps the Western powers could have intervened but, quite aside from other considerations, they were occupied by the unfolding Suez Crisis. British and French paratroopers had landed in Egypt to try to reclaim control of the canal on 5 November. By 11 November, the Soviets were back in control in Budapest, at the cost of around 2,500 Hungarian lives.

On 22 November, the Central Workers Council called for a national assembly of delegates from various workers councils across the country to be held in the Népstadion. A ring of 400 Soviet tanks around the stadium forced the meeting to be held elsewhere. The fighting may have been over, but limited resistance went on. A month to the day after the Uprising had begun, an hour of silence was staged across Budapest. And then, on 4 December, there was a demonstration to commemorate those who had died during the Uprising that included a silent procession of women dressed in black to the tomb of the unknown soldier. That night, candles were lit in almost every window in Budapest, despite attempts by the authorities to prevent their sale. The battle, though, was lost.

Honvéd had been drawn against Athletic of Bilbao in the European Cup and they used that as an excuse to get their players out of Budapest, rearranging the tie so they would play the away leg first, on 22 November.

---

[11] In *Hungary 1956* (Alison & Busby, 1976).

They based themselves in Brussels and, to remain sharp, began playing a series of friendlies in Austria, Germany and France. Finding themselves temporarily without a manager, they turned to the great freelancer Béla Guttmann, whose time at Vicenza had come to an end in the summer. He and Puskás had the previous year patched up their differences from Guttmann's first stint at the club. Guttmann's first competitive game in the post came at Athletic, where Honvéd went down 3–2.

MTK were not involved in European competition that season, but they also got out of Budapest. 'On 1 November, the MTK players were gathered together and were taken to Vienna in massive Chevrolet cars,' said Bödör. 'An article in *Népsport* said the players had been stolen. But I was left here. I lived nowhere near the centre of town. The next day, I was sent a message through the kit man that the team had left and I should go to the Ministry of Foreign Affairs because my passport was there.

'It was by the banks of the Danube, a long way from me, but the next day I rode my bike there and picked up my passport. On 4 November, I went to Óbuda and hitch-hiked. A cargo van picked me up. They were going to Győr, and all the way coming towards us down that road were tanks, so many tanks. I was thinking, "What on earth is going to happen?"

'They took me as far as they could and dropped me at a station on the Ebenfurth line. I caught a train and the next morning, 5 November, arrived in Vienna. Everybody was checked very carefully at the border, but they knew me as an MTK player. In Vienna, I went to the police and told them I was looking for MTK. They rang a couple of the big hotels where they might have been staying, found them, put me in a taxi and I arrived in time for breakfast. "Why did you come?" Károly Sándor asked. "Our share of the match fees will be less."'

* * *

After losing to Athletic, Honvéd continued their European tour uncertain when or where they'd be able to play the second leg of the tie against Athletic. Towards the end of November, Grosics received a telegram from Spain asking him to join Honvéd as both their goalkeepers were injured. A car picked him up and drove him towards the Austrian border. He was followed by plain-clothed Soviet officers but they didn't intervene, not even when tank traps in the road forced him to get out and walk the last few miles. A car met him on the other side of the border and drove him to Vienna from where he took a flight to Madrid. The following day he flew on to Barcelona where he played that night in a 4–3 win. Honvéd then moved on to Italy.

Östreicher, a fixer and political operator of great skill and imagination, had somehow also managed to get the players' wives out in November. That eased some of the immediate pressure to return home, but the situation remained confused. 'We were carrying money around in paper bags,' Östreicher said. 'We had no idea what was going to happen in Hungary.'[12]

They ended up playing the second leg against Athletic in Brussels on 20 December and drawing 3–3, in part because, just after half-time, the goalkeeper Lajos Faragó suffered a recurrence of the injury that had led to Grosics's call-up. Sebes, though, always wondered whether all of Honvéd's players really wanted to win, or whether they preferred the freedom to accept an offer they had received from Flamengo to tour Brazil for $10,000 a game.

The players held a meeting in the lobby of the Cosmopolitan Hotel in Brussels. There were three factions: Puskás, Czibor and Östreicher all wanted to go, Lajos Tichy and László Budai did not, while Bozsik

---

12 Róbert Zsolt, *Puskás Öcsi* (Szabad tér, 1989).

and Grosics were waverers. In the end, only Tichy, Ferenc Machos, István Solti and Tibor Palicskó stayed behind.

MTK ended up going on a 40-day tour, which included games against Manchester City and Wolves. 'The whole world was talking about the situation,' Bödör said. 'My family was back in Budapest. We had no telephone in the house, but they lived outside the city centre so they were fairly safe.'

The national Under-21 team, meanwhile, was in Switzerland, preparing for a UEFA competition, although Mándi, who had been coaching them, remained in Budapest. Sebes was despatched to Geneva and to Brussels to try to persuade the Under-21s and Honvéd to return home. In neither case was he successful. He then tried to get the MLSZ to sanction Honvéd's tour which, as he saw it, would have saved some face and bought a little time. He failed in that as well, and resigned from the sports ministry in January 1957.

Sándor Barcs, the president of the MLSZ and an MTK fan, went to Austria to persuade MTK to return home. As an incentive, they were promised there would be no customs checks on the way home. 'I never considered staying away,' said Bödör, 'but [Károly] Sándor didn't come home. That's when I was cemented in the team at outside-right. These decisions were never discussed, but it never occurred to me to stay away.' Sándor and Mihály Lantos both decided to accept offers to join up with Honvéd on their tour of South America and flew to Casablanca to meet their new teammates while they waited for visas. Guttmann also brought in the forward Ferenc Szusza, who had played for him at Újpest.

Honvéd arrived in Brazil on 9 January 1957. They played five games against Flamengo, two in Rio, one in São Paulo and two in Caracas, Venezuela, winning two, losing two and drawing one.

Guttmann decided to stay, which conveniently helped him to avoid a court case back in Milan about his car crash. On 1 March, three days before Dezső Solti stood trial alone, Guttmann signed a contract to become manager of São Paulo.

Visa problems meant the rest of the squad returned in two groups, but they got back to Vienna in the last week of February. Barcs had been replaced as MLSZ president by Márton Nagy, who decided a show of strength was necessary. His threats of sanctions, though, merely helped persuade many to stay away. Grosics returned and was sent to play for Tatabánya. Bozsik had been offered a coaching job by Atlético in Madrid but his father had recently died and he felt a commitment to his mother and four brothers back in Hungary. He was allowed to stay on at Honvéd but they were so weakened that they would have been relegated in 1957 had the MLSZ not decided to spare them the embarrassment by enlarging the first division.

Puskás, Czibor and Kocsis, though, all defected and so did Östreicher, who became technical director of Real Madrid. The three players were banned, but Czibor and Kocsis were eventually signed by Barcelona. Östreicher persuaded the Madrid president Santiago Bernabéu to sign Puskás, even though he was nearly three stones overweight. He would help them to five league titles and three European Cups.

None of the Under-21 side ever went home, and with that the glorious culture that had sprouted from the seeds planted by John Tait Robertson and Jimmy Hogan, the vision of Edward Shires and Alfréd Brüll, was eradicated. The increasingly authoritarian tendencies of the late 1930s and war years had begun the destruction, and the nationalisation of the Communists may have finalised that break with the past anyway, but this was the decisive thrust.

Not only did Hungary lose three of its greatest players, perhaps its greatest administrator and yet another of its greatest coaches, but there was no bridge to a new generation: amid the chaos of the aftermath of the Uprising, the 40-year golden age of Hungarian football came to an end.

CHAPTER EIGHT
ELEGY IN AMSTERDAM

2 May 1962. The flat open bowl of the Olympisch Stadion in Amsterdam, a venue that already has a special place in football history: it was here in 1928 that Uruguay had won their second successive Olympic gold. The stands packed with men in hats and ties, most of them smoking. Adverts familiar, and yet old-fashioned enough to belong to another age, for Bols, Amstel, Shell and Martini. A pitch muddied in a way it never would be for a final today.

Real Madrid in a deep purplish blue. A Benfica free kick, headed clear. Alfredo Di Stéfano, blond hair flapping over a balding scalp, lofting the ball over a high defensive line, Ferenc Puskás scurrying on, lither and quicker than in his later years in Hungary, and crashing a finish past Costa Pereira before three defenders can catch him. Five minutes later, Di Stéfano again, surging forward, to Puskás who from 25 yards hits an awkward shot that bounces past the Benfica goal-keeper. Mário João, the right-back, hugs himself as he turns back to the centre circle, his head bowed. The five-time champions lead the defending champions 2–0.

But there are still 67 minutes to play and, after two of them, Eusébio, with his strange, high-kneed, pointed-toe technique, scuds a free kick goalwards from just outside the box. It bobbles, José

Araquistáin saves, and José Águas fires in. Eight minutes later, Eusébio holds the ball up on the edge of the box and lays it off for Domiciano Cavém, who belts a shot into the top corner: 2–2, and there are still only 33 minutes gone. Soon, though, Madrid take the lead again, Puskás picking up a loose ball on the edge of the box, creating space and drilling a shot into the bottom corner to complete his hat-trick, his second in a European final. And Madrid could easily be 4–2 up before half-time, Paco Gento beating Mário João on the outside and crossing for Luis del Sol, whose header loops over Costa Pereira but bounces back off the bar.

Five minutes after the break, Ângelo Martins dispossesses Puskás midway inside the Benfica half. Germano hits it long and the ball comes to Mário Coluna just outside the box. He is able to turn and his low shot beats the right hand of Araquistáin: 3–3. Cavém picks up Di Stéfano, whose influence wanes. Fitter and stronger, Benfica begin to run Madrid ragged.

Another Benfica break, Eusébio cuts in from the right. Pachín, leaden-footed, cannot follow a surge to his left and brings him down: penalty. Eusébio, who had left Mozambique for Portugal only a year earlier, converts with a calm side-foot. Five minutes later, he is tripped again, just outside the box. The free kick is worked on to his right foot and he hammers a shot under Araquistáin.

It finishes 5–3 and Benfica retain the European Cup. At the final whistle, Puskás exchanges shirts with Eusébio. It is a moment fraught with symbolism, the passing on of the baton from the veteran to a player 14 years his junior.

Neither, though, would ever win another European Cup. An era ended in Amsterdam that day, but it had less to do with Eusébio supplanting Puskás as the greatest player in Europe than the passing of a style of play. The following year, Benfica lost in the final to Nereo

Rocco's AC Milan[1] and the era of *catenaccio* had begun. Football would never be as free-flowing and open again. Structure became key, even after *catenaccio* had yielded by the end of the decade to the Total Football of the Dutch.[2] Football was entering its modern age and as it did so, Hungary was left behind. What happened in Amsterdam stands now as an elegy for the golden age, and not just because Puskás scored a hat-trick. Three months earlier, Emil Östreicher, the sporting director who had assembled that Madrid squad, had taken the decision, one he would regret for the rest of his life, to leave the Bernabéu for Torino. More pertinently, the Benfica manager was Béla Guttmann. As players well aware how central he had been to their success chaired him from the field after their celebrations, they were also carrying a style of play, a way of thinking about the game.

* * *

At São Paulo, Guttmann had taken over from Vicente Feola, who became his assistant. As Dori Kürschner had discovered at Flamengo, that could be awkward, but Feola was a far more relaxed, genial character than Flávio Costa, a *bon vivant* who would often fall asleep on the bench during training. Brazilian football, anyway, had moved closer to Hungarian football in the two decades since Kürschner's arrival. Guttmann found a world that thanks to Flávio Costa's development of Kürschner's ideas, was not unfamiliar to him. The 4–2–4, the shape

---

[1] For more on that final and its ramifications, see Miguel Delaney's article 'AC Milan 2 Benfica 1' in *The Blizzard*, Issue Ten.

[2] For more on this process see my book *Inverting the Pyramid* (Orion, 2008). Total Football itself can be seen as a more physically aggressive variant of the football Hogan practised; although it evolved along a different path, it too had its origins in the Scottish passing game. For more on that and the continuing influence of the theories of Total Football on the modern game see *The Barcelona Legacy* (Blink, 2018).

towards which Hungarian football had been slowly progressing as József Zakariás dropped deeper and deeper in midfield, was already accepted. Guttmann's role was not to introduce a new formation but to lessen the self-indulgence that so often slowed attacks, drilling his players in playing more quickly and more directly. His calls of 'ping-pang-pong' and 'ta-ta-ta', encouraging greater rapidity of passing, became catchphrases.

Guttmann led São Paulo to the Paulista championship in 1957 and although he then returned to Europe with Porto, Feola carried on his work. Feola was subsequently appointed national coach and, introducing the world at large to 4–2–4, led Brazil to World Cup glory in 1958. To call it a Hungarian triumph would obviously be an overstatement, but Brazil's revolutionary style had been laid down by one Hungarian and honed by another.

By then Guttmann seems to have accepted his fate was to be a wanderer, never staying anywhere long enough for his ideas and his manner to become abrasive or repetitive. 'The third year is fatal,' he said. 'A coach dominates the animals, in whose cage he performs his show, as long as he deals with them with self-confidence and without fear. But the moment he becomes unsure of his hypnotic energy, and the first hint of fear appears in his eyes, he is lost.'

Portugal saw Guttmann at his peak. He helped Porto overhaul a five-point deficit to pinch the title from Benfica, who promptly appointed him themselves. He sacked 20 players on his arrival but, promoting youth, won the league in both 1960 and 1961. More significantly, in 1961 in Bern, which seven years earlier had been the graveyard of Hungarian dreams, Guttmann led Benfica to victory over Barcelona in the European Cup final, ending Real Madrid's five-year domination of the competition. Nobody doubted how significant Guttmann had been to the win.

'Guttmann was obsessed with discipline,' said Mario Coluna. 'Maybe that was the secret of his success. It was good to give us discipline. If he hadn't done that, maybe we would never have achieved what we did. The players were afraid of him and had a lot of respect for him. He would fine the players for the smallest thing… We had to be very careful. Guttmann was always advising us. He used to repeat that footballers should only have sex once a week.'[3] As the players celebrated in the dressing room there was no champagne; Guttmann had prohibited alcohol.

A day after that game, Guttmann gave a competitive debut to Eusébio,[4] whom he had signed after a chance meeting with a former São Paulo player, José Carlos Bauer, in a barber's shop in Lisbon. Bauer alerted him to an extraordinary talent playing for Sporting's feeder club in Maputo (then Lourenço Marques), the capital of Mozambique; Benfica hijacked the deal and so landed the greatest player in their history. 'By signing Eusébio,' Guttmann said, 'I was able to play Mario Coluna deeper, more as a wing-half than an inside-forward. He did not like it at first because he did not score so many goals, but he became my best player.' Like Hidegkuti, his creative potential was enhanced by a deeper starting position.

Eusébio was only 20 when he inspired Benfica to their second European Cup. Guttmann by then seemed able to adjust his players' mood at will. At half-time in the final, with his side 3–2 down, as he made the decisive shift to Cavém's role, he went round congratulating his players, telling them, 'We've got this sewn up.' Mario Coluna said

---

[3] Ben Lyttleton, *Match of My Life European Cup Finals* (Know the Score, 2006).

[4] In a Taça de Portugal game against Vitória de Setúbal that the authorities refused to reschedule despite Benfica playing in the European Cup. Benfica lost the leg 4–1 (but won 5–4 on aggregate), with Eusébio both scoring and having a penalty saved by the Vitória goalkeeper Félix Mourinho, the father of José.

the words made him feel about half a metre taller. Even with the looming threat of *catenaccio* from Italy, who knows what might have been achieved had Guttmann stayed? But he didn't. He fell out with the board that summer over their refusal to give him a bonus for his successes in Europe and, it's said, cursed the club on his way out, telling them they would not win another European trophy for 100 years. Fifty-seven years later, despite appearing in eight further finals – and despite Eusébio praying for forgiveness at Guttmann's grave in Vienna before the 1990 European Cup final – they still have not.[5]

Guttmann wandered on, to Peñarol,[6] the Austria national side, back briefly to Benfica, Servette, Panathinaikos, Austria Wien and Porto before he finally settled back in the city where he had always felt most at home: Vienna. Aged 75, he bought an apartment near the opera house on Walfischgasse, going to the coffee house every day to drink a *Melange*, something he had dreamed of wherever he was living. He died in Vienna six years later, in 1981.

In the end, with his two European Cups (plus six domestic league titles[7] and a Mitropa Cup), Guttmann was probably the most successful of all the Hungarian coaches, but what makes the great diaspora so important is not the trophies so much as their influence. Run down the list of World Cup winners and ask which was not in some way a product of the culture that flourished in Budapest in the early 1920s. Given the wave of Hungarians who coached there, Árpád Weisz, Ernő Erbstein and István Tóth only the most notable, Italy in 1934 and 1938 certainly was. Uruguay in 1950 had been

---

[5] For a far more detailed discussion of the curse and whether Guttmann actually said what he is supposed to have said, see Bolchover, *The Greatest Comeback*.

[6] For more on his slightly unhappy time in Montevideo, see Martin da Cruz's article, 'The Thwarted Revolutionary', in *The Blizzard*, Issue Twenty-Eight.

[7] Or, being precise, five national titles and a Brazilian state title in the era before a national championship there.

directly shaped by Imre Hirschl. West German football owed a lot to Kürschner, the Konráds and Alfréd Schaffer. Brazilian football took off after Kürschner's arrival. Argentinian football was changed forever by Hirschl. How might French football have developed without József Eisenhoffer?

Even England, insular and sceptical of foreign ideas as ever, owe their World Cup success to the reassessment of the game forced after the 6–3 defeat to Hungary in 1953. It's no coincidence that Alf Ramsey, England's manager in 1966, had played in the humiliation at Wembley.

And then there are all the others: Márton Bukovi in France and Yugoslavia, Lajos Czeizler, Imre Schlosser and Kálmán Konrád in Sweden, György Orth, Guttmann and Czeizler in Portugal, Géza Toldi in Denmark, Jenő Medgyessy, Ferenc Plattkó and Orth across Latin America, György Szűcs in Iran, Imre Pozsonyi in Spain and Poland, the many who in various ways shaped the game in Austria, Switzerland and Turkey, Hogan himself then Weisz in the Netherlands...

The list seems almost limitless. They were a great mix of personalities, the charmers and the storytellers, the drinkers and the thinkers, the generous and the avaricious, the morose, the irascible, the extrovert and the brave, and they all drew their inspiration from Jimmy Hogan and the school he had founded at MTK. But perhaps what is most remarkable about that generation is that it had such a profound effect on how football is played despite the fact that so many suffered untimely deaths: Weisz at Auschwitz, Csibi Braun in a labour camp in Ukraine, Tóth and Kertész at the hands of the SS, Eisenhoffer from wounds sustained in an air raid, Kürschner from a virus in Rio, Schaffer from who knows what in the railway carriage near Prien am Chiemsee, Erbstein at Superga.

Football was seeded by the great British diaspora of the late 19th and very early 20th century, the sailors, shipbuilders, industrialists, entrepreneurs, teachers and bankers who took it round the world. But it was cultivated by the interwar Hungarian diaspora. What Edward Shires, John Tait Robertson and Jimmy Hogan created in Budapest was improved and refined and carried across Europe and South America. It was an extraordinary culture, concerned both with the aesthetic and the pragmatic, endlessly inventive, one whose turbulent origins meant it was never still, its emissaries fleeing always a turbulent centre. It survived the ravages of Fascism, just, to have its golden period in the early 1950s but already by then Communism had struck at its roots. But it could not survive the Uprising and that final, most decisive emigration.

The golden age of Budapest football is long gone, but its influence lives yet. Hungary taught the world to play; we're all the protégés of Jimmy Hogan now. And in some precise through-ball, well-delivered pass or moment of improvisation, perhaps, when the game is at its most appealing, we hear still some strain of old Budapest, of the game of the coffee houses and the *grunds*, of that most beautiful and tragic of footballing cultures.

ACKNOWLEDGEMENTS

No book is ever written alone and this one demanded more assistance than most. A curtain fell over Hungary in 1945 and it is only recently that historians have begun to probe behind it. Many of the details in this book came from files that had not been opened in almost a century. In addition, Hungarian is not a language that readily yields its secrets to an English eye.

I could direct, prompt and ask questions but, essentially, I was blind, led by four of the most diligent and energetic researchers imaginable. Enormous thanks to Matt Watson-Broughton, Hajni Déak, Henrik Hedegűs and Gábor Sisak for their work variously sifting through archives, tracking down interviewees, arranging interviews and translating. This book couldn't have been written without them. In Budapest, Tamás Dénes, Péter Szegedi, Gábor Andreides, Dániel Bólgar, Zsolt Gyulas, Tibor Szegő, Tamás Bodrogi, György Kósa, József Uri, György Szöllősi, Marika Lantos, Lajos Szabó, Judit Blaha, István Szomolányi, Tamás Hegyi, Gyula Pataki and Gábor Laszip were more helpful than they had any need to be, as was Tamás Karati in New York.

To all those who gave their time to be interviewed about their memories of fathers, uncles, grandparents, other more distant relatives, teammates and acquaintances, and to all the various assistants in archives, records offices and cemeteries, a huge thank you.

I was conscious from the start that I was standing on the shoulders of giants. The work of Gunnar Persson on Hakoah, Dominic

Bliss on Ernő Erbstein, David Bolchover on Béla Guttmann, Matteo Marani on Árpád Weisz, Dietrich Schulze-Marmeling on the role of Jews in German football and Péter Szegedi on Hungary in the inter-war years was of enormous benefit.

Thanks also to Aleksandar Holiga in Croatia; to Gunnar Persson in Sweden; to Martín Da Cruz in Uruguay; to Ednilson Valia and Cassiano Gobbet in Brazil; to Martín Mazur, Araceli Aléman, Esteban Bekerman and Sam Kelly in Argentina; to Sid Lowe in Spain and to Tom Williams in France. Thanks to Philippe Auclair for providing access to the archives of *France Football* and *l'Équipe* in Paris. And further thanks to Gunnar Persson for his help in Sweden and to David Bolchover for being so generous with advice and contacts.

At Blink, thanks to Matt Phillips for having faith in a project many would have deemed excessively recondite, to Beth Eynon for pulling everything together, and to my copy-editor Ian Greensill and proof-reader Justine Taylor. And thanks also to my agent David Luxton, even if he hasn't yet got me a deal to write the definitive guide to *Silent Witness* (for which Wilson is very much available).

Thanks more generally for advice and support to Jon Adams, John Brewin, Miguel Delaney, Ruth Dunleavy, Raphael Honigstein, Dan Magnowski, Jack Pitt-Brooke, Josh Robinson, and to all the various colleagues and teammates who've endured me banging on about obscure Hungarians over the years.

Kat Petersen, as well as scouring the manuscript with her usual ferocious eye, performed a vital service in going through German sources – and this time without even the delight of *El Gráfico* covers as recompense. A massive thanks you.

BIBLIOGRAPHY

Álvarez, Luciano, *Historia de Peñarol* (Aguilar, 2014)

Archetti, Eduardo, *Masculinities* (Bloomsbury, 1999)

Barcs, Sándor (ed), *Száz éves az MTK-VM sportklub* (MTK, 1988)

Bayce, Rafael, '*La evolución de los sistemas del juego*', *100 años de fútbol*, no. 22, (Editores Reunidos, 1970)

Benson, Colin, *The Bridge* (Chelsea Football Club, 1987)

Bliss, Dominic, *Erbstein: The Triumph and Tragedy of Football's Forgotten Pioneer* (Blizzard, 2014)

Bognár, Sándor, Iván Pető and Sándor Szakács, *A hazai gazdaság négy évtizedének története 1945–1985* (Közgazdasági és Jogi Könyvkiadó, 1985)

Bolchover, David, *The Greatest Comeback* (Biteback, 2017)

Borenich, Péter, *Csak a labdán van bőr* (Magánkiadás, 1983)

Claussen, Detlev, *Béla Guttmann, a világfutball edzőlegendája* (Akadémiai Kiadó, 2015)

Csaknády, Jenő, *Die Béla Guttmann Story* (Bintz-Dohany, 1964)

Csatár, István, Eghia Hovhannesian and György Oláh (eds), *Pest-Pilis-Solt-Kiskun vármegye és Kecskemét th. jogu város adattára* (1939)

Da Cruz, Martin, 'The Thwarted Revolutionary', *The Blizzard*, Issue Twenty-Eight (2018)

Delaney, Miguel, 'AC Milan 2 Benfica 1' in *The Blizzard*, Issue Ten (2013)

Dénes, Tamás, Mihály Sándor and Éva B Bába, *A magyar labdarúgás története* (Campus, 2016)

Dénes, Tamás and Péter Szegedi, *Az 1938-as magyar vb-ezüst* (Akadémiai, 2018)

Dibenedetto, Luca, *El balon fiuman* (Senza, 2004)

Ericson, Georg and Åke Stolt, *Inlägg från Åby* (DEWE-Forläget, 1977)

Fekete, Pál, *Orth és társai* (Sport, 1963)

Figes, Orlando, *A People's Tragedy* (Viking, 1997)

Fodor, Henrik (ed), *25 év. A Magyar Testgyakorlók Köre története 1888–1913*, (Minerva, 1913)

Fox, Norman, *Prophet or Traitor?* (Parrs Wood Press, 2003)

Freud, Sigmund, Sándor Ferenczi. Eva Brabant, Ernst Falzeder, Patrizia Giampieri-Deutsch, *The Correspondence of Sigmund Freud and Sándor Ferenczi, Volume 2: 1914–19* (Harvard University Press, 1993)

Galuppo, Fernando, *O time do meu coração: Sociedade Esportiva Palmeiras* (Leitura, 2009)

Garrido, Atilio, *Maracaná: La historia secreta*, (Atilio Garrido, 2014)

Garrido, Atilio and Joselo González, *El gol del siglo* (El País & Tenfield, 2000)

Glanville, Brian, *Champions of Europe* (Guinness, 1991)

Gluck, Mary, 'The Budapest Coffee House and the making of "Jewish Identity" at the Fin de Siècle', *Journal of the History of Ideas*, April 2013, Volume 74, no. 2

Grüne, Hardy, *Die Trainerlegende* (Agon Sportverlag, 2001)

Gunther, John, *Inside Europe* (Hamish Hamilton, 1936)

Hadas, Miklós, 'Football and Social Identity: The Case of Hungary in the Twentieth Century' in *The Sports Historian*, Volume 20 (2000), Issue 2

Hamilton, Aidan, *An Entirely Different Game* (Mainstream, 1998)

Hámori, Tibor, *Puskás, Legenda és valóság* (Sportpropaganda, 1982)
Régi gólok, edzősorsok (Lapkiadó Vállalat, 1984)

Hegyi, Iván, *Magyarok nagy pályán* (Sprint Kiadó, 2010)

Hesse, Uli, *Tor!* (WSC, 2002)

Horak, Roman and Wolfgang Maderthaner, 'A Culture of Urban
Cosmopolitanism: Uridil and Sindelar as Viennese Coffee-
House Heroes' in *European Heroes*, edited by Richard Holt, J.A.
Mangan and Pierre Lanfranchi (Routledge, 1996)

Horowitz, David, 'Hakoah in New York (1926–32): A New
Dimension for American Jewry', *Judaism* 25, summer 1977

Johnston, Harry, *The Rocky Road to Wembley* (Sportsmans Book
Club, 1954)

Jones, Ron (with Joe Lovejoy), *The Auschwitz Goalkeeper* (Gomer,
2013)

Kelemen, Gábor L., *Gól a halál kapujában* (Sportpropaganda, 1981)

Kitchen, Martin, *The Coming of Austrian Fascism* (Routledge, 1930)

Liptai, Ervin, Endre Bassa and József Gassi (eds), *A magyar
antifasiszta ellenállás és partizánmozgalom* (Kossuth, 1987)

Lomax, William, *Hungary 1956* (Alison & Busby, 1976)

Lowe, Sid, *Fear and Loathing in la Liga* (Yellow Jersey, 2013)

Lyttleton, Ben, *Match of My Life European Cup Finals* (Know the
Score, 2006)

Mallász, Gitta, *Talking With Angels* (Daimon, 2011)

Marani, Matteo, *Dallo scudetto ad Auschwitz* (Imprimatur, 2014)

Meisl, Willy, *Soccer Revolution* (Phoenix, 1955)

Molnár, Ferenc, *A Pál utcai fiúk* (Móra Könyvkiadó, 1906)

Nagy, Béla, *Fradi – Football Century* (Futballmúzeum, 2005)

Nordahl, Gunnar, *Guld och gröna planer* (Bonniers Folkbibliotek,
1954)

Pálfi, György and János Vachó, *Fekete könyv* (Hungarian General Sports Library, Issue 1)

Patai, Raphael, *The Jews of Hungary* (Wayne State UP, 1996)

Persson, Gunnar, *Stjärnor på flykt* (Norstedts, 2004)
'The Exile', *The Blizzard*, Issue Twenty-Three, 2016

Romsics, Ignác, *Bethlen István. Politikai életrajz 1874–1946* (Magyarságkutató Intézet, 1991)

Ronay, Barney, 'The Bomb and the Bowler Hat', *The Blizzard,* Issue Three, 2011

Rózsaligeti, László, *A Nagy Honvéd* (Alma Mater Zala Bt., 2013)

Sánta, Gábor, '"*Vigasztal, ápol és eltakar*": *A budapesti kávéházak szociologiai és pszichológiai természetrjza a századfordulón*,' *Budapesti Negyed* 12–13, nos. 2–3 (1996)

Schidrowitz, Leo (ed), *Geschichte des Fußballsportes in Österreich*, (Verlag Rudolf Traunau, 1951)

Schulze-Marmeling, Dieter, *Der FC Bayern, seine Juden und die Nazis* (Werkstatt,2013)

Skrentny, Werner, '*Von Serbien nach New York, von Budapest nach Stockholm: die Odysee der Konrad-Zwillinge*', in *Davidstern und Lederball*, ed. Dieter Schulze-Marmeling (Werkstatt, 2003)

Smith, Stratton and Eric Batty, *International Coaching Book* (Souvenir, 1966)

Spector, Scott, 'Modernism without Jews: A Counter-Historical Argument' in *Modernism/Modernity* 14, no. 4 (2006)

Stibbe, Matthew, 'Enemy Aliens, Deportees, Refugees: Internment Practices in the Habsburg Empire, 1914–1918' in the *Journal of Modern European History*, Nov 2014, Vol. 12 Issue 4

Szegedi, Péter, *Az első aranykor: A magyar foci 1945-ig* (Akadémiai, 2016)

Taylor, Peter, *With Clough by Taylor* (Sidgwick & Jackson, 1980)

Taylor, Rogan, *Puskás on Puskás* (Robson, 1998)

Toldi, Géza (with Axel Hansen), *Fodboldnavn paa flygtningepas* (Martin, 1962)

Török, Ferenc, *Mandula* (Nyik-Ki, 1999)

Újvári, Péter, *Magyar Zsidó Lexikon* (1929)

Ungváry, Krisztián, *The Siege of Budapest* (Yale University Press, 2006)

Veres, István, *Apám mellett, apám helyett* (Kurucz Gábor, 1994)

Veres, Péter, *A paraszti jövendő* (Jövő, 1948)

Vignes, Spencer, *Lost in France* (History Press, 2007)

Viharos [Ödön Gerő], *Az én fovárosom* (Révai Testvérek, 1891)

Wilson, Jonathan, *The Anatomy of England* (Orion, 2010)

> *Angels with Dirty Faces* (Orion, 2016)
>
> *The Barcelona Legacy* (Blink, 2018)
>
> *Inverting the Pyramid* (Orion, 2008)
>
> *Nobody Ever Says Thank You* (Orion, 2011)
>
> *The Outsider* (Orion, 2012)

Zsolt, Róbert, *Puskás Öcsi* (Szabad tér, 1989)

INDEX

Credit: Alil Haydar Yesilyurt

Jonathan Wilson is the founder and editor of *The Blizzard*. He writes regularly for the *Guardian*, *Sports Illustrated*, and *World Soccer*, and his work also appears in the *Independent*, the *Sunday Times*, and the *New Statesman*. He is the critically acclaimed author of a number of sports titles, including *Inverting the Pyramid: A History of Soccer Tactics*, which was football book of the year in the UK and Italy and was shortlisted for the William Hill Sports Book of the Year.